THE HEALTH CARE CONSUMER GUIDE

Robert Gann is Director of The Help for Health Trust, a charity which provides people with the information they need to become active partners in their own health care. Training originally as a librarian, he worked in the National Health Service for fifteen years. As Health Information Manager for Wessex Regional Health Authority, he established innovative information services on self-help groups, HIV/AIDS and waiting lists.

As a freelance writer on health issues, he has carried out a number of editorial and writing assignments for the British Medical Association, including reports on living with risk, pesticides and health, coping with stress, and rights and responsibilities of doctors and patients. He has been a consultant on information for health promotion to the World Health Organization and the British Council. He is married with three young sons and lives in Salisbury, Wiltshire.

Some other Faber health titles

THE FERTILITY AND CONTRACEPTION BOOK
Julia Mosse and Josephine Heaton

ALZHEIMER'S DISEASE: THE LONG BEREAVEMENT
Elizabeth Forsythe

MULTIPLE SCLEROSIS: EXPLORING SICKNESS AND HEALTH
Elizabeth Forsythe

SLEEP AND DREAMING
Jacob Empson

DRUG USE AND ABUSE
James Willis

FOOD FACTS AND FIGURES
Jill Davies and John Dickerson

UNDERSTANDING YOUR CHILD
Richard Woolfson

EVERYWOMAN: A GYNAECOLOGICAL GUIDE FOR LIFE
Fifth Edition *Derek Llewellyn-Jones*

FABER POCKET MEDICAL DICTIONARY
Elizabeth Forsythe

CERVICAL CANCER
Judith Harvey, Sue Mack and Julian Woolfson

SAFER SEX
Peter Gordon and Louise Mitchell

ANOREXIA NERVOSA: THE BROKEN CIRCLE
Ann Erichsen

AGORAPHOBIA
Ruth Hurst Voce

YOUR CHILD'S HEALTH
Ivan Blumenthal

The Health Care Consumer Guide

Robert Gann

faber and faber
LONDON · BOSTON

First published in 1991
by Faber and Faber Limited
3 Queen Square London WC1N 3AU

Photoset by Parker Typesetting Service, Leicester
Printed in Great Britain by Clays Ltd, St Ives plc

A CIP record for this book is available from the British Library.

ISBN 0 571 14298 2

For Thomas, Jack and Joseph with love

Contents

Acknowledgments

This book is based on the experiences of running Help for Health, a consumer health information service for the Wessex Region. Many of the needs for information and the resources available to meet them have been identified in my everyday work with Help for Health. I am indebted to my colleagues Marilyn Jamieson, Anne Anderson, Mavis Filder, Ann Davies and Ian Dillow for their contribution to the success of Help for Health, and thereby to the substance of this book.

Information is all about communication and sharing, and many people have been generous with their contacts and suggestions for the content of the book. In particular I am grateful to fellow workers in health information services in the UK and abroad: Sally Knight, Gill Needham and Mig Muller, Jackie Chapman and Lyn Mastoris, Jane Sweetland, Stephen Grace, Balbine Callou in Paris, Hugh and Marian Faulkner in Italy, Robin Orr and Tracey Cosgrove at the Planetree Center, California, and Alan Rees in Cleveland, Ohio. I would also like to express my appreciation to the many self-help groups and voluntary organizations who have provided information for the book, and to the Consumers' Association and the British Medical Association for use of their excellent publications. I am fortunate in having Roger Osborne as my editor at Faber and Faber. His genuine knowledge and enthusiasm for the subject have made this a better book than the one I first offered him.

As always I owe the most to Jane. As a lawyer, Community Health Council member and voluntary organization chairperson, she has been my constant source of robust advice. She has selflessly extended her social life to give me quiet evenings with the word-processor. I would never have done it without her.

Introduction and How to Use This Book

This book is about information: the information we all need to be active health care consumers. Having information is the first step to every healthy choice we make: weighing up the risks and benefits of treatment, choosing a healthier lifestyle, using the health service, joining a self-help group, claiming welfare benefits.

The term 'health care consumer' is used to include all members of the public who use or consume health services. Those services might be provided by family doctors, hospitals, community care and the private sector. But equally they include the informal care provided by self-help groups, families and friends, and the self-care which we provide for ourselves. For this reason the term 'health care consumer' is preferred to 'patient'. Most people would only regard themselves as patients when actually receiving professional health care. On the other hand we are users or consumers of health care almost every day of our lives.

As consumers we also need information almost every day of our lives. However, some groups of health care consumers need more information than others: people with disabilities or suffering from chronic illnesses such as diabetes; parents; pregnant women; the terminally ill; the elderly and their families and friends. This book is intended to give these people, in particular, access to the information they need to use the services to which they are entitled.

The shape of this book follows the picture of health care in the UK today (and in most other countries). The balance was expressed graphically by Drs John and Elizabeth Horder in a celebrated diagram produced over thirty years ago. It is as valid today as it was in 1954.

Most health care – as much as 80 per cent – is self-care and informal care. This is the care which we provide for ourselves, our friends and families, using appropriate home remedies, buying over-the-counter medicines, and drawing on the resources of self-help groups and information services to increase our knowledge and confidence in dealing with the health problems of everyday life. Self-care and our active participation in our own health is covered in SECTION 1.

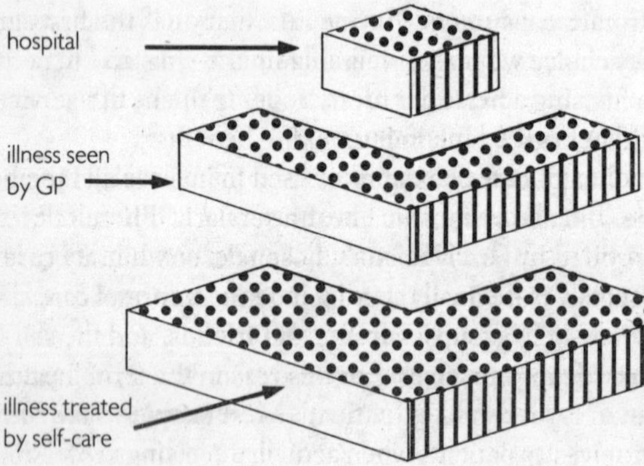

The relative proportions of illness treated by hospital care, primary care and self-care. Although this diagram was first produced over thirty years ago, the picture is equally true today (Source: *Practitioner*, 1954)

There comes a stage (about five times a year for most people) when we feel a health problem is beyond our own competence and we need to seek professional advice through our general practitioner. Advice may be all we need, or we may need to use the GP as the gatekeeper to a range of other options (prescribed drugs, other members of the health care team, diagnostic tests, hospital treatment). Primary care comprises about 15 per cent of all episodes of health care and is discussed in SECTION 2.

Today more and more people with chronic illnesses and disabilities are being cared for in the community. The care they receive comes from the GP and other members of the primary care team, from social services, from voluntary organizations, and above all from their own family and friends (informal carers). If people are to live a full and independent life in the community, they need information on the range of services and financial support available to them. This is given in SECTION 3.

Despite the attention given to it, and the resources spent on it, hospital care is a very small part of the total health care picture (about 5 per cent). But when we are admitted to hospital (and most of us are at some stage in our lives) we are likely to be particularly worried and feel particularly vulnerable. It is at this time that information can reduce anxiety and smooth the path to recovery. Hospital care is covered in SECTION 4.

As consumers, we all exercise choices at many levels of the health care process. But sometimes we have particularly difficult decisions to make. Problems in decision-making can occur when there is a lack of consensus in medical thinking, and we may have to make up our minds without clear advice from professionals. Or we may feel prepared to act against properly cautious medical advice because we feel the risks are worth taking for the possible benefits which may ensue. Examples are choices of place of birth, or unproven therapies for cancer and AIDS. These special areas of choice are discussed in SECTION 5.

It is increasingly possible that we may need to use health services overseas. Each year British holidaymakers take 15 million trips abroad. The growth of multinational companies means that it is now routine for employees to spend periods overseas. The establishment of the Single European Market in 1992 will lead to a much greater migration of labour within the European Community. When we travel overseas we have particular information needs. We may think we know how the health care system works in the UK, but do we know which types of treatment are free to UK citizens abroad, or who to turn to for help and advice? SECTION 6 provides some of the answers to questions on health services overseas.

As well as advice provided by GPs and other health professionals there is now a bewildering number of health information services available to the public. These include the information available through generalist services like public libraries and Citizens' Advice Bureaux, as well as specialist health education services, healthlines, etc. These services are often underused because people are unaware of the resources available and how to benefit from them. SECTION 7 provides a guide through the information maze so that you can find information for yourself to complement the advice given by your doctor.

Within each chapter there are many suggestions on sources of further information. But no consumer guide would be complete without a full resources section which provides a subject guide to self-help organizations and publications. Self-help Resources (SECTION 8) is at the end of the book for easy reference.

1 Self-Care

While this book aims to provide information about personal health care, it is important to remember that good health is not solely an individual matter. Having a superbly healthy body while surrounded by a filthy environment where sick and disabled people are neglected would be a perverse idea of 'health'. We can only enjoy good health when it is shared by our whole community.

Our health in the Western world has been improving for 200 years. Until quite recently the commonly held view has been that these improvements are the result of scientific medicine. Recent public memory, at least until the arrival of AIDS, is of the apparent demise of epidemics, declines in maternal and infant mortality, and more people living into old age.

In fact, improvements in death rates in Europe and the USA have not coincided with medical advances. Over 75 per cent of the decline in the death rate since 1875 had occurred *before* medicine's most significant discoveries became available. Then the discovery of antibiotics in the 1930s ushered in a period during which the decline in the death rate accelerated. But subsequently the trend of several centuries came to a halt, and for the next fifteen years there was no appreciable increase in life expectancy. Strangely enough, this period coincided with the advent of high-technology medicine. Death rates only began to fall again in the 1970s. In the USA this was due to a drop in deaths from heart disease and stroke, and coincided with a reduction in the use of tobacco, decreased consumption of fats and increased exercise among Americans. A little way behind, these trends are now being felt in the UK and other developed countries too. In other words, recent continuing improvements in health were beyond the reach of medicine, and only came about through a better-educated and better-informed public choosing to adopt healthier lifestyles. This combination of public policy and personal involvement is crucial to maintaining and improving standards of health care.

Healthy Individuals in Healthy Communities

Today's politicians set great store by individuals taking responsibility for their own lives. This is a healthy philosophy when it recognizes the competence of ordinary people to deal with a wide range of problems for themselves, instead of relying on professionals and the medical system. Indeed commentators like Ivan Illich suggest that the medical establishment is actually a threat to health and that the 'medicalization of life' leads to widespread iatrogenic disease (illness caused by medical procedures – side-effects of drugs, infections acquired in hospitals, and so on). For Illich the only possibility of a 'recovery of health' lies with the individual's capacity to understand, control and cope with his or her own health, and ultimately suffering and death.

This book is largely concerned with giving people the information they need to become active participants in their own health care. In our enthusiasm for the informed and active individual it is important not to forget that our freedom to make these health choices is only possible because of tremendous advances in public health, particularly in the nineteenth century. The UK Public Health Movement founded by Chadwick and other social reformers was very effective in combating communicable diseases through the provision of better housing, a safe water supply and effective sewerage systems. In his influential analysis of the contribution of medicine to health, Thomas McKeown has shown how the high death rates of the past were largely due to infectious diseases, inadequate nutrition and unhealthy living conditions. The most significant illnesses were tuberculosis, chest infections and water and foodborne diarrhoea. From the second half of the nineteenth century, improved nutrition and improved hygiene were already making a marked impact on people's susceptibility to infection, even before widespread immunization. In our own time, the World Health Organization has always been at pains to emphasize the importance of society and the environment to health.

The new public health

In the late twentieth century we may have conquered many of the old threats to health, but the emergence of new diseases (in particular AIDS) and the recognition of the continuing links between social deprivation and ill health have led to a new public health movement. The 1980 Black Report on inequalities in health (published by Penguin in 1982) showed quite clearly that although there have been huge advances in health generally, there are still significant discrepancies in health between different sections of the population, between different social classes, different parts of the country and different racial groups. Obviously our social conditions are still central to our health.

All District Health Authorities in Britain now have a DIRECTOR OF PUBLIC HEALTH. He or she is responsible for the prevention of disease and promotion of health, more specifically:

- policies for health education and health promotion
- the control of communicable diseases (including AIDS)
- production of an annual report on the health of the local population

For more information on the role of the Director of Public Health and public health policy contact your District Health Authority.

Health for All

In 1978 the World Health Organization held an international conference on primary care at Alma Ata in the USSR. Out of the conference came the WHO goal of Health for All by the year 2000, and the agreement (by 134 nations) of the Declaration of Alma Ata. The declaration was the basis of much subsequent work in public health and health promotion worldwide, and gave official recognition to the emerging movement for participation of ordinary people in their own health care. It states quite explicitly that 'The people have a right and duty to participate individually and collectively in their own health care.'

Subsequent statements from WHO recognize the limitations of high-tech medicine in making real improvements in health and see the hope for the future in people themselves:

'Health science and technology have come to a point where their contribution to the further improvement of health standards can make a real impact only if people themselves become full partners in health protection and promotion.'

'Health for all will be achieved by people themselves. A well-informed, well-motivated and actively participating community is a key element for attainment of the common goal.'

The Health for All targets are important because they emphasize the way in which almost all political decisions can have health consequences. Healthy policy comes not only from within the NHS, but from elected government at national and local level. As individuals we can have a personal influence on our own health, not only in the way we behave but also in the way we vote.

CENTRAL GOVERNMENT has a responsibility to:

– assign to the National Health Service adequate resources
– consider the health consequences of taxation (for example, on alcohol and tobacco)
– use legislation to promote health (for example, seat belts)

– influence the availability of products which affect health (for example, through agricultural subsidies)

LOCAL GOVERNMENT has a responsibility to:

– maintain safe environments, free from pollution and contaminants
– ensure that children receive an education which enables them to participate in decisions about their own health
– ensure sufficient and suitable housing
– provide adequate and accessible leisure facilities
– ensure domestic and public environments which minimize the risk of accidents and injuries

Politics is largely about priorities. It is the aim of the WHO Health for All declaration to ensure that the health of the population is given a high priority in government planning and expenditure.

Green Health

In the same way that all shades of political opinion lay claim to self-help and consumer power, so every party today is coloured green. Environmental concerns are high on the National Health Service agenda too. The NHS is a major consumer of world resources, using between 6 and 7 per cent of the UK gross national product. With its 1 million employees and 1,700 hospitals, it has a major impact on the environment in using energy, creating waste and developing land. In a new campaign launched in 1990, the Department of Health urged health authorities to implement environment-friendly policies wherever they are sensible and affordable. These are policies which are worth pursuing, not only in the NHS, but in any employing organization. After all, the health of the planet is crucial to the health of its inhabitants. Health authorities are not obliged to pursue green policies, but you can use public meetings and the consultative process that health authorities go through in planning services to influence change in this direction.

Issues worth considering include transport, energy consumption, recycling, deforestation and pollution.

For more information on caring for the health of the environment, get in touch with FRIENDS OF THE EARTH 26–8 Underwood Street, London N1 7JQ Tel: 071-490 1555.

You can contact your District Health Authority (see page 34) and local authority to find out whether they have a 'green' policy. If you are an employer or a trade unionist, see how these policies could be implemented in your organization.

Keeping Healthy

Our health and well-being can be undermined by our behaviour as a community (for example, when this results in poverty or pollution), and also by our behaviour as individuals. Health educationalists usually distinguish three levels of health promotion:

PRIMARY: the prevention of disease
SECONDARY: helping the recovery from illness
TERTIARY: optimizing health when living with a long-term illness or disability

Each of these approaches involves providing people with the information they need to make healthy choices about their own lives. Before we can adopt a healthy lifestyle we need to be aware of the real risks to our health. The popular perception of the risks of life can bear little relation to the real hazards to our health. Media coverage of tragedies and popular panics can lead us to overestimate our risk of dying in a plane crash, contracting bovine spongieform encephalopathy, or being bitten by a Rottweiler. Yet despite all the efforts of health education campaigns, some people continue to smoke, to eat high-fat diets and to drive when they have been drinking. These are the real risk factors.

The most accessible, popular guide to personal risk management is the *BMA Guide to Living with Risk* (Harmondsworth: Penguin, 1990). As the guide shows, 85 per cent of people die from three causes: heart disease (48 per cent of all deaths); cancer (25 per cent); and respiratory diseases (11 per cent). Deaths among young people are largely due to accidents. Seventy per cent of deaths in 25-year-old men are caused by accidents and violence, in particular accidents on the road, many associated with alcohol.

If there is one clear message which emerges from an examination of the real risks of life, it is the hazards of smoking. Smoking is the greatest single self-imposed risk to health. The Royal College of

Physicians has estimated that out of 1,000 young men in England and Wales who smoke:

– 1 will be murdered
– 6 will be killed on the road
– 250 will be killed before their time by tobacco

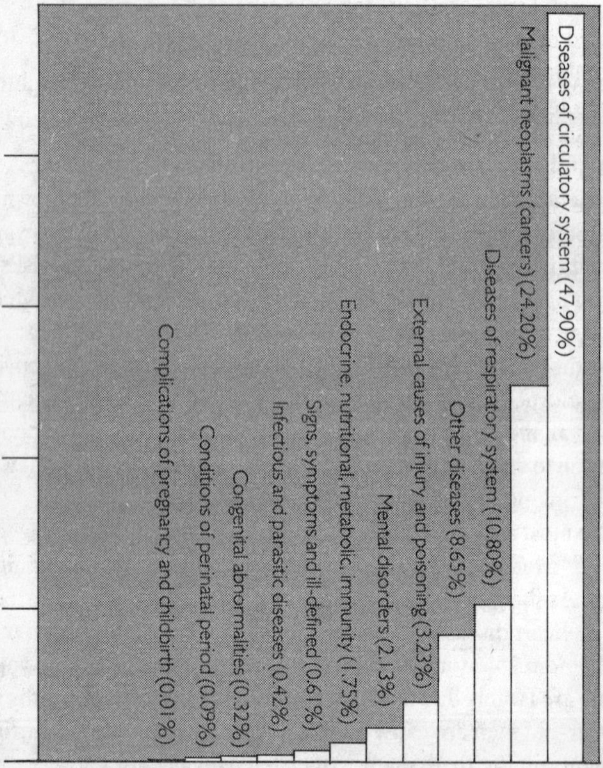

Causes of death in England and Wales in 1986. Heart disease and other diseases of circulation account for almost half of all deaths, and cancer accounts for a further quarter (Source: OPCS Mortality Statistics)

Many of us spend a lot of time worrying about small risks over which we have no control, when we can do a great deal to avoid or minimize the risks which are important. The *BMA Guide* gives some basic guidelines for personal reduction of the risks to health.

– Stop smoking
– Keep weekly alcohol intake to below twenty-one units for men and fourteen units for women (a unit is a glass of wine, single measure of spirits or half a pint of beer)
– Avoid being overweight
– Cut down on fatty food
– Eat plenty of fibre
– Limit your salt and sugar intake
– Take care in the sun
– Take regular exercise (at least twenty minutes three times a week)
– Learn to relax
– Practise safe sex
– Observe health and safety practices at work
– Don't drink and drive
– Always wear seat belts and ensure children are restrained in cars
– For women – have a regular cervical smear test, and examine your breasts monthly

Coping with Minor Illness

We all expect and accept periods of ill health. One study of women in a Scottish new town found that over a three-week period 94 per cent of them reported some illness. This figure is very similar to another piece of research which found that 95 per cent of the people studied suffered from some complaint over a fortnight, yet 35 per cent described themselves as in perfect health. Obviously

Results of a survey into minor ailments

- While the British population believe themselves to be healthy, they reported an average of five ailments each in any two weeks, about one every two or three days
- Over a two-week period, a third of the children and a quarter of the adults under survey had a skin problem, a quarter of the children had a respiratory problem, and a quarter of the adults were in pain
- People are able to distinguish between minor ailments and those requiring professional advice. Nine out of ten ailments were dealt with by individuals themselves without needing to visit the doctor. One of the greatest information needs consumers have is at what stage symptoms are beyond the scope of self-care, and when professional advice should be sought
- Half the ailments did not receive any treatment. They were just tolerated and went away. If people used a medicine at all it was much more likely to be an over-the-counter remedy than something on prescription. Only 13 per cent went to see their doctor or dentist

Right What is done about minor health problems. Only 13 per cent of people consult their doctor for a minor health problem. Most use an over-the-counter or prescribed medicine, or simply do nothing and wait for the problem to go away (Source: *Everyday Health Care*, Proprietary Association, 1987)

some ill health (acute self-limiting problems such as headaches, stomach upsets, colds) is regarded as quite normal.

In 1985 the Proprietary Association of Great Britain (representing manufacturers of over-the-counter medicines) funded an independent market research survey into how British people treat the minor ailments of daily living. The study demonstrated that self-care is the single largest component of health care in the UK. Individuals and their families can handle the overwhelming majority of episodes of ill health without the need for professional help.

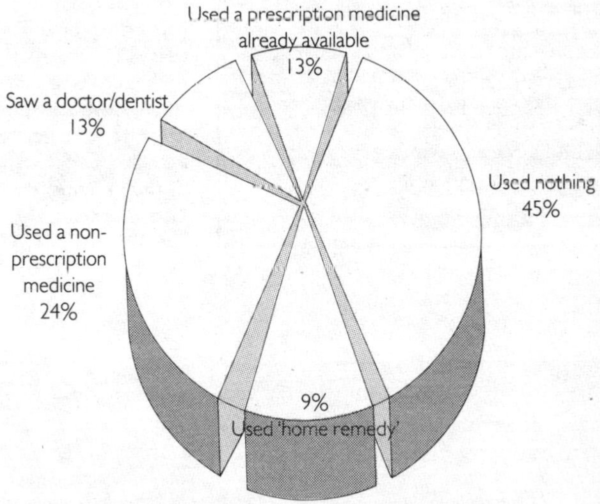

Note: Adds up to 104% because more than one action was taken in some cases. Home remedies include hot water bottle, lemon/honey drinks, ice bags, etc.

Some 'home doctor' books

The following give practical advice on appropriate self-care and when to consult the doctor:

Take Care of Yourself: a practical do-it-yourself guide to medical care by D. M. Vickery (London: Unwin, 1980)

Home Doctor: an A–Z guide by V. G. Daniels (Cambridge Medical Books, 1986)

The New Macmillan Guide to Family Health edited by Tony Smith (London: Macmillan, 1987)

The Complete Guide to Symptoms, Illness and Surgery by H. Winter Griffith (Wellingborough: Thorsons 1987)

The BMA Complete Family Health Encyclopaedia (London: Dorling Kindersley, 1990)

Right Average two-week incidence of minor illness. Over an average fortnight a quarter of us have a skin problem and nearly a quarter are in pain. More than a third of children have a skin problem and a quarter of them a cough or cold (Source: *Everyday Health Care*, Proprietary Association, 1987)

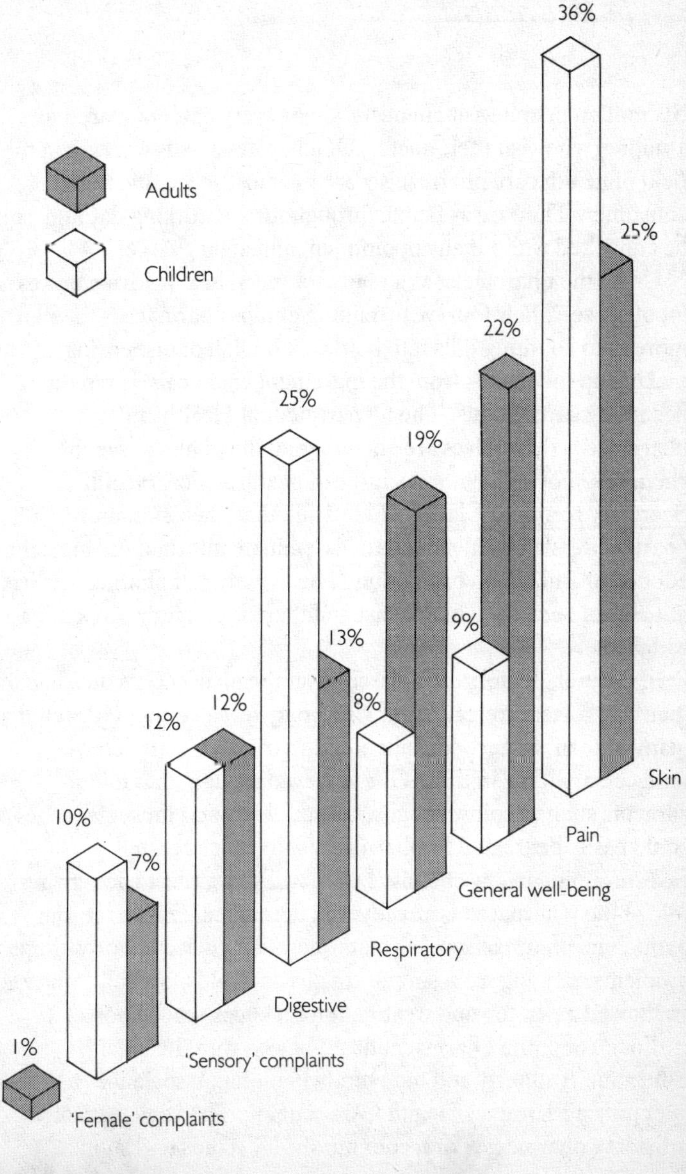
Adults
Children
36%
25%
22%
25%
19%
13%
9%
8%
12%
12%
10%
7%
1%
Skin
Pain
General well-being
Respiratory
Digestive
'Sensory' complaints
'Female' complaints

The Pharmacist

Six million people visit chemists' shops every day, compared to 1 million who visit their doctor. Of all professionals working in the field of health care pharmacists are the most accessible to the consumer. They are available throughout the working day and can be consulted without an appointment and at no charge.

Using the pharmacist as a ready source of health advice makes a lot of sense. Their four-year training equips pharmacists for a lot more than counting pills into bottles. The skill of dispensing, making up medicines from the ingredient chemicals, is rapidly becoming superfluous. The Department of Health and pharmacists themselves are encouraging the public to see the chemist's shop as a natural source of health advice. Health Secretary Kenneth Clarke said in 1990 that 'the community pharmacist is an ideal person to disseminate information on health education and health promotion. The expertise of pharmacists has not always been used in the past and there is certainly scope for a wider role.'

In general, doctors are pleased to let the pharmacists do some of their work. Research at Aston University revealed that GPs felt that many of their surgery consultations are trivial or completely unnecessary. One in three GPs surveyed thought that minor ailments such as colds, coughs, mouth ulcers and muscular aches could easily be treated by pharmacists. In fact, as casual eavesdropping in any chemist's shop will show, the advice-giving role of the pharmacist is already well developed. Over a ten-day period one pharmacist received requests for advice on forty-three problems, ranging from simple coughs and colds to a child who had swallowed a pen top and treatment for a knock-kneed horse!

Since 1986, the Pharmaceutical Society, with the Health Education Authority and the Family Planning Association, has been operating a Pharmacy Health Care scheme. The project involves providing pharmacies with counter display stands and supplies of free leaflets for customers to take away. Over 10 million leaflets have been distributed through pharmacies to the public on major health care topics including smoking, heart disease, alcohol, family planning, drug misuse, cancer and AIDS. The scheme is voluntary and pharmacies do not have to use all or any of the material they are sent. Formal evaluation of the scheme shows a very high take-up rate, with pharmacists reacting very positively to this support for their health education role. However, on-the-spot visits by the Consumers' Association found large variations in the number and type of leaflets on display. On over half their visits the researchers did not find any leaflets at all. The quality of advice varies as does access to the pharmacist and the degree of privacy available.

Using the pharmacist

There is therefore some room for improvement, particularly in the areas of privacy and access to professional advice, but you can still make good use of the pharmacist's knowledge and experience. Qualifying as a pharmacist involves a three-year degree course in pharmacy followed by a year of supervised practical experience. Since the early 1980s pharmacy training courses have included giving advice to the public, since about three-quarters of registered pharmacists practise in chemists' shops. To practise in the UK pharmacists have to register with the Pharmaceutical Society.

Almost all community pharmacists are contracted by the local Family Health Services Authority to dispense prescriptions under the NHS.

Drugs are divided into three categories:

– GENERAL SALE LIST (GSL) medicines such as paracetamol which can be sold over the counter in ordinary shops
– PHARMACY (P) medicines which can be sold only under the supervision of a pharmacist
– PRESCRIPTION ONLY MEDICINES (POM) which can be supplied only against a doctor's prescription

If you discuss your symptoms with the pharmacist he or she may be able to suggest a Pharmacy (P) medicine for your condition which you did not even know was available. The pharmacist may also be able to suggest an unbranded generic product which is an identical but cheaper alternative to a brand-name drug. It is also worth checking with the pharmacist whether a medicine prescribed by the doctor may actually be cheaper to buy over the counter. With prescription charges at over £3, a number now are.

Prescription charges

People in the following categories are exempt from prescription charges:

- children under 16 years old
- students under 19 in full-time education
- people over retirement age
- people on income support and family credit
- war pensioners
- pregnant women
- women who have had a child in the past year
- people with some specific medical conditions, including diabetes, epilepsy, stomas, myasthenia gravis, Addison's Disease and thyroid conditions

Otherwise you will have to pay £3.05 for each item on prescription. If none of the above applies to you and you need a lot of medication, you may be able to reduce prescription costs by getting a pre-payment certificate. You use this like a season ticket to pay for prescriptions.
⇒ DSS leaflet P11, available from post offices.

Patient Information on Medicines

Most homes have at least ten types of medication in the bathroom cabinet. Research by the Proprietary Association has found that most people have six to eight over-the-counter preparations (painkillers, indigestion remedies, cough and cold medicines, skin ointments, antiseptics) and at least two prescribed drugs.

Over the next few years we can expect to find increasing numbers of drug packets containing explanatory leaflets on how the medicines work, their side-effects and what to do should these develop. Most over-the-counter drugs are already sold in the manufacturer's packaging with instructions, and this should soon be the case with prescribed drugs too. Fewer and fewer pills are now dispensed in little brown bottles with illegible labels and there is a growing trend towards original pack dispensing. In part this is due to the requirements of the Consumer Protection Act 1988 which clarifies the responsibility of pharmaceutical companies for defects in their products. Ensuring that drugs are issued by pharmacists in the original packs helps to make the medicines tamper-proof, protects them from the environment, and makes them harder to counterfeit. The patient receives the drug in the condition in which it was packaged, with its batch number and expiry date (just the sort of information which is on any packaged food in the supermarket, but until recently not on many medicines). Patients also recognize their drug better if it is in a distinctive package rather than an anonymous brown bottle. And original pack dispensing should be quicker for the pharmacist, allowing him or her to spend more time in giving health education and advice.

As well as protecting the legal position of manufacturers, original pack dispensing also makes it possible for all drug packages to include information sheets for patients. In fact, from 1992, all pharmaceutical manufacturers will be obliged to provide 'patient package inserts' (PPIs). European Community Directive 89/341 makes compulsory the inclusion of a patient information leaflet in the packaging of a medicinal product, unless all the information required can be given on the outside of the pack itself. Leaflets should be in 'clear, understandable language' and give the reasons for the use of the drug, when it should not be used (contra-indications), instructions for use, possible side-effects, storage and expiry date.

Understanding drug information

This improvement in consumer information is not before time. Studies have shown an alarming public ignorance about medicines and a corresponding failure on the part of the medical profession and pharmaceutical companies to convey this vital information simply. Many of the classic phrases used on the labels of prescribed drugs are poorly understood by patients, according to work carried out by Professor Charles George in Southampton. 'Complete the prescribed course', 'Do not exceed the stated dose', and 'See a doctor if the symptoms persist' have all caused problems, particularly for patients whose reading is poor, or who are not fluent in English. Most medicines are taken by elderly people (the over-75s average twenty-four prescription items per head each year, compared with five per head for those under 65). Many elderly people find the size of print on medicine labels too small to be legible.

The Plain English Campaign has also identified many problem areas, and gives as an example the following typical label:

> A non-greasy, water-miscible cream with a marked anti-pruritic and analgesic action. The special base achieves intimate contact with moist surfaces, has a drying effect on exudative skin conditions and is particularly suitable for application to exposed surfaces.

In a 1986 survey of 9,000 Boots customers more than half did not know when or how to take their drugs, and 80 per cent had not been warned of side-effects. Ninety per cent said they wanted more information on the risks of medication.

In one experiment, 1,000 pharmacists were asked to distribute information leaflets to patients who were prescribed penicillins, anti-inflammatory drugs and beta-blockers. The vast majority of the patients welcomed the leaflets. Awareness of possible side-effects almost doubled. But, contrary to the expectations of some doctors, this did not cause patients to visit their GP with spurious or imagined complaints. In fact the leaflets seemed to reassure patients that some mild side-effects are nothing to worry about.

Patient-FASS

In Sweden it is a legal requirement for doctors to inform patients of the possible side-effects of drugs. This is part of the Swedish Health and Medical Services Act 1982 which provides that health services should be 'founded on respect for the self-determination and privacy of the patient, that care and treatment must as far as possible be designed and conducted in consultation with the patient, and that the patient must as far as possible be informed of his state of health and the treatment methods available'. Explanatory leaflets are widely available for most drugs and in addition there is a comprehensive manual of pharmaceutical information available to the public.

Patient-FASS is based on the same information that goes into the professional *FASS* (Pharmaceutical Specialties in Sweden), the official listing of all drugs registered with the Swedish National Board of Health. But *Patient-FASS* is simplified to make the information understandable to the general public, and also includes additional general chapters on Drugs and the elderly, Drugs and children, How to take medication, How drugs interact, etc. Launched in 1983, *Patient-FASS* is now published every other year. The first edition sold 375,000 copies, more than any other book in Sweden that year, including the Bible. Sales to date are over 600,000. The book is sold in Sweden in bookshops and pharmacies, and reference copies are usually to be found in libraries and doctors' waiting rooms. (*FASS* is produced by LINFO PO Box 5522, s-114 85, Stockholm, Sweden.)

In the absence of an official UK version of *Patient-FASS* there is a number of popular pharmacopoeias (directories of medicines) available from libraries and bookshops. They will give you the scientific and brand name of drugs, their uses, dose, precautions and any side-effects:

Medicines: a guide for everybody by Peter Parish, 6th edition (Harmondsworth: Penguin, 1987)

The BMA Guide to Medicines and Drugs (London: Dorling Kindersley, 1988)

Medicines: the comprehensive guide (London: Bloomsbury, 1988)

Self-Help Groups

It is not only when dealing with comparatively trivial complaints that self-care is the most important part of health care. Most people with longer-term chronic illnesses and disabilities (arthritis, diabetes, multiple sclerosis and others) are for the most part looking after themselves or are being looked after by family and friends. Dr John Fry has summed this up as follows:

> Self-care is the first true level of health care and comprises numerically the major portion of the system. There are more people caring for their own complaints than there are attending health professionals. Self-care taking place within the family context dictates to a degree the whole pattern of health care.

When living with a long-term health problem, people tend naturally to seek contact with others in the same position. When people who feel they have a common problem meet together to support and encourage each other, a self-help group is born. The boom in self-help groups has been a major phenomenon of our times. Indeed social commentator John Naisbitt has identified self-help as one of the ten most important 'megatrends' that shape our lives today. In Naisbitt's words, when there is rapid 'high-tech' innovation in society, people tend to set up counterbalancing 'high-touch' networks of human contact. The growth of self-help groups is a response to the isolation, depersonalization and breakdown of human values in industrial societies in general, and in technological medicine in particular.

An indication of the importance of the self-help phenomenon is the way in which all shades of political opinion claim it for their own. The political Right links it with the Victorian values of Samuel Smiles: hard work, personal initiative and the overcoming of problems and adversity by one's own efforts rather than by relying on the state. The Left prefers the concept of mutual aid, best expressed by the anarchist writer Prince Petr Kropotkin – ordinary people coming together to share problems and overcome them without reliance on professional hierarchies. Interestingly, Kropotkin seems to have foreseen the problems faced by information services on self-help, when he wrote at the turn of the century: 'The countless societies, clubs and alliances which have lately grown up in such numbers that it would take many years simply to tabulate them are another manifestation of the same ever-working tendency for association and mutual aid.'

How many self-help groups?

Self-help is an international movement, although there are many more groups in the USA and Northern Europe than in Southern European countries with their stronger traditional family networks. Estimates suggest that there are at least half a million self-help groups with a total of 14 million members in the USA. In West Germany the number of groups doubled from 30,000 to 60,000 in the four years between 1980 and 1984. In Flanders, over 700 self-help groups were registered at the national information centre, Trefpunt Zelfhulp, in 1985.

Within the UK there has always been a strong tradition of voluntary activity in health care. The 1978 Wolfenden Committee on the Future of Voluntary Organizations traced this activity back to eighteenth-century paternalism and patronage through charity. Voluntary organizations continued to act as major providers of health services (through voluntary hospitals, etc.) until well into the twentieth century. The advent of the National Health Service did not diminish the importance of voluntary organizations: there was just a reorientation of roles. Voluntary bodies increasingly have an emphasis on provision of specialist services to complement statutory services and there has been a growth in pressure groups and mutual aid organizations.

We tend to lump all these organizations together under the heading 'self-help groups'. In fact there are at least three generations of voluntary health care activity in the UK. Before the

Second World War almost the only organizations for people with specific handicaps were those for the blind and the deaf. Then in the 1950s a wide range of organizations was established by the parents of handicapped children (such as the Spastics Society and MENCAP). Today these are considerable charitable companies, with large budgets, staffing and premises. In turn the 1960s and 1970s saw the flowering of true self-help organizations run as mutual aid groups by people with a common problem. Many were linked with the emerging women's movement and disability rights campaigns. Today there are many community health groups, which instead of focusing on a particular illness or disability, bring together people in their own community to tackle some of the social and environmental problems which might be detrimental to health. Community health projects, such as the Waterloo Health Project and the Albany Health Project in London, or the Whiteway Health Project in Bath, have tended to concentrate on issues such as the take-up of welfare benefits, safe play spaces for children and support for isolated mothers.

It is almost impossible to give an accurate figure of how many self-help groups and similar voluntary organizations there are in the UK. In 1983 Penny Webb identified over 2,000 groups in London.

The most comprehensive register of self-help groups in the UK is the database that we maintain at the Help for Health information centre at Southampton General Hospital (see page 27). Here there are details of over 1,000 national organizations and 2,000 local groups within the Wessex region of 3 million people. In a city the size of Southampton (250,000 population) you would expect to find at least 250 organizations, so in the whole of the UK there could be as many as 50,000 groups ranging from major national bodies down to small contact groups for rare handicaps which might have half a dozen members.

What do self-help groups do?

The classic definition of a self-help group is that provided by the American sociologists Katz and Bender:

> Self-help groups are voluntary, small group structures for mutual aid and the accomplishment of a special purpose. They are usually formed by peers who have come together for mutual assistance in satisfying a common need, overcoming a common handicap or life disrupting problem and bringing about desired social or personal change.

But what could you expect if you contacted a self-help group or went along to a meeting? People go to self-help groups:

– to meet fellow sufferers and to get and give support
– to get information on the condition the group is based on
– to get ideas on how to cope and where to get help elsewhere
– to have time to talk

In terms of practical activities, a study of cancer self-help groups published in the *British Medical Journal* showed that all groups undertook some of the following:

– GROUP MEETINGS that are open to anyone who comes along, sometimes with a speaker
– SMALLER DISCUSSION GROUPS that enable people to talk more intimately about things which concern them
– A TELEPHONE LINE manned by volunteers or by the person in whose home it is. For some people this will be their sole contact with the group
– HOME OR HOSPITAL VISITING carried out by volunteers from the group
– PRACTICAL HELP such as transport, help with shopping, collecting prescriptions, etc.

Finding a self-help group

With so many self-help groups around it is likely that somewhere there will be one for your problem. But the fact that there are so many, and that new ones spring up and old ones die away every year, can make it very difficult to find the right group at the right time.

DIRECTORIES There are several useful directories of national organizations which you should find in public reference libraries:

The Health Directory (London: Bedford Square Press, 1990)
Voluntary Agencies (London: National Council for Voluntary Organizations, 1989)
The Self-help Guide: a directory of self-help organizations in the UK (London: Chapman and Hall, 1988)
People Who Help (London: Profile Productions, 1990)
Directory of British Associations (CBD Research, 1990)

Remember that self-help group contacts change very rapidly and so the best directories are updated annually. Of the above, *The Health Directory* is probably the best buy. You may find directories of local organizations produced by your library, Community Health Council, Council for Voluntary Service or health promotion department. The Self-help Resources section at the end of this book gives details of self-help groups for the major health problems.

SELF-HELP DATABASES The most comprehensive computer database of self-help groups is HELPBOX, the information system developed by Help for Health (Grant Building, Southampton General Hospital, Southampton SO9 4XY Tel: 0703 779091). The database contains details of 1,000 national groups, 2,000 local groups in Hampshire, Wiltshire, Dorset and the Isle of Wight, 2,000 self-help books and 1,500 self-help leaflets. The database is designed to run on any personal computer with hard disk storage and is used not only at Help for Health but also at the National

Self-help Support Centre and many of the new health information centres which are springing up around the UK (pages 292–7).

LOCAL INFORMATION CENTRES In many local areas there are SELF-HELP SUPPORT CENTRES or CLEARING HOUSES. These centres provide practical services such as meeting rooms, typing, printing facilities; they can help with training and getting new groups off the ground; and they act as a good source of information on local groups.

In most cases these support centres form part of a local COUNCIL FOR VOLUNTARY SERVICE (CVS). You should find these in most towns and there are usually countywide umbrella bodies for voluntary activity too. Your public library will be able to give you the addresses as well as details of individual local groups.

The best example of the self-help support centre is the SELF-HELP TEAM in Nottingham (20 Pelham Road, Sherwood Rise, Nottingham NG5 1AP Tel: 0602 691212). The Self-Help Team have gained international renown for their work in supporting existing self-help groups in Nottingham and helping to get new groups going. Their publications are well worth getting hold of: the information pack *Starting Off* is invaluable for anyone thinking of starting a self-help group, not only for those in Nottingham. There are also booklets on using local radio, giving talks to professional workers and guidelines for good listening. Team leader Judy Wilson's practical guide to self-help, *Self-Help Groups: getting started, keeping going*, was published by Longman in 1986.

NATIONAL AND INTERNATIONAL INFORMATION CENTRES

THE NATIONAL SELF-HELP SUPPORT CENTRE 26 Bedford Square, London WC1B 3HU Tel: 071-636 4066, was set up in 1986 with a brief to support the work of local centres and increase awareness of self-help at a national level. The Centre has produced a directory of local self-help support projects and publishes a quarterly newsletter called *MASH: Mutual Aid and Self Help*.

For information on community health projects, there is the NATIONAL COMMUNITY HEALTH RESOURCE 15 Britannia Street, London WC1X 9JP Tel: 071-837 2426.

For information on self-help groups for rare handicaps and syndromes, contact:

IN TOUCH TRUST 10 Norman Road, Sale, Cheshire M33 3DF Tel: 061 905 2440. This remarkable organization is run from the home of the founder, Ann Worthington, and in particular links up the parents of children with rare mental handicap and chromosome abnormalities. Even if there is no group available, it is often possible to link up individual parents.

CONTACT A FAMILY 16 Strutton Ground, London SW1P 2HP Tel: 071-222 2695. This support organization links up families of children with all sorts of disabilities through local self-help groups. CAF also runs the CONTACTLINE telephone information service on 071-222 2211.

For information on the self-help scene worldwide (but particularly in Europe) contact the INTERNATIONAL INFORMATION CENTRE ON SELF-HELP AND HEALTH E. van Evenstraat 2 C, B-3000, Leuven, Belgium. This World Health Organization centre promotes and publishes research, links up projects in different countries, holds workshops and publishes a newsletter.

2 General Practice and Family Health Services

The family doctor or general practitioner (GP) occupies a key position in health care. Most everyday diagnosis and treatment is carried out by the GP. If your condition needs the attention of a specialist it is the GP who must make a referral for NHS treatment. The GP can also act as a way in to the network of community care services described in Section 3. And the role of the GP in screening and health promotion is receiving increased emphasis in the changing health service. The GP is the central member of the primary care team, a team of professionals from various health disciplines who work from a GP surgery or health centre. Other members of the team include the district nurse, health visitor, practice nurse, community psychiatric nurse, chiropodist, therapists and social worker. Their role is described later in this section, as are the services provided by dentists and opticians. Dentists and opticians, like GPs, are independent self-employed practitioners who can have a contract with the Family Health Services Authority to provide services within the NHS.

The role of the GP differs from one practice to another. GPs are variously seen as counsellor, technician, father-figure, pill-dispenser, adviser and a host of other things. Our expectations of our doctors don't always coincide with their own view of themselves and their role in society. The aim of this section is to help you to get the most out of your GP and the family health service. You can only do this if you have the right information, and GPs are now encouraged to provide this on a much wider basis.

The Organization of the National Health Service

To most people the NHS is a complex and bewildering institution. But if you are going to make the best use of it, you need to know something about its overall organization.

In England the NHS is divided into fourteen Regional Health Authorities. Wales constitutes a single Region, with nine District Health Authorities (see below). In Scotland there are fifteen Health Boards and in Northern Ireland four Health Boards. The areas covered by each are shown on the map (right). These regions are responsible for the strategic management of the NHS.

Each Region contains a number of District Health Authorities (DHAs), 190 in all. These operate the hospitals and are in general control of the day-to-day running of the health service.

Your GP is independent and self-employed. But GPs are contracted to their Family Health Services Authority.

Right Map of the National Health Service Regions. The UK is divided into Regional Health Authorities for the management of NHS services. There are fourteen English Regions, plus Scotland, Wales and Northern Ireland. The Regions are further divided into District Health Authorities (in England and Wales) or Health Boards (in Scotland and Northern Ireland)

1 Northern RHA
2 Yorkshire RHA
3 Trent RHA
4 East Anglian RHA
5 North West Thames RHA
6 North East Thames RHA
7 South East Thames RHA
8 South West Thames RHA
9 Wessex RHA
10 Oxford RHA
11 South Western RHA
12 West Midlands RHA
13 Mersey RHA
14 North Western RHA
15 Wales
16 Scotland
17 Northern Ireland

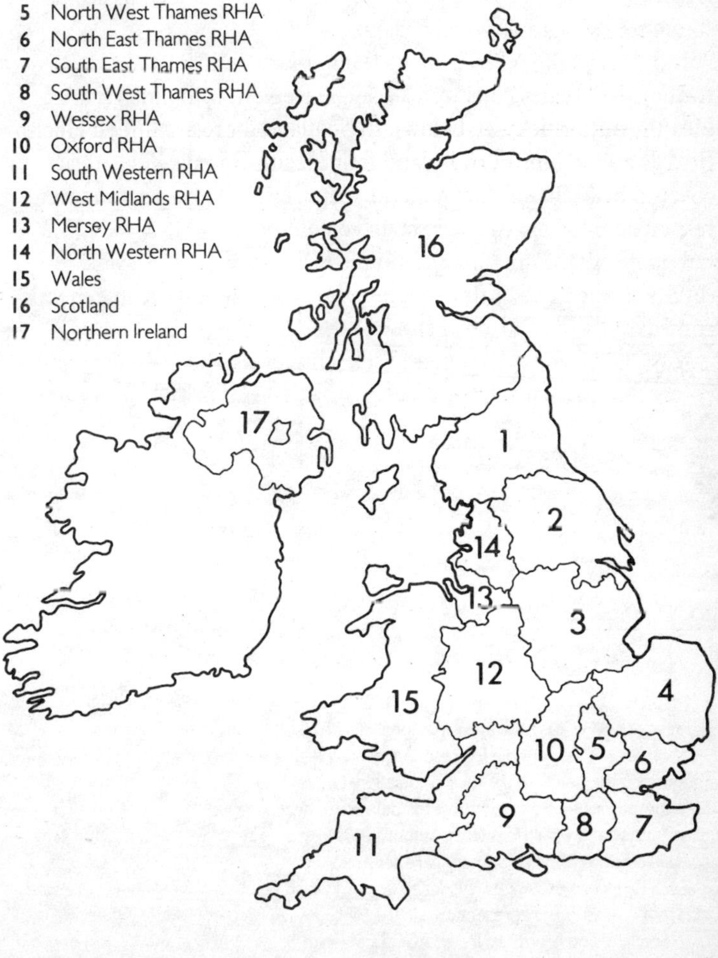

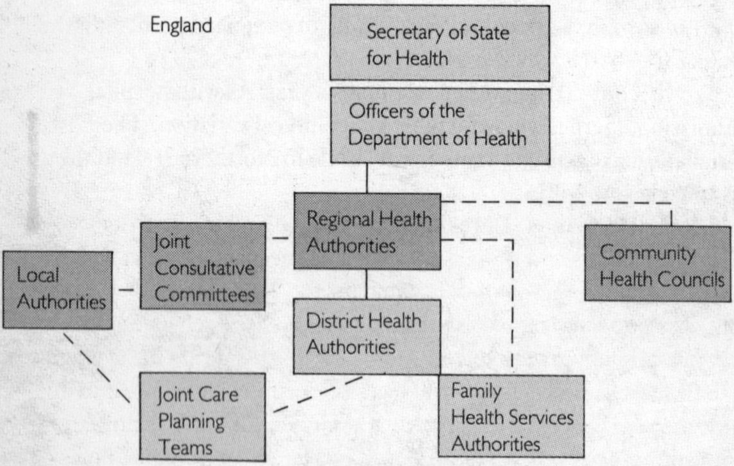

The tiers of NHS administration. Regional Health Authorities are responsible for resource allocation and monitoring the health of the local population. District Health Authorities are responsible for delivery of health care, with Family Health Services Authorities having a specific responsibility for primary care services.

Each DHA has a Community Health Council which acts as the consumer representative in the NHS.

In Scotland and Northern Ireland, District Health Authorities are called Health Boards, and Community Health Councils are called Local Health Councils.

Who Goes to See the GP?

There are just over 30,000 GPs in the UK, with an average list of 2,000 patients each. The number of GPs is increasing (in 1970 there were only 24,000) and the number of patients per doctor is falling (in 1970 it was 2,400).

We visit our GP on average 4.4 times a year. As with hospital admission, there is a considerable geographical variation. The East Anglians make only 3.1 visits a year, while in Northern Ireland the average is 5.3.

Most visits to the GP are for short-term complaints such as throat infections and skin disorders. These are usually dealt with by a prescription for antibiotics, ointments, etc. Each year GPs write out over 400 million prescriptions, an average for each patient of 7.5 prescriptions a year (*Social Trends*, HMSO, 1990). The average GP (if there is such a thing) will have 100 people consulting him in any one year for high blood pressure, another 100 for arthritis, 30 for asthma, 20 for diabetes, and over 450 for chronic mental illness. Between 4 and 5 million people a year consult their GP because of conditions such as anxiety and depression. Two hundred and fifty people out of 1,000 will experience symptoms of mental illness at any one time. Of these 230 will consult their GP and 140 will be prescribed psychotropic drugs. Only a small number (6 out of 250) will need to be admitted to a psychiatric hospital. GPs are also seeing many patients with long-term term or 'chronic' disorders. In the 1978 *General Household Survey* over half the men and nearly three-quarters of the women interviewed reported that they had a health problem all the time or one that kept recurring.

What Patients Want from Their GP

It seems that the main reasons that patients visit their GP are first, because the GP is the gatekeeper to treatment (prescription drugs, referral to specialists, etc.), and second, because they are seeking reassurance. A survey on what patients want from their doctor, carried out by London GP Dr David Ryde, had the following findings:

What patients want from their GP

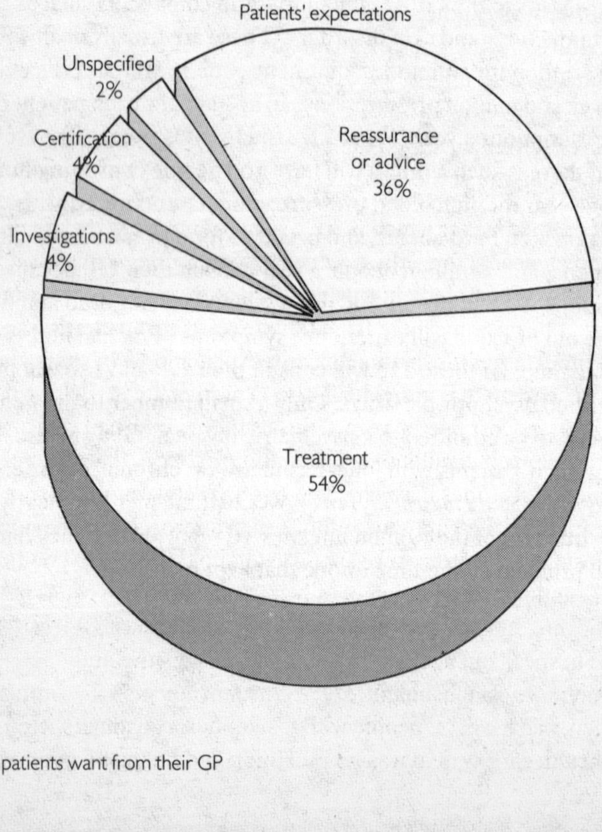

What patients want from their GP

In 1989 the Consumers' Association carried out a survey of patients to find out what improvements they wanted from their GP. The results were published in *Which?*, October 1989. The improvements patients wanted are shown below.

	%
More time explaining about illness	91
More time listening to patients	89
Free health check-ups	89
More information about hospitals/specialists	84
More time explaining about drugs	82
A more helpful receptionist	80
Shorter waits at the surgery	79
A choice of which hospital to go to	77
A nurse at the surgery	71
More home visits	71
More convenient surgery hours	69
Minor surgery at the practice	68

Other options, for which there was less support, were advice about diet; access to medical records; nicer waiting areas; availability of complementary therapies; and always seeing your own doctor. The clear message from this survey is that patients want more time, more information, clearer explanations. In short, they want to be treated as individuals and to participate in their own health care. Most people regard this as more important than improvements in facilities such as waiting areas.

Patients' attitudes have changed enormously over the past generation. In the 1950s an authoritarian approach was the norm for most GPs. Doctors were supposed to hold the key to good health, and patients were generally treated, and behaved, as passive supplicants. In the 1960s sections of the middle class, at least, began to speak out against the seemingly insensitive and impenetrable establishment, and rights movements were born (women, blacks, gays, people with disabilities, consumers, etc.). The health care system was no exception and has come in for a good deal of criticism. Although most of the criticism has been aimed at impersonal hospital systems, primary care has not escaped unscathed. A Consumers' Association survey in 1989 found that only 38 per cent of patients felt 'very confident' that their GP knew what was wrong with them.

The new medical *perestroika* is certainly helping to erode professional mystiques and barriers. But interestingly some commentators are now arguing that a certain mystique is an important part of the healing process. The power of the doctor as a therapeutic agent in his or her own right is reflected in placebo studies, where patients given a dummy drug often make good recoveries just because the medicine is prescribed by the doctor. Today many middle-class patients, in particular, are demanding a greater openness and acceptance of professional limitations on the part of GPs. Ironically it may be the very same patients who are turning to complementary practitioners for the charismatic, 'witch doctor' quality which they miss in their own family doctor.

Promoting Better Health

At the end of 1987 the British government published its programme for improving primary health care under the title *Promoting Better Health.* This White Paper (Cm 249) and the connected legislation, the Health and Medicines Act 1988 and the NHS and Community Care Act 1990, have as key objectives:

– to make services more responsive to the consumer
– to give patients the widest range of choices in obtaining high-quality primary care services
– to promote health and prevent illness
– to improve value for money
– to raise standards of care
– to enable clear priorities to be set for family practitioner services

It is not surprising to find *Promoting Better Health* aiming to raise standards – any proposals for reform would hope for that. What is more interesting is the quite explicit commitment to a consumer-orientated service, and the assumption that this can be achieved by increased competition.

> The Government believes that no opportunity should be lost to increase fair and open competition between those providing family practitioner services. To that end consumers should have ready access to much more information about the services provided, and the remuneration of practitioners should be more directly linked than at present to the level of their performance.

But what does this mean in practice?

Information for patients

Family Health Services Authorities (FHSAs) are now obliged to provide more comprehensive information about local GP practices. LISTS OF GPS specifying the doctor's sex, qualifications and year of qualifying, as well as details of surgery opening hours, services provided and arrangements for emergencies, are compiled by the FHSAs and made available to the public in places like public libraries.

Practices are now producing their own PRACTICE LEAFLETS giving details of the practice staff and services provided. At the moment doctors are not allowed to advertise. The government is discussing with the General Medical Council ways of removing this restraint, to give patients more information.

To enable patients to make use of this information, it is becoming easier to CHANGE GP. Patients no longer have to approach their existing GP and the FHSA before registering with a new doctor.

Screening and health promotion

The declared aim of the government changes in primary care is to give prevention of illness and health promotion a new emphasis. It seems that patients want this too. According to a survey published in the *British Medical Journal* (1984) most patients think GPs should be interested in health promotion, but most think their own GP is not.

The new GP contracts introduced in April 1990 give doctors a special fee for giving an initial HEALTH CHECK-UP to patients

Payment to GPs for achieving targets

There are two levels with the upper level of achievement giving the GP three times the payment of the lower.
Cervical cytology:
Higher payment 80% uptake
Lower payment 50% uptake
Childhood immunizations:
Higher payment 90% uptake
Lower payment 70% uptake

registering for the first time with an NHS doctor (this does not include children under 5). GPs can also claim a fee for advertised HEALTH PROMOTION CLINICS (such as for giving up smoking, alcohol reduction or stress management) as well as clinics for chronic health problems (such as diabetes, asthma or hypertension).

The old system of service fees for CHILDHOOD IMMUNIZATIONS and CERVICAL SMEARS is being replaced by payments for achieving targets.

GPs have expressed concern about the ethics of a system which pressurizes doctors to undertake procedures (for example, whether to vaccinate a child) when there may be clinical doubts. In addition, GPs in areas with a very mobile population fear that they will have difficulties in meeting these targets.

Choosing Your GP

Finding the right GP

Everybody has a right to a GP, and most people at some stage need to choose a new one (see 'Changing your GP', page 48). New legislation is designed to give more choice, but many people do not have a real choice and most others do not exercise theirs.

Except in an emergency, you need to be registered with a GP before you can receive treatment, so it is important to register with one as soon as you can. Here's where to look for information about GPs in your area.

– Check the FAMILY HEALTH SERVICES AUTHORITY (FHSA) MEDICAL LIST. All NHS GPs are registered with the local Family Health Services Authority. The FHSA produces a list of all the GPs in its area, and you can look at this at the FHSA offices (in the phone book under Family Health Services Authority or Family Practitioner Services). Libraries, Citizens' Advice Bureaux, Community Health Councils and main post offices should also have copies. Under the new NHS legislation, FHSAs are obliged to provide more detailed information in these lists (see pages 41–2). For example, it might be important for you to know about women GPs in the practice, whether family planning services or maternity care are provided, and whether there is an appointment system.
– More detailed DIRECTORIES OF GP SERVICES are sometimes produced by local consumer groups and similar bodies. A good example is *Avon Health*, a telephone directory-sized publication giving details of all health care services in the county of Avon (available from Blue Sax Publishing, 122 Howard Road, Westbury Park, Bristol BS6 7XA). The compilers sent a questionnaire to all local GPs and have used them to put together a parish-by-parish guide to GPs. The doctors give information not only about hours, clinics, etc. but also about complementary therapies, counselling, patient participation groups, and so on. In some parts of the

country, groups campaigning on specific issues have carried out surveys to identify GPs sympathetic to their approach. For example, some branches of AIMS (Association for Improvement in the Maternity Services) have produced directories of GPs sympathetic to home births (see page 182).

– Public reference libraries should have a copy of the *Medical Directory*. This lists the qualifications, research interests and articles published by most doctors in the UK. So it can be useful if you want a GP with a special area of interest or experience. You can also use it to get an idea of a GP's age, as date of qualification is given. The *Directory* is in alphabetical order by doctor's name. There is no index by place or by medical specialty, so you will have to find the names of local GPs in the FHSA list first, and then use the *Medical Directory* to give you a more detailed picture.

– All GP practices now produce PRACTICE LEAFLETS, giving details of the doctors, hours, clinics, etc. Visit a few local surgeries and pick up a brochure so that you can make comparisons.

What to look for

THE TYPE OF PRACTICE

– SINGLE-HANDED GPS: these are usually found in rural areas (or alternatively in inner-city areas) where the catchment area is not big enough to warrant a group practice or other doctors are not attracted to the area. Single-handed practices are unlikely to offer a wide range of services.

– GROUP PRACTICES: typically these range from two to six partners, working together as a small business. If your own GP is unavailable you can usually see one of the other partners.

– HEALTH CENTRES: these house one or more group practices in premises owned by the health authority. They generally provide a wider range of services, such as health visiting, chiropody, dental care. The centres may be more modern buildings with facilities for minor surgery on the premises.

APPOINTMENT SYSTEMS Ideally the practice should operate an appointments system, by which you can telephone the receptionist and arrange a specific time to see your doctor. Even with an appointments system you will probably still have to wait in the surgery. Appointments may be five minutes apart, and of course some consultations last longer than the allocated time. However, in some special circumstances, if you are waiting with a child, for example, the GP may fit you in before your place in the queue.

An alternative system is the OPEN SURGERY where patients simply turn up and wait to be seen. This can be useful if you have not been able to make an appointment in time. However, surveys have shown that people wait longer to see the doctor in open surgeries than those with appointment systems. Many practices operate both systems with, for example, appointments in the morning and open surgery in the evenings.

People sometimes complain that they cannot get an appointment when they need one. If your problem is not urgent you cannot demand that the GP sees you the same day. If your health would be threatened by waiting a day or more, you can insist that the receptionist explains the situation to the doctor. It is then up to the doctor whether to see you that day or make a later appointment. At a group practice you can often get an appointment sooner if you are willing to see one of the other doctors, rather than your own GP.

HOME VISITS Whenever possible you should go to the surgery to see your doctor. If you feel you cannot go to the surgery, telephone and ask for a home visit. If possible phone before 10 am so that the doctor can plan his or her visits. Explain the symptoms as fully as you can, and the doctor will decide whether a home visit is justified. Home visits are made between morning and evening surgery. The GP is not obliged to visit you at home. According to their terms of service, GPs must visit patients at home 'if the condition of the patient so requires'. It is up to the GP to make this assessment, although failing to visit when necessary could be a breach of the terms of service, or negligence.

OUT-OF-HOURS VISITS are home visits made in the evening or at weekends. A GP must ensure that there is medical cover available during these hours, but obviously cannot be on call all day every day. There are two ways in which out-of-hours cover may be provided:

– ROTA SYSTEMS whereby partners or doctors from neighbouring practices take it in turns to accept out-of-hours calls.
– DEPUTIZING SERVICES whereby the GP employs a commercial organization (such as Air Call) to deal with out-of-hours calls, using deputizing doctors. Most services insist on some general practice experience from the doctors used.

When choosing your GP you may wish to check whether you are likely to see one of the partners on an out-of-hours call, or a deputizing doctor.

Doctors may also use LOCUMS (for example, to cover for sickness). Locums are not employed by the GP in the same way as a hospital doctor is employed by the health authority, but the GP's responsibility to provide a competent standard of health care extends to the locum. If the treatment you receive from a locum is not up to standard, it is your GP who is in breach of his or her duty of care.

Registering with a GP

In order to receive care from a GP when you want it (rather than in an emergency) you must register and have your name on the GP's list. Take your medical card which shows your NHS number along to the practice you have chosen and tell the receptionist you wish to register. If you have lost your card contact your Family Health Services Authority for a new one. Some practices have pre-registration interviews, to give you a chance to meet the doctor before deciding whether to register. The GP is not obliged to take you as a patient, although he or she is unlikely to refuse unless the list is full. When you have registered the FHSA will send you a new medical card, and your medical records will be sent on to your new GP. Children under 16 need to be registered by their parents. Just as you can be registered with a different GP to your spouse, so you can register your children with a different GP to your own. However, it may be easier for a doctor to understand and treat a problem if he or she knows the whole family.

If you are going to be in the area for less than three months (while on holiday or temporary business for example) you can ask a GP to accept you as a TEMPORARY RESIDENT. You remain on the list of your own GP but can be treated by the temporary GP should the need arise.

If you cannot find a GP willing to accept you, contact the FHSA. They will probably give you a list of GPs to try and ask you to contact at least three yourself. If you still cannot get accepted the FHSA will allocate you to a GP. The GP is obliged to accept you – at least on a temporary basis.

Changing your GP

Most people get a new GP because they have moved house or because the old GP has moved, retired or died. A small proportion change because they are dissatisfied with the doctor. You can change GP without giving a reason, although the new GP is likely to ask why you no longer wish to be with your present doctor. At present there are two ways of changing:

– Find a new GP willing to take you on, then go along to your present GP and tell him or her you wish to change. Ask him or her to sign your medical card, and then take it to the new doctor to sign. You are then registered with the new doctor immediately.
– If you do not want to ask your present GP yourself, you can write to the FHSA saying you wish to change and enclosing your medical card. The FHSA will return the card with a slip attached giving you permission to approach a new GP. In the interval between applying to the FHSA and being placed on the new doctor's list your present GP is still responsible for your treatment.

The government is now introducing a system to make it easier to change GP. Under the new system you can go straight to a new GP and ask to be taken on, without having to take leave of your old GP first.

Do you have a real choice?

In reality most people are not very methodical when it comes to choosing their family doctor. The NHS White Papers *Promoting Better Health* and *Working for Patients* assume that patients choose GPs on the basis of the service they provide, and that increased competition will raise standards. But a survey of people who had recently registered with a GP in Reading, published in the *British Medical Journal* in 1989, showed a marked lack of 'consumerist' behaviour: 44 per cent of patients simply registered with the practice nearest to home; 23 per cent had the practice recommended by friends and colleagues; 16 per cent had other people in the family already registered there. Only 4 per cent of people said they had made a comparison between practices in order to decide which was best for them.

In order for market mechanisms to work, consumers need not only to have information but also to possess the motivation to exercise choice, a range of alternatives from which to choose, the competence to make a rational choice, and the opportunity to implement their choice once it has been made. In fact most people are not particularly motivated to exercise choice. Their need for GP care is spasmodic and minimal, and they do not spend much time in seeking alternatives. For those with a chronic condition requiring more regular contact with the doctor, familiarity and trust is a powerful motivation to stay put. Although there are 30,000 GPs in UK the range of choice is really quite limited. Most people only have access to half a dozen or so rather similar practices in the area where they live. In rural areas there may be only one. For their part GPs may be unwilling to accept further patients because of limits on list size or geographical boundaries of the practice.

Although consumers are perfectly competent to make choices on issues like surgery hours, appointment systems, etc. a real consumer choice would also be based on an assessment of clinical competence and quality of care. Patients are unlikely to have the information to make choices of this kind, and even if they did, not many would feel able to exercise the choice. And finally, the need to register with a GP is an obstacle to totally free choice. Unlike consumers of other goods and services, patients are unable to sample alternatives for a while or use a different supplier when they think it is appropriate. Most people choose the doctor nearest home, register, and stay with them for as long as they remain in the area. GPs are usually only willing to cover a defined geographical area. If you move outside this area, you will have to register with a new GP.

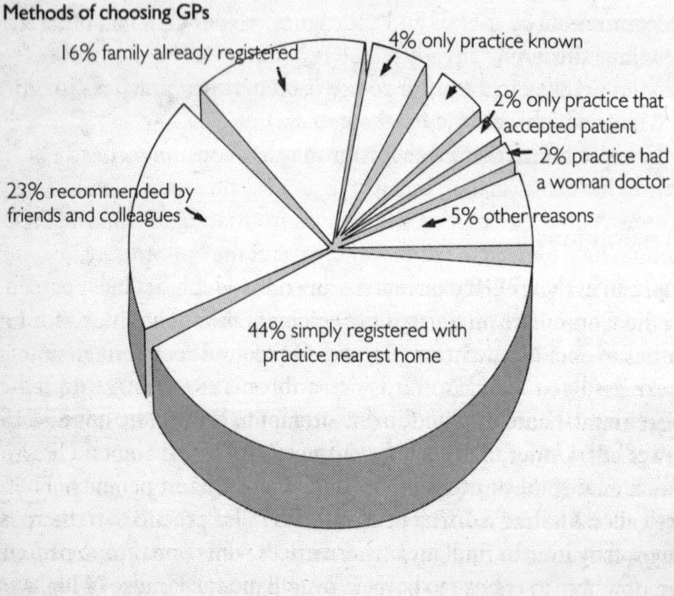

The methods adopted for choosing a GP

Using Your GP

Most people visit their GP for diagnosis and treatment of ill health. Apart from diagnosis and treatment, services offered by a GP can vary widely from practice to practice. The changes in the NHS aim to encourage GPs to run more clinics and preventive medicine sessions, to remunerate them for doing so, and to provide their patients with information about what is available. Typically your GP might offer:

Prescriptions
Health check-ups
Cervical smears
Health promotion clinics
Contraception
Immunization
Minor surgery
Medical examinations for seat belt exemptions, etc.
Maternity services (see pages 176–84)
Complementary therapies (see pages 215–16)

Prescriptions

You can ask your GP to prescribe any drug which has been passed by the Committee on Safety of Medicines, although it is up to him or her to decide whether its use would be of value. In recent years there has been a trend towards prescribing GENERIC DRUGS rather than brand-name products, in an attempt to reduce the huge NHS drugs bill. Under the new GP contracts, all GPs will be told how much money they can spend on medicines for their patients. These are called 'indicative' drug budgets: if GPs overspend then there is an investigation to find out why. Practices with over 11,000 patients are now able to choose to have an overall practice budget with which to buy treatment for their patients. The budget will have to pay for non-emergency operations, diagnostic tests and drugs. Whether your GP is in a FUND-HOLDING PRACTICE or whether he is governed by an indicative drug budget, he will certainly think more carefully about unnecessary prescribing. GPs will be less likely to prescribe palliative medicines – like cough, cold and indigestion remedies – and you may find you have to buy them over the counter at the chemist (see 'Using the pharmacist', page 17).

A reduction in unnecessary prescribing, which is costly and can even harm patients (see page 212) should be a positive aspect of GP drug budgets. A less welcome effect could be that patients needing expensive medication may find it harder to get a GP to take them on. The average cost of prescribed drugs per person in 1989 was £39. But the medication for a patient with hypertension costs on average £80 a year, and for arthritis £110 a year (*Which?*, October 1989). The potential impact on a GP's drug budget of taking on a patient with HIV infection or AIDS would be considerable. The cost of zidovudine treatment alone is more than £5,000 per patient per year. And on top of this could be the costs of other treatments for AIDS symptoms, which are increasingly being required in general practice. The BMA Foundation for AIDS, amongst others, has expressed concern that taking on a patient with AIDS could involve the GP in wrangles with the FHSA and local hospitals over the responsibility for prescribing and for meeting the high treatment costs (see Section 5).

A recent report has suggested that black and Asian families may not be receiving their share of prescriptions from family doctors because they do not always register with a doctor and tend to be less ready to visit the doctor when ill. As a general rule deprived areas, especially those in the North, have a higher expenditure on drugs. According to official data for 1988/9 Salford Family Health Services Authority has the highest annual spending figure on medicines at £49.80 for each registered patient. This figure is 50 per cent higher than the lowest spender, Oxford, with £33.10 a head. However, two of the most deprived areas in the UK (Lambeth, Southwark and Lewisham; and Camden and Islington) spent respectively £35.30 and £35.70, well below the national average of £39. The report suggests that this is because ethnic minority families in these areas are getting fewer prescriptions. The study also shows that NHS expenditure on drugs has risen from £20 million in 1950 (5 per cent of total NHS resources) to £3 billion today (more than 10 per cent of resources).

GPs can only prescribe a limited amount of a drug at any one time, and many drugs have only a limited shelf life. So if your treatment is continuous you will need to get REPEAT PRESCRIPTIONS from your doctor. Your GP will probably be able to give you a repeat prescription card naming the drugs you have on repeat prescription. You can then leave this with the receptionist for signing by your doctor without needing to make an appointment to see him or her. Remember that this will take a day or so, so do not leave it until you are down to your last pill to ask for a repeat prescription. Most GPs have a limit on the number of repeat prescriptions they will issue. Your GP may ask you to make an appointment to see him or her after about six months.

Check-ups and screening

The new GP contracts say that all NEWLY REGISTERED PATIENTS must be given a written invitation to attend for a check-up within twenty-eight days of their acceptance on the list. The doctor must record and carry out:

MEDICAL HISTORY

– Illnesses, immunizations, allergies, hereditary problems, medication, tests carried out in the past
– Social factors, including employment, housing and family
– Lifestyle, including smoking, diet, exercise, alcohol, use of drugs

PHYSICAL EXAMINATION

– Blood pressure, height, weight and urine sample

Similar check-ups (THREE-YEAR CHECKS) must now be offered to all patients between the ages of 16 and 75 who have not been seen in the surgery within the previous three years. These checks also give the GP the opportunity to see whether patients have had immunizations and smears.

Both sorts of check need not necessarily be carried out by the GP. In some practices, the practice nurse will do the job. If the patient is unable to come to the surgery because of a physical condition the health check is made in the patient's home.

Beyond these GP check-ups, the type of screening available varies from one part of the country to another. The Department of Health recommends that all women between 20 and 60 should have a CERVICAL SMEAR TEST every five years. Some health authorities recall women for cervical smears every three years; in others it is five. In many parts of the country there are mobile BREAST SCREENING UNITS which allow women to have their breasts checked by mammography. WELL WOMAN CLINICS (and occasionally well man clinics) also provide the opportunity for people to have free health 'MOTs'. You can find out about the availability of screening locally from your Community Health Council. Other check-ups are only available on the NHS if your GP thinks they are warranted. An examination for an employer or for insurance purposes is not covered by the NHS – you or the company will have to pay.

PRIVATE MEDICAL COMPANIES, such as British United Provident Association (BUPA) and Private Patients Plan (PPP), have their own screening clinics. These offer a more extensive check-up than is usually available on the NHS, but unless you are covered by an insurance scheme or through your work, you will have to pay (about £200 for a full health screen). Independent screening clinics are listed in *The Directory of Private Hospitals and Health Services*, published regularly by Longman and available in medical libraries and larger public reference libraries.

The new GP contract also means that ALL PATIENTS OVER 75 must have an annual health check in their own home. This consultation should include an assessment of their mobility, continence, mental and physical condition and social environment. These visits can be undertaken by practice nurses.

Contraception

Around two-thirds of the 4.5 million people who contact the NHS for contraception visit their GP. One-third go to family planning clinics. As some health authorities are cutting back on their family planning clinics and encouraging women to go to their GP, the number of patients consulting their GP for family planning is likely to rise. If you want to use your GP for family planning, make sure he or she is on the Contraceptive Service List. The FHSA lists give this information, and most GPs do have this qualification. The advantage of going to your GP is that he or she knows your whole medical history. You can also get advice during an ordinary surgery; no one in the waiting room knows why you are there.

Some women prefer to go to a FAMILY PLANNING CLINIC. Although family planning clinics are also available to men, in reality men seem reluctant to visit clinics on their own, and not very frequently with their partner. In most cases contraception remains the responsibility of women. Clinics have more specialized experience and there is a greater chance of seeing a woman doctor if required. Family planning clinics also have the advantage of providing condoms, which GPs do not do. Many clinics also provide youth advisory sessions, 'morning after' contraception, sterilization/vasectomy counselling and operations, cervical smears and breast checks. Some also offer pregnancy testing, abortion advice and referral, sub-fertility advice, psychosexual counselling, and well-woman services. You can find out your nearest clinic from your GP (although you don't need a referral, and you can approach a family planning clinic direct without going to your GP), from the phone book (under Family Planning), from your local Community Health Council, library or Citizens' Advice Bureau. The FAMILY PLANNING INFORMATION SERVICE 27–35 Mortimer Street,

London WIN 7RJ Tel: 071-636 7866 has a list of every family planning clinic in the UK, and also publishes a range of leaflets on different methods of contraception.

Abortion

Although some doctors are opposed to abortion and many women may feel reluctant to approach their GP, it is still worth contacting your own GP as the first step if you become pregnant and feel you would like an abortion. If you go to your doctor (or to a family planning clinic) within seventy-two hours of possible conception you could ask for a 'morning after' pill. If your GP is sympathetic to your wish for an abortion he or she should be able to:

– give counselling, provide information on the alternatives, and help you to make up your mind and come to terms with your decision
– sign the necessary form saying that you fall within the terms of the Abortion Act
– make you an appointment at the hospital. If you will be more than ten weeks pregnant by the time you go to hospital you should consider 'going private'. The legal limit for abortions is now twenty-four weeks, but the earlier you can have the termination the better.

Half the women seeking abortions end up going outside the NHS. Nursing homes and clinics carrying out abortions must be licensed by the Department of Health. You can find licensed clinics under Pregnancy in the Yellow Pages. Otherwise contact the head offices of the two main abortion charities:

– BRITISH PREGNANCY ADVISORY SERVICE Austy Manor, Wootton Wawen, Solihull, West Midlands B95 6BX
Tel: 05642 3225
– PREGNANCY ADVISORY SERVICE 11–13 Charlotte Street, London WIP 1HD Tel: 071-637 8962
– BROOK ADVISORY CENTRES offer help and advice to young people on personal problems, contraception, etc. They also make

referrals for abortions, wherever possible to NHS hospitals. Most centres are in London but they are also in Birmingham, Bristol, Coventry and Edinburgh. Details from Brook Advisory Centre, 233 Tottenham Court Road, London W1P 9AE Tel: 071-323 1522.

– WOMEN'S HEALTH AND REPRODUCTIVE RIGHTS INFORMATION CENTRE (WHRRIC) should be able to advise you on NHS abortion facilities in your area. Contact WHRRIC 52–4 Featherstone Street, London EC1Y 8RT Tel: 071-251 6332.

The New Our Bodies, Ourselves, edited by Angela Phillips and Jill Rakusen (Harmondsworth: Penguin, 1989) has a comprehensive section on how to get an abortion, techniques used, etc. Also recommended is *The Fertility and Contraception Book* by Julia Mosse and Josephine Heaton (London: Faber and Faber, 1990).

Immunization

Your child can be vaccinated under the NHS against a number of potentially serious infectious diseases.

There is a very small risk that a child may suffer a reaction to a vaccination which could lead to permanent injury. The most publicized risk is brain damage following whooping cough vaccination. Studies have suggested that there is a chance of about one in 100,000 that a full three-course dose of whooping cough vaccine might cause brain damage. Against this must be balanced the fact that whooping cough itself can be an extremely unpleasant and life-threatening illness in young children. Between 1976 and 1983 at least fifty-nine children died from whooping cough in England and Wales. Advice is given to GPs by the Department of Health on when they should not vaccinate for whooping cough. The vaccine should never be given to children in the following categories:

- when they have a fever
- if they have had a severe reaction to the first or second dose
- if they are subject to fits or convulsions

Vaccination timetable recommended by the Department of Health

3 months	Triple vaccine (diphtheria, tetanus and whooping cough) Polio (by mouth)
4½–5 months	Triple vaccine (second dose) Polio (second dose)
8½–11 months	Triple vaccine (third dose) Polio (third dose)
12–18 months	MMR (measles, mumps and rubella)
4–5 years	Diphtheria, tetanus and polio boosters
10–13 years	Rubella (girls only)
13 years	BCG vaccination against tuberculosis
Adults	May require tetanus vaccination after wounds. Women who have not had the rubella (German measles) vaccination or are not already immune can have the vaccination in adulthood.

Make sure your GP knows of any problems of this kind when you are considering vaccinations for your child. There is a useful guide to the vaccinations available, their effectiveness and the pros and cons, in *Which?*, July 1986.

The BMA Guide to Living with Risk (Harmondsworth: Penguin, 1990) takes vaccination as a particularly good example of the way in which we all weigh up risks and benefits when making decisions in our everyday lives. A summary is given of a number of studies on the risk of brain damage following vaccination.

You can get vaccinations for travelling abroad on the NHS if they are recommended by the Department of Health (see page 246). Your GP can charge for other vaccines before you travel.

Medical examinations

GPs carry out medical examinations to determine eligibility for some welfare benefits (see Section 3) and also for exemption from the need to wear a seat belt on medical grounds. There is a charge for the latter, although disabled people and those on Income Support are exempt. For more information get the leaflet *Seat Belts, the Law and You* from DSS offices or Citizens' Advice Bureaux. GPs also carry out medical examinations for insurance purposes. This has become a contentious area, particularly concerning HIV and AIDS. See further discussion of this on pages 71 and 191.

For more advice on choosing and using GPs

Choices in Health Care by Elaine Farrell (London: Optima, 1989)

Making the Most of your Doctor by Jennifer King, David Pendleton and Peter Tate (London: Thames Methuen, 1985)

A Patient's Guide to the National Health Service (Consumers' Association/Patients Association, 1983)

Patients' Rights leaflet from Association of Community Health Councils of England and Wales, 30 Drayton Park, London N5 1PB (also available in Welsh, Hindi, Punjabi, Gujerati, Urdu, Cantonese, Turkish, Vietnamese and Greek)

Communicating with Your GP

Gathering information is a very important part of the general practice consultation. This is a two-way process. Your description of the symptoms is crucial to the diagnosis, and in return the GP's advice is a key element in your participation in the treatment.

Before you visit your GP, decide exactly what you want to know about your condition. It can be helpful to write down a list of questions. *Making the Most of your Doctor* (see box, page 59) suggests the following check-list of things to discuss with your doctor.

– What has been happening to you
– How it has affected your daily routine
– What you think may be wrong with you
– What you are afraid of
– What you want your doctor to do
– What you want to know
– What you have tried already

The most likely treatment your GP will offer is some form of medication. This will lead to the following questions:

WHAT AND HOW?	HOW IMPORTANT?	WHAT SIDE-EFFECTS?	HOW LONG?
What kind of tablets are they? How can they help me? How should I take them? How can I tell if they work?	How important is it to take the tablets? What may happen if I don't take them?	Do they ever cause trouble? Do they have side-effects? Can I drive after taking them? Can I take other medicines with them? Can I drink alcohol while I am taking them?	How long will I need to continue with the tablets? What shall I do with tablets I don't need? Will I need to see you again? What will you want to know when I see you?

This is obviously a lot to remember to ask. But if you don't get to ask your doctor all these questions, you can check with your pharmacist (see page 16).

You may find it helpful to note down the advice your GP gives you. You could even tape-record the consultation, but ask the doctor if he or she has any objection first. Some doctors may find this inhibiting, but taping the consultation would probably lead to more careful advice-giving, as well as forming a record to which you could refer back in your own time.

You may feel more confident with a relative or friend to accompany you, but again it would be worth checking that the doctor has no objection first. Some people are worried that they will be branded as difficult patients if they ask too many questions, but this should not deter you from finding out what you need to know. Many doctors welcome patients as sources of information. After all, patients with long-term chronic disorders who may be members of self-help groups are experts in their own right.

Despite the best intentions of doctor and patient, important information is not always communicated effectively. Most information is given verbally and the evidence of many research studies suggests that patients then forget what they are told. In one study patients had forgotten half of what the general practitioner had said to them within five minutes of the consultation. It is not difficult to see why patients fail to take in information given to them. They are in alien surroundings, perhaps in pain, almost certainly worried. The doctor may be from a different background, age, gender, class, race. As Carolyn Faulder puts it in her book *Whose Body Is It: the troubled issue of informed consent* (London: Virago, 1985), 'This puts patients at a distinct disadvantage when it comes to voicing their preferences or doubts to someone who speaks with a different accent, almost in a different language, and who is surrounded by the trappings of authority.'

One solution to the problem of communication is the provision of printed literature which can be taken away by patients, assimilated in their own time, shared with relatives (who may be deeply affected by the illness), and referred to again when required. All GP surgeries are now obliged to provide a leaflet about the practice (see page 42). There is considerable scope for the extension of this idea to leaflets about the management of common health problems.

Most general practice consultations are for minor illnesses which could be treated adequately using self-care measures. For children under 16, over half the consultations are for six common symptoms (stuffy nose, sore throat, coughs, vomiting, diarrhoea, and minor injuries). In 1980 a research team at St Thomas's Hospital in London produced a booklet for patients on coping with these problems. It was edited by the leader writer of the *Daily Mirror*, tested for readability with a group of young mothers, and its use evaluated in general practice. There was more self-care and a significant fall in the number of visits to the GP amongst families who had received the booklet.

A number of other research studies have confirmed the value of information booklets as an aid to communication between doctors and patients. The fact that many doctors are now giving out patient information leaflets is clear from a survey of the use of written material by GPs, published in the *British Medical Journal* (19 March 1988). All the GPs in the survey had used a leaflet at some stage. The most popular were diet sheets, used by 90 per cent of the doctors. Eighty-one per cent had displays of leaflets in their waiting rooms. None had produced their own leaflets. Instead, the GPs relied on leaflets from other sources, in particular drug companies. There was a recognition that the information included in drug company leaflets might not be impartial, but the GPs found it difficult to obtain material from other sources, such as self-help groups.

The medical establishment is becoming increasingly aware of the need to improve communication with patients. A leader in the *Lancet* ('Write for your patient', 27 May 1989) declares:

> The days of paternalism are over – it is no longer acceptable to leave people in ignorance of prognosis, treatment, and the social

consequences of their disease. After all, why should patients not have the same rights to information and counselling as people whose problems are legal or financial? The spread of self-help groups that encourage patients to play an active part in their own care means that accurate and detailed information about disease must be available.

The Royal College of General Practitioners recognized this growing concern by setting up a Patient Liaison Group. One of its main concerns has been the provision of information to patients. In 1988 the Group's chairperson, Susan Clayton, listed some of the ways in which GPs can improve the information available to their patients:

– Providing a collection of leaflets in the surgery
– Running their own patient library
– Working with local public libraries to ensure that a stock of good health books is available to the public
– Providing a welfare rights assessment package on a microcomputer in the practice
– Improving the display of posters available in the waiting room
– Providing information about statutory services and self-help groups
– Setting up patient participation groups

The health care consumer body, the College of Health, came up with a similar check-list in 1989:

– It should be the rule, rather than the exception, for medical schools to teach communication skills. Patients, carers and self-help groups could be brought in to help
– Information about common diseases, operations, and diagnostic procedures should be available in language ordinary people understand
– Consultants and GPs should monitor their own communication skills, using video and audio recordings
– Patients should be encouraged to tape-record their consultation

and listen to it again in the more relaxed atmosphere of their own home
– All drugs should be dispensed with explanatory leaflets for lay people
– Doctors should provide notices in the waiting room saying they would like to answer patients' questions
– Hospitals and GPs should keep up-to-date registers of self-help groups

These are all recommendations, and it is clear that while some doctors take them seriously, others ignore them. It is in this kind of area that consumer choice is supposed to work. You should be in a position to ask your doctor for printed information. You can tell your doctor that this is provided by many GPs with benefit to patient and doctor. Your final sanction of course is to move to a practice where communication is considered important.

Information and Participation

In general practices around the UK there are many practical examples of giving patients information and enabling them to participate in their own care.

Patient libraries

Some practices have set up patient information libraries. The Dib Lane surgery in Leeds first established a library in 1981. The library started with a core collection of 250 books and gradually built up to its present stock of over 500 books and a small collection of audiotapes. The practice is fortunate in having the services of a librarian, Clare Pace, who looks after the library on a part-time basis. A detailed analysis of a year's use shows over 700 borrowings in the year, with women predominating. The most popular book then was *Breast is Best* by P. and A. Stanway. Many of the borrowers said they normally rarely read books but as one of the partners, Dr Chris Varnavides, says, 'For those patients who want to share in the responsibility for their condition, the library can help. Books can reinforce the advice given by the doctor, and answer questions the patient may be afraid to ask.'

Funding for patient libraries has come from a variety of sources. The Dib Lane library was initially funded by a Regional Health Authority research grant, but is now funded from within the practice. Dr David McKinley's practice in Clitheroe, Lancs set up their library as a charity called the Medical Education Foundation to which patients and local funding bodies have contributed. In Hertfordshire, the pioneering Health Information Service at the Lister Hospital, Stevenage, has been using a grant from the national Office of Arts and Libraries to put a collection of patient information books into a network of GP practices. The medical magazine *Medeconomics* has given practical advice to doctors on setting up a patient library and ensuring that it qualifies for

The most popular books in the Dib Lane patients' library include:

Everywoman by D. Llewellyn-Jones (London: Faber and Faber, 1989)
The New Our Bodies, Ourselves edited by A. Phillips and J. Rakusen (Harmondsworth: Penguin, 1989)
Pregnancy and Birth Book by M. Stoppard (London: Dorling Kindersley, 1985)
Breast is Best by P. and A. Stanway (London: Pan, 1983)
Keep your Baby Safe by J. Asher (Harmondsworth: Penguin, 1988)
Self-help for Your Nerves by C. Weekes (London: Angus and Robertson, 1984)
Anxiety and Depression by R. Priest (London: Optima, 1983)
Caring for an Elderly Relative by K. Thompson (London: Optima, 1986)
The Joy of Sex by A. Comfort (London: Quartet, 1988)
Relaxation tapes from Relaxation for Living, 29 Burwood Park Road, Walton on Thames KT12 5LH

charitable status ('GPs try novel approach to education in the surgery', *Medeconomics*, April 1986).

Welfare rights advice

Research by the Disablement Income Group shows that patients expect their GP to be able to give them advice on welfare rights. In some places GPs are meeting those expectations. Patients attending Lisson Grove Health Centre in London receive not only medical advice but also a detailed breakdown of their entitlement to DSS benefits. Professor Brian Jarman and his colleagues spent three years designing a welfare rights assessment computer programme after a survey of the health centre's 7,000 patients made it clear that a disturbing number of ailments could be traced to financial stress and that many patients were not receiving the benefits to which they were entitled.

Roughly two-thirds of the population consult their GP at least once a year, so the GP is exceptionally well placed to detect those in financial need and give advice. The Lisson Grove team now give benefit advice to several thousand patients a year and the system has now been installed in a number of other practices. It is worth asking whether your practice has information leaflets.

It is not only GPs who are working to extend their role in advice-giving. Health education and advice work is an important part of the role of the HEALTH VISITOR (see page 75), particularly when she visits patients in their own homes. In some areas, health visitors have set up 'advice clinics'. When an advisory health clinic for elderly people was opened in Bloomsbury, London, the health visitors found that over half the problems presented had a social cause, usually lack of money. A social worker now joins the health visitors at the clinic to give specialist advice. In East Dorset a health visitor coordinates the activities of a Health Mobile, an information van which takes health promotion advice out around the Bournemouth area. Computerized health checks are also provided on the van. In the Wythenshawe area of Manchester health visitors staff a regular information stall in the local flea market.

Patient participation groups

Patient participation groups have become increasingly common since the 1970s. The first successful group was established in Berinsfield, Oxfordshire in 1972, with the objective of allowing the views of patients to be heard by doctors. The Berinsfield group was closely followed by the Aberdare Patients Committee in Mid-Glamorgan and the Whiteladies Practice Association in Bristol.

There are now 100 or so in existence. They vary a lot in their role, but typically they are involved in:

– Consumer feedback: a voice in planning and running the practice
– Health promotion activities
– Production of information literature, practice guides, etc.
– Voluntary community care: transport, fetching prescriptions, etc.
– Fund raising for the practice

For those thinking of setting up a patient participation group, there is a now a great deal of literature on the subject. A good starting-point is an article by Tim Paine, 'Set up a patient participation group', in *British Medical Journal* 1987, 295: 828–9. A more detailed but very readable study of the whole PPG scene is *Promoting Health through Participation* by Anne Richardson and Caroline Bray (London: Policy Studies Institute, 1987).

Dr Paine suggests the following steps for setting up a group:

– Read up on the subject
– Consult the GPs, other members of the practice team, and other patients
– Contact the NATIONAL ASSOCIATION FOR PATIENT PARTICIPATION Helen Lyus, 13 Manor Drive, Surbiton, Surrey KT5 8NE Tel: 081-399 4122, and ask for their newsletter, starter pack and contact addresses for other groups
– Invite a member of an established PPG to speak at a meeting
– Set up a small steering group involving at least one of the GPs
– Approach the practice, the health authority and local companies and charities for some running expenses
– After a couple of years review progress and try to involve new blood. It can be easy for the group to lose momentum after the initial enthusiasm has worn off.

Access to Medical Records

One of the most obvious ways of improving communication between patients and doctors is for doctors to allow their patients to see what is written in their medical records. A growing number of GPs are doing this. At Balsall Heath Medical Centre in Birmingham patients have had open access to their records for over ten years. The GPs believe that this is an important demonstration of openness and trust between doctor and patient:

> A non-English speaking Asian woman told us through an interpreter that, although she could not understand a word in her records, the fact that she was handed them by the receptionist when she came for the consultation with her husband made her feel a person in her own right.

There are also important practical benefits. Allowing patients to check their own records provides an opportunity for errors and out of date information to be picked up. In Oxfordshire a group of patients were sent their case notes to check. One in five had to alter factual errors. A London GP asked his patients to update their files: 12 per cent found mistakes, including one woman who was described as having had an abortion when she had specifically refused one. In addition, records sometimes contain quite unjustified, subjective comments. The Freedom of Information Campaign reports one doctor's letter on a file which is reputed to have said, 'I have seen the patient, I have seen his wife, I have seen the two kids, and I have seen the pet rabbit. In my opinion the most intelligent of the lot is the rabbit.' It is unlikely that the GP would have written this if he knew that the files could be read by the patient.

There is a good case for allowing patients not only to see their records but actually to look after them. Every 1,000 records take up 17 feet of shelf space in the surgery and 10 per cent of records cannot be found when the patient comes to see the GP. The practice of allowing pregnant women to keep the record of their antenatal care at home is well established. All members of the primary care team can then see the notes on home visits and in the surgery, communication between the different professionals is improved and going through the record is an excellent basis for the patient to discuss any concerns with the doctor or midwife. Many countries, including France, Germany and New Zealand, have had parent-held child health records for some time (in the case of France since 1945). Studies in Oxford and Newcastle are showing support for the idea in the UK as well. This freedom of information is slowly coming to hospitals too. Tameside General Hospital won the 1990 Campaign for the Freedom of Information award for a primary nursing experiment which gives patients access to their nursing notes.

There is no doubt that public opinion is in favour of patient access to medical records. A Consumers' Association survey showed that 91 per cent of patients wanted to see their notes. This supported the findings of a survey commissioned in 1987 by the Data Protection Registrar, which found that 86 per cent of respondents thought that people should 'always' or 'usually' have the right to see their records. Even patients faced with the disclosure of a serious prognosis want the truth. A study of 167 multiple sclerosis patients published in the *Lancet* (6 July 1985) found that the great majority favoured knowing their diagnosis. Yet many had not been told this by the doctor. They had found out by overhearing a chance remark, or by surreptitiously reading their own notes.

The medical profession is less enthusiastic. The BMA accepts that sharing information with patients is an important part of patient care. But it is also worried about possible distress which might be caused to patients by seeing their records, and has argued that the decision on whether to show information to patients should be a matter of clinical judgement. Those doctors who have always allowed patients to see their records feel that it is only a very small proportion of patients for whom reading their notes would not be a good idea. Dr Bird in Birmingham puts the figure at only about sixteen patients out of the 4,500 on his practice list.

If your medical records are held on computer you have a legal right to see them under the Data Protection Act. However, the Access to Health Records Act, which comes into force in November 1991, extends the right of access to computerized medical records to manual files. The Act establishes the right of access to all health records for individuals to whom they relate (or their representatives). It also provides for the correction of inaccurate records. Doctors are not to disclose any part of the record if it is likely to cause serious mental or physical harm to the patient.

Another piece of legislation dealing with access to medical information, the Access to Medical Reports Act, came into force in January 1989. This Act gives people the right to see medical reports prepared by their doctor for employment or insurance purposes. The doctor must wait for twenty-one days before sending the report to the employer or insurance company, in order to give the patient time to see it. The patient can ask to see the report before it is sent or up to six months after it has been supplied. For further information about medical examinations for insurance see pages 59 and 191.

Complaints about GPs

Complaints about general practitioners are dealt with by the FAMILY HEALTH SERVICES AUTHORITY (as are complaints about other 'family practitioners', that is, dentists, opticians and chemists). The address of your FHSA is on the front of your medical card but you can also get it from the phone book, local library, Citizens' Advice Bureau or Community Health Council.

Only allegations of BREACH OF CONTRACT can be investigated formally by the FHSA. This means that while complaints relating to, for example, failure to respond to an out-of-hours call, are covered by the FHSA, complaints relating to the attitude or behaviour of a practitioner are not. Complaints about non-contractual matters (abusive behaviour, sexual advances, drunkenness, etc.) must be made to the GENERAL MEDICAL COUNCIL 44 Hallam Street, London W1N 6AE Tel: 071-580 7642.

If you are complaining to the FHSA, you should address your complaint to the GENERAL MANAGER. If you find it difficult to put your complaint in writing, FHSA staff can advise you. Your Community Health Council would also be able to help you to phrase your letter. You can find the address and phone number of your local CHC in the phone book under Community Health Council. If you are unable to write because of disability you can tape-record your complaint at the FHSA office.

Your complaint must be made to the FHSA no later than THIRTEEN WEEKS after the event which caused it (for dentists it is either six months after the end of the treatment which caused the complaint or thirteen weeks after you became aware of the cause, whichever is sooner).

You can complain on behalf of OTHER PEOPLE in some circumstances. You can complain on behalf of a child or where a patient has died. You can complain for someone who is too old or ill to do it themselves, if they give their written consent.

A LAY CONCILIATOR appointed by the FHSA will try to clear up any misunderstanding, by talking to you and the practitioner informally. If this does not work then you may have the right to a formal investigation.

FORMAL INVESTIGATIONS are carried out by a committee of equal numbers of FHSA lay members and practitioners, with a non-professional chairman. You can present your own case or have someone else (for example, a friend or your CHC secretary) do it for you. A copy of the report of the findings will be sent to you and the practitioner concerned.

If the complaint is PROVED the practitioner may be given a warning and/or have pay deducted. You are not entitled to compensation: for that you would have to sue the practitioner in the courts. However you can claim expenses for the hearing from the FHSA.

If you disagree with the decision, the FHSA will tell you how you can APPEAL. Appeals are made to the Secretary of State for Health. The Ombudsman or Health Service Commissioner cannot investigate claims about practitioners.

The Primary Care Team

Although the GP is the gatekeeper to health care, you are likely to come across other health professionals who collectively are known as the primary care team.

District nurses

District nurses are particularly involved with the care of patients after they are discharged from hospital, and in the care of elderly people in their homes. The district nursing service is sometimes called home nursing or community nursing (although the latter more accurately describes both district nursing and health visiting). District nurses carry out a wide range of practical nursing care, including changing dressings, administering drugs and giving bed baths. A district nurse may be attached to one or more GP practices, working with their patients but employed by the District Health Authority rather than by the partners. She will report to a nurse manager within the DHA. District nurses have an additional qualification after their basic nurse (RGN) training.

Visits from a district nurse are most commonly arranged by the GP. However, district nursing help can also be arranged by a social worker, home help, relatives, etc. You can speak to the nurse directly at the surgery or health centre, or you can go through the Community Nursing Office (this should be listed in the phone book under the name of your District Health Authority).

Nurses are referred to as 'she' in this book and it is in fact very likely that the nurse will be a woman. Currently, 8 per cent of qualified nurses in the UK are men, and most of these work in hospitals or in management. There are a few male district nurses and health visitors, but still not many.

Health visitors

Like district nurses, health visitors are trained nurses with an additional qualification. But unlike district nurses they do not wear uniform or carry out hands-on nursing care. The main role of the health visitor is to give health advice and to monitor the welfare of the family. Much of her work is with babies and young children, but there are also health visitors who work with elderly people and the younger disabled. The health visitor takes over the care of the mother and baby from the midwife, and will make regular visits to the family at home until the child starts school. Health visitors have an important health education role, and can advise on a range of topics from immunization and breastfeeding to diet and family planning. They should also be able to give information about self-help groups (or at least be able to find out for you) and basic welfare benefit advice.

The health visitor may work from a health centre, GP's surgery or clinic. You do not have to be referred to the health visitor by your GP: simply phone the surgery and ask to speak to the health visitor. If your GP does not have a health visitor you can still contact one through the Community Nursing Office (in the phone book under the name of your District Health Authority).

Community psychiatric nurses

Community psychiatric nurses (CPNs) provide support and counselling to people with mental health problems, so that they can continue to live in the community. They can also administer drugs. A CPN is usually assigned to a patient by the GP, and will then visit the patient in his or her home. Some health authorities have an open referral system, which means that someone who feels in need of help can contact a CPN directly. Contact the Community Health Council to see whether such a scheme operates in your area.

Other community nurses

Increasingly GPs are employing their own PRACTICE NURSES. These work with the GP in the surgery and carry out health checks, injections, etc.

In the USA it is common to find NURSE PRACTITIONERS, but they are less widespread in the UK. Nurse practitioners have extended training to allow them to perform many of the tasks usually performed by a doctor. You can consult a nurse practitioner directly. Contact your CHC to see whether there are any practising locally.

There are SPECIALIST NURSES who can advise on topics such as diabetes, stoma care and incontinence. Some work in hospitals but you can also be referred by your GP. These specialist clinics are increasingly held in general practice.

In most health authorities there are teams of MARIE CURIE NURSES who provide support for terminally ill cancer patients in their homes. This can be arranged through the GP or district nurse, or by contacting Marie Curie Cancer Care, 28 Belgrave Square, London SW1X 8QG Tel: 071-235 3325.

Community midwives

Midwives are trained to provide care throughout pregnancy, childbirth and postnatally on their own responsibility; to recognize problems which require referral to a doctor; and to provide women with advice, information and emotional support. They are practitioners in their own right and are allowed to prescribe drugs without the sanction of a doctor. Most midwives train in general nursing and then go on to do a specialist midwifery qualification. However, it is possible to qualify as a 'direct entry' midwife without undergoing training as a nurse first.

Midwives work in hospital obstetric units and in the community. Like community nurses, community midwives are usually attached to a GP surgery or health centre, or may work with a group of GPs. For more information on the choices available in childbirth see 'Having a Baby' in Section 5.

Chiropodists

Chiropodists treat problems of the foot such as corns, calluses and ingrowing toenails. Chiropodists qualify after three years' training and can then become state registered, using SRCh after their name. Only state registered chiropodists can work within the NHS. They work in the community, usually from a health centre, and also in hospital where they may treat foot problems secondary to another condition (such as diabetes).

Chiropody under the NHS is available to women over 60, men over 65, schoolchildren, pregnant women and disabled people. Some people are referred to a chiropodist by their GP but you can approach the chiropody service direct. Because of the limits on eligibility for chiropody under the NHS, and long waiting lists, many people consult chiropodists privately. To find a private chiropodist, look under Chiropodist in the Yellow Pages, or write to the SOCIETY OF CHIROPODISTS 53 Welbeck Street, London W1M 7HE Tel: 071-486 3381 and ask for details of local practitioners.

Occupational therapists

Community occupational therapists (OTs) can visit patients in their home to assess disability, advise on ways of coping with activities of daily living, and recommend aids and equipment. They can also arrange for the installation of aids and adaptations to the home. Community OTs work for the local authority social services department, and can be contacted through your local authority or town hall.

Community physiotherapists

Most physiotherapists work in hospitals (see page 144) but in some areas there is a Community Physiotherapy service. A GP would be able to arrange physiotherapy in the home if such a service exists in your area.

Speech therapists

Speech therapists work with patients who have speech problems following strokes, head injuries, etc. They also work with handicapped children, and treat speech impediments such as stammering. Hospitals have departments of speech therapy, but speech therapists also work in the community, in clinics and health centres.

Community dietitians

Most dietitians work in hospitals, but there are also community dietitians working in health centres, etc. Dietitians have an important role in health education, particularly with ethnic minorities and people on low incomes.

Social workers

About a quarter of GPs have a social worker attached to their practice, and in some areas the local social services office is housed in the health centre. The GP may suggest you see the social worker for practical advice and help with welfare rights and community services. For more information on community care see Section 3.

Dentists

Dentists can choose whether to work privately or to have an arrangement with the Family Health Services Authority, whereby they see patients under the NHS. Dentists work in three ways in the NHS:

– As GENERAL DENTAL PRACTITIONERS, to whom most people go for treatment. They are also known as family dentists, or just dentists.
– In DENTAL DEPARTMENTS IN HOSPITALS, where patients may be referred for specialist treatment by their GP or family dentist.
– Within the COMMUNITY DENTAL SERVICE, based in health clinics and carrying out school dental examinations.

Choosing a family dentist

You can go to any dentist for a check-up or a course of treatment. You do not have to register as a patient as you do with a GP. There are of course advantages in the continuity of treatment which you will get if you stay with one dentist, and many dentists have a system of recall where they remind patients that a check-up is due.

Family Health Services Authorities maintain lists of dentists in their area who do NHS work. This dental list is available at FHSA and CHC offices, and should also be kept in libraries and post offices. The dental list will tell you the names of dentists, the address of the surgery and times. Dentists are also listed in the Yellow Pages under 'Dental Surgeons'. The government is now encouraging the production of dental practice leaflets, along the same lines as those now available for general medical practices.

Dental charges

When making your appointment for dental treatment, make sure you tell the dentist that you want to be treated on the NHS or else you may find yourself being charged as a private patient. Unless you come within one of the categories for free treatment (see below) you will have to pay some of the costs of treatment, even if this is carried out under the NHS. And your dentist is entitled to charge you if you fail to keep an appointment without notifying him or her.

Dental check-ups and treatment are free for:

– all children under 16
– young people of 16–18 who have left school, for everything except dentures
– young people under 19 in full-time education
– pregnant women, or mothers with babies under one year
– people receiving Income Support or Family Credit

Others on low income may still be able to get help with the costs, even if they cannot get completely free treatment. ⇒ DSS leaflet D11, *NHS Dental Treatment*, available from DSS offices and post offices. To claim ask your dentist for form F1D and send the completed form to Agency Benefits Unit, DSS, Longbenton, Newcastle-upon-Tyne NE98 1YX. If you have already paid, go to the DSS and ask for form AG5 to reclaim the charges.

Unless you can get free treatment or help with the costs, you will have to pay about three-quarters of the cost (the remaining quarter is covered by the NHS and reclaimed by the dentist). The most you can be asked to pay for a whole course of treatment is £150. Dental check-ups used to be free but there is now a charge of £3.45 (despite the emphasis on preventive dentistry in the *Working for Patients* White Paper). Since October 1990 dentists have been obliged to provide patients with a treatment plan, giving details of costs, which patients can take away and consider before proceeding with treatment.

Emergency dental treatment

If you need emergency dental treatment you can ask any dentist to accept you as an NHS patient for emergency treatment. Not all dentists will deal with emergencies outside surgery hours, and they are not obliged to provide out-of-hours cover in the way a GP must. In an emergency, try to contact your usual dentist first. In some areas dentists have organized rotas to deal with emergency patients. In some health authorities there is an emergency dental service operating from health authority premises. If you cannot get help through these channels, and you need treatment to stop bleeding or excessive pain, you can go to your GP or a hospital Accident and Emergency department.

Home visits

If you have been accepted for treatment and your condition makes it impossible for you to get to the dental surgery, your dentist must visit you at home, provided this is not more than five miles from the surgery. There is no extra charge for this.

Complaints about dentists

If you are not satisfied with your treatment, complain first to the dentist. It may simply be a matter of correcting earlier work (such as an ill-fitting denture) without extra charge.

If you are still dissatisfied with the standard of service a complaint should be made to the FAMILY HEALTH SERVICES AUTHORITY (see page 72).

Complaints about the Community Dental Service should be made to the District General Manager of the District Health Authority, not to the FHSA.

If you have a complaint to do with an accusation of improper personal, ethical or professional behaviour you should contact the GENERAL DENTAL COUNCIL 37 Wimpole Street, London W1M 8DO Tel: 071-486 2171. The General Dental Council can also deal with complaints about private treatment.

For more information about using dental services see the National Consumer Council book, *You and Your Dentist: a guide to patients' rights* (HMSO, 1987).

Opticians

Opticians are another group of practitioners who contract with Family Health Services Authorities to provide services under the NHS.

– OPHTHALMIC OPTICIANS test eyesight and examine eyes for any medical problems. They can prescribe lenses to correct sight problems but must refer medical problems to your GP. These opticians are sometimes called OPTOMETRISTS.
– DISPENSING OPTICIANS can have spectacles made up or adjust frames, but they cannot prescribe.
– OPHTHALMOLOGISTS are not opticians but doctors specializing in treatment of eye disorders.
– ORTHOPTISTS work with ophthalmologists, usually in hospital eye departments, to correct children's squints and other eye defects.

Sight tests

You can go to any optician for a sight test; as with dentists, there is no need to register with a particular one. Free sight tests are now only available to people:

– under 16
– under 19 and in full-time education
– on Income Support or Family Credit
– with a valid DSS exemption certificate
– registered blind or partially sighted
– diagnosed diabetic or with glaucoma
– aged 40 or over and the brother, sister or child of a glaucoma patient

Other people have to pay a charge of about £10. The cost may vary from one optician to another, so it is worth shopping around.

The charge for eye tests was introduced in April 1989. Since then the number of eye tests has fallen by a fifth (2.5 million tests in England and Wales). A survey in *Which way to health*? (June 1990) found that two in five people said they would go for an eye test less often now there is a charge. There is also confusion about the charges. Two in five people who were actually exempt from the eye test charge thought they had to pay.

Obtaining glasses

When you have had your eyes tested you may be given a prescription. You can then use the prescription to obtain glasses, either from the optician who examined you or by taking it to another registered optician or supplier of glasses. There is now a wide range of glasses available in department stores and spectacle shops, but if you go to one of these your prescription must not be more than two years old. These suppliers cannot supply glasses to children under 16 nor lenses for partially sighted or registered blind people. The prices of frames are usually clearly marked but make sure you ask about the *complete* cost, including the kind of lenses you are having.

NHS VOUCHERS FOR GLASSES Some people are eligible for vouchers to help with the cost of buying new spectacles. You are entitled if you are:

– under 16
– under 19 and in full-time education
– on Income Support or Family Credit

You may also be entitled to a voucher if you need a particularly powerful or complicated lens. Tell the optician if you think you are entitled to a voucher when you sign the sight test form. You can choose glasses that cost more than the voucher and pay the difference yourself.

Complaints

If you have a complaint about the standard of service given by an optician complain to the FAMILY HEALTH SERVICES AUTHORITY (see page 72).

If the complaint is about the optician's conduct you should contact the GENERAL OPTICAL COUNCIL 41 Harley Street, London W1N 2DJ Tel: 071-580 3898.

3 Care in the Community

In recent years more and more people with a disability, or those affected by ageing or chronic physical and mental ill health, are being cared for 'in the community'. This means that they and their carers need to find their way through an often baffling maze of community services, provided by statutory and voluntary organizations.

In 1988, the Office of Population Censuses and Surveys (OPCS) published the first national survey of the extent of disability in Great Britain for twenty years. The report revealed the enormous size of this sector of health care:

– 6.2 million adults in Great Britain have a disability
– About 400,000 disabled adults are living in some kind of residential establishment. This means that well over 5 million people with disabilities are living at home, and being 'cared for in the community'
– Put another way, 14 per cent of all adults in private households have a disability
– Most disabled people are also elderly. Half are aged 70 or over, and almost 70 per cent are over 60
– There are more disabled women than men. This is partly because women tend to live longer than men
– The North, Wales and Yorkshire have the highest rates of disability. London and the South-East, East Anglia and the South-West have lower than average rates

Disability is rarely clear-cut. It is a continuum of severity, with many people disabled in more ways than one. The OPCS survey identifies ten levels of disability and provides 'pen-pictures' of typical cases who are likely to be cared for in the community.

The commonest set of causes of disability are musculo-skeletal complaints (including arthritis and back problems) which affect 46 per cent of disabled people in private households. Next come ear complaints affecting 38 per cent, and eye complaints affecting 22 per cent. Mental disabilities are the most common amongst people in residential care (56 per cent, including senile dementia which affects 26 per cent).

Examples of levels of disability in OPCS survey

Level 1: A man, 59, deaf in one ear, has difficulty hearing someone talking in a normal voice
Level 2: A man, 75, often forgets what he is doing, or loses track of what's being said in the middle of a conversation. He has poor hearing
Level 6: A woman, 40, is epileptic, cannot read a short newspaper article, and is often confused about the time of day
Level 10: A man, 55, has had a stroke, and cannot walk at all, feed himself or get out of a chair without help

The OPCS calculates that there are approximately the following numbers of people in the different categories of disability:

Level 1	1,198,000
Level 2	840,000
Level 3	750,000
Level 4	704,000
Level 5	708,000
Level 6	545,000
Level 7	486,000
Level 8	396,000
Level 9	365,000
Level 10	210,000

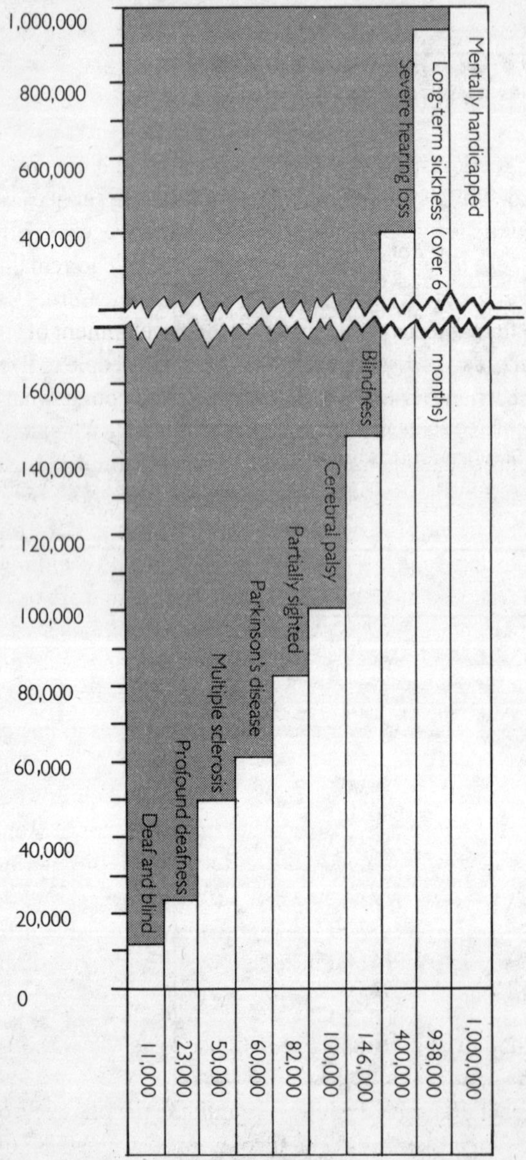

The most commonly experienced disabilities

Who's Caring for People?

However good hospital care is, most people would not choose to live in hospital. The development of community care services in recent years, and the future direction indicated by the recent Griffiths Report, seeks to ensure that more people are able to remain in their homes or return to them. The 1989 White Paper, *Caring for People*, has as its first objective, 'To promote the development of domiciliary, day and respite services to enable people to live in their own home whenever feasible and sensible.' Of course what 'community care' means in practice is that people who are affected by problems of ageing, mental illness, mental handicap or sensory or physical disability, are for the most part looked after by their families and friends (the so-called 'informal carers'). Six million carers in Britain look after a relative or friend who is elderly, ill or disabled. Many spend long hours on the practical work of caring. Some experience great stress; some are elderly themselves. Often they receive little or no help. These carers are the backbone of community care in Britain and most other countries. Without them the state would have to bear greatly increased costs in its health and social services.

There is no doubt that very many disabled and elderly people and their carers do not receive the kind of financial, practical and emotional support outlined in the Carers' Needs programme. A second OPCS report (*The Financial Circumstances of Disabled Adults Living in Private Households*, HMSO, 1989) paints a picture of widespread deprivation and need amongst people with disabilities living at home.

– 4.5 million disabled adults live in households where there is no earner
– 75 per cent of disabled adults – 4.3 million people – rely on state benefits as their main source of income, at an average of £65 a week
– Only 31 per cent of disabled people were in paid employment,

and only 2 per cent of those with severe disabilities
– Over 70 per cent of disabled adults were on incomes which were three-quarters or less of average earnings; 35 per cent were on incomes below half the national average.

The data for the OPCS survey was collected in 1985. Since then the situation has worsened considerably. The Disability Alliance estimates that over a million disabled people are now worse off because of the major changes in social security benefits introduced in 1988.

Recently a group of organizations involved in caring, including Age Concern, the Alzheimer's Disease Society and the Carers' National Association, produced a ten-point plan listing carers' needs:

1 **Recognition of their contribution** and of their needs as individuals in their own right
2 **Services tailored to their own individual circumstances,** needs and views, through discussions at the time help is being planned
3 **Services which reflect an awareness of differing racial, cultural and religious backgrounds** and values, equally accessible to carers of every race and ethnic origin
4 **Opportunities for a break,** both for short spells (an afternoon) and for longer periods (a week or more), to relax and to have time to themselves
5 **Practical help** to lighten the tasks of caring, including domestic help, home adaptations, incontinence services, and help with transport
6 **Someone to talk to** about their own emotional needs, at the outset of caring, while they are caring, and when the caring task is over
7 **Information** about the available benefits and services, as well as how to cope with the particular condition of the person cared for
8 **An income which covers the costs of caring** and which does not preclude carers taking employment or sharing care with other people
9 **Opportunities to explore alternatives to family care,** both for the immediate and long-term future
10 **Services designed through consultation with carers,** at all levels of policy planning

Carers' needs: a 10-point plan for carers King's Fund Informal Caring Programme, 126 Albert Street, London NW1 7NF

Meeting the Need for Information

Disabled people and their carers do not get all the help they need because of an inadequate system of social security and community care. But they also miss out because often they do not know about the support which is available to them. They lack the information identified as a fundamental need in point 7 of the Carers' Needs plan. Help is available from a bewildering array of sources: health service, social services, social security, voluntary organizations and the private sector. Many disabled people can tell of lengthy experiences negotiating the maze of agencies and services. The Community Care White Paper became law in June 1990 as part of the NHS and Community Care Act, although the government has since announced that its implementation will be slower than originally expected because of concerns about the impact on the level of poll tax or community charge. The new Act places great emphasis on a 'mixed economy' of care with an increased role for voluntary organizations and the private sector. But it intends to make access to these services easier by making locally based 'case managers' responsible for putting together an individually tailored 'package of care' for every disabled person.

In fact, since 1986 local authorities have been obliged to provide information on services to disabled people. Section 9 of the 1986 Disabled Persons (Services, Consultation and Representation) Act says that a local authority has a duty to provide to any disabled person who receives its services, information about other organizations which can provide help. Such information might include details of voluntary groups, transport schemes, leisure opportunities, respite care, etc.

Local authorities are trying to meet this requirement, usually through their Social Services Department, but there is no doubt that many are making slow progress. Disabled people and their carers still have to rely on a multitude of information sources. This section of the book brings together the help available to disabled and elderly people living at home. Further advice is available from the self-help groups for specific problems listed on pages 310–20. The following are indispensable sources of further information on the care of disabled people living in the community:

BOOKS

Disability Rights Handbook (Disability Alliance, 25 Denmark Street, London WC2H 8NJ Tel: 071-240 0806. Published annually in April).
DRH is the most up-to-date and comprehensive guide to rights, benefits and services for all people with disabilities and their carers.
Caring at Home by Nancy Kohner (National Extension College, 18 Brooklands Avenue, Cambridge CB2 2HN Tel: 0223 316644, 1988)
Detailed guide to benefits and services available to carers, with practical advice on the practicalities of day-to-day care.
Directory for Disabled People by Ann Darnbrough and Derek Kinrade (5th edition, Cambridge: Woodhead Faulkner, 1988)
The most detailed guide to services and opportunities for disabled people, with sections on topics such as holidays, leisure, sex and legislation, as well as the usual information on benefits and statutory services.
Guide to the Social Services (Family Welfare Association, 501–5 Kingsland Road, London E8 4AU Tel: 071-254 6251. Published annually)
A standard reference book for over 100 years, covering personal social services, social security, the NHS and other statutory services.

ORGANIZATIONS

AGE CONCERN Astral House, 1268 London Road, London SW16 4EJ Tel: 081-679 8000
A centre for information on everything to do with elderly people. Age Concern also services a network of 1,400 independent local

groups which can offer a wealth of advice and practical support to elderly people and their carers.

CARERS' NATIONAL ASSOCIATION 29 Chilworth Mews, London W3 3RG Tel: 071-724 7776

An information and advice service for carers, which puts carers in touch with one another and raises awareness of carers' needs.

DIAL UK Victoria Buildings, 117 High Street, Clay Cross, Chesterfield S45 9DZ Tel: 0246 250055

DIALs are information and advice services run by disabled people for disabled people (see page 304 for more on DIALs). If you have difficulty tracing your local DIAL, DIAL UK is the national office and will be able to put you in touch with your nearest local service.

DISABLED LIVING FOUNDATION 380–4 Harrow Road, London W9 2HU Tel: 071-289 6111

Best known as the UK's major source of information on aids and equipment for people with disabilities, DLF also provides information on the whole field of disability including incontinence and clothing.

DISABLEMENT INCOME GROUP Millmead Business Centre, Millmead Road, London N17 9QU Tel: 081-801 8013

The main functions of DIG are research and acting as a pressure group. Local DIG groups can be authoritative sources of advice on welfare rights.

ROYAL ASSOCIATION FOR DISABILITY AND REHABILITATION (RADAR) 25 Mortimer Street, London W1N 8AB Tel: 071-637 5400

RADAR is a coordinating body with over 400 member organizations in the field of disability. Useful publications include a booklet, *If only I'd known that a year ago: a guide for newly disabled people, their families and friends*.

Who's Who in Community Care

Many people are confused about just who is responsible for the various elements of community care. They may have a vague notion that help is available from 'the social' without really knowing what this means or who to contact. The similarity between the names of the two major agencies (Department of Social Security, and Social Services Department) does not help.

Department of Social Security

The Department of Social Security (DSS) administers most of the financial help available to people with disabilities. The former Department of Health and Social Security was split into two separate departments (the Department of Health and the Department of Social Security) in 1988. You may still hear the Department of Social Security referred to as 'the DHSS' (or less charitably as 'the SS'). The address of your local office still appears in the phone book under Health and Social Security, Department of. In Scotland, however, the entry is under 'Social Security'. Some areas have separate offices for national insurance and for income support (formerly supplementary benefit). If you are not sure which office you need, just phone up and ask.

You can also contact the Department of Social Security on FREELINE SOCIAL SECURITY. Dial 0800 666 555 free of charge between 9 am and 4.30 pm Monday to Friday. Advice in Urdu is available on 0800 289 188.

Social Services Departments

Many of the practical services available to disabled people are provided by Social Services Departments. These are local authority departments (County Council or Metropolitan Borough). To find your local office look under the NAME OF YOUR LOCAL

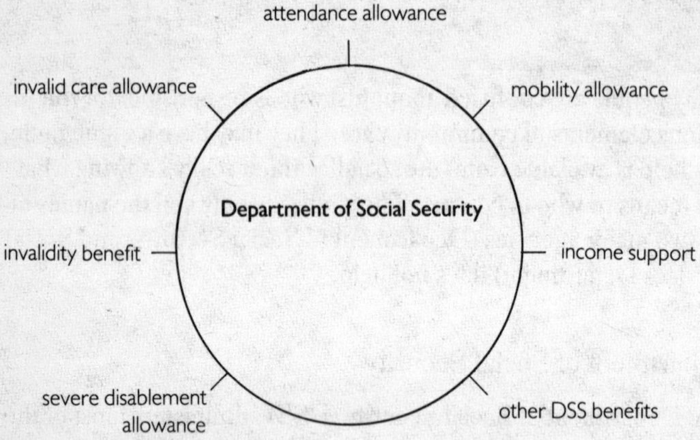

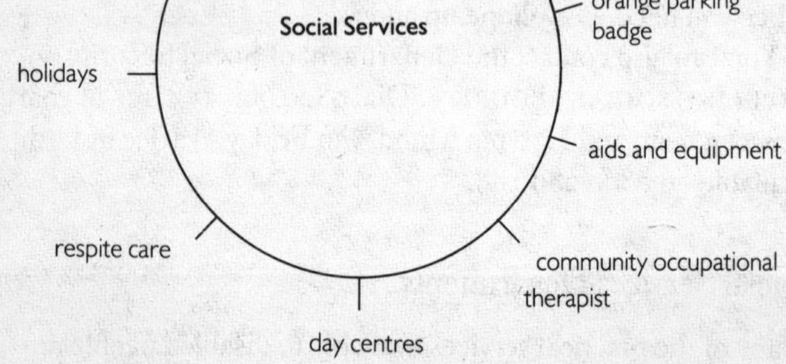

The community care agencies

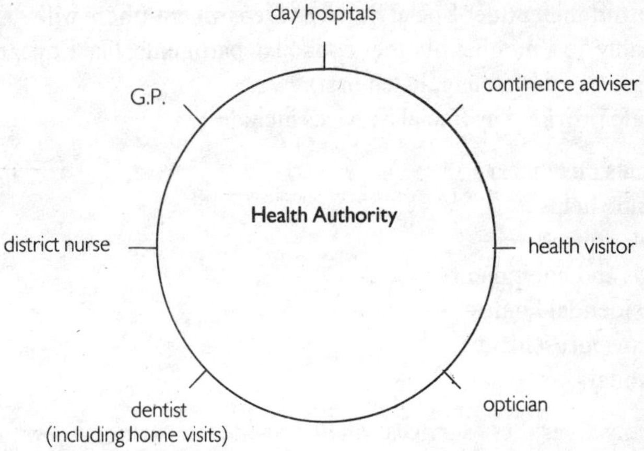
day hospitals
G.P.
continence adviser
Health Authority
district nurse
health visitor
dentist
(including home visits)
optician

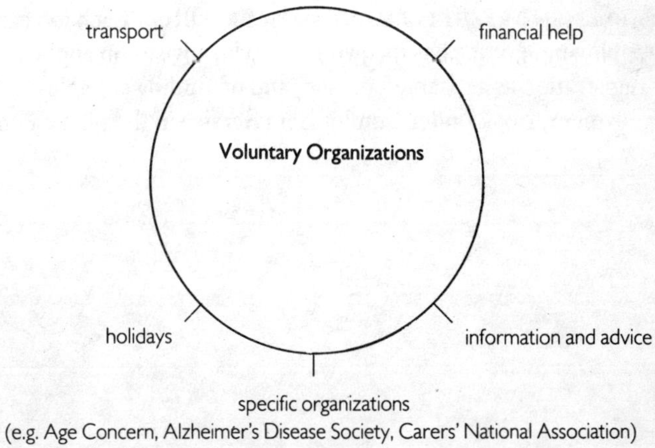
transport
financial help
Voluntary Organizations
holidays
information and advice
specific organizations
(e.g. Age Concern, Alzheimer's Disease Society, Carers' National Association)

AUTHORITY (for example, Wiltshire County Council) in the phone book and then under Social Services Department (there will probably be a number of other council departments, like Education, Libraries and Planning, listed first).

Help provided by Social Services includes:

- Meals on wheels
- Home helps
- Day centres
- Aids and equipment
- Residential homes
- Transport schemes
- Holidays

In many areas these services will be provided in partnership with voluntary organizations.

Department of Employment

The Department of Employment has a particular responsibility for advice on the employment needs of disabled people, through the DISABLEMENT RESETTLEMENT OFFICER (DRO). Each job centre or employment office has its own DRO who advises on applications for registration as a disabled person, and on finding suitable employment. Look under Employment Service in the phone book.

Benefits for Disabled People and Their Carers

If you are ill or disabled you may be eligible for a number of benefits. The following is a brief guide. For more detailed advice get a copy of the *Disability Rights Handbook*, or talk to your local DSS office, Citizens' Advice Bureau or DIAL. The DSS leaflets mentioned at the end of each section give more information and tell you how to apply. There is also a more detailed sixty-page booklet, *Equipment and Services for People with Disabilities* (HB6). They are available from DSS offices and some post offices. Benefit rates are those in operation in April 1990, but there are usually annual increases.

Sick Pay and Sickness Benefit

Employers are responsible for paying STATUTORY SICK PAY (SSP) to employees for up to twenty-eight weeks in any period of sickness. To qualify you must earn enough to pay National Insurance contributions. The amount you get is either £39.25 or £52.50 per week, depending on your average weekly earnings, and payments are taxable.

If you are not eligible for SSP you can claim SICKNESS BENEFIT from the DSS for the same period, provided you have enough National Insurance contributions. Sickness benefit is £35.70 a week, plus £22.10 for an adult dependant (wife, husband, or a person looking after your child).

⇒ DSS leaflet NI 16, *Sickness Benefit*.

Invalidity Benefit

After twenty-eight weeks' incapacity for work, you should claim Invalidity Benefit. It lasts for as long as you remain incapable of work, and can be paid until you reach 65 (women) or 70 (men). The benefit is worth more than Sickness Benefit. You get £46.90, with an additional £28.20 for each adult dependant, and £9.65 for each child. There is a further addition (Invalidity Allowance) of £3.10 – £10 per week depending on your age.

⇒ DSS leaflet NI 16A, *Invalidity Benefit.*

Severe Disablement Allowance

If you do not qualify for Invalidity Benefit because you have not paid enough National Insurance contributions, you may be able to claim Severe Disablement Allowance (SDA). SDA was introduced in 1984 to replace non-contributory invalidity pension. You get £28.20 a week, with an additional £18.85 for an adult dependant and £9.65 for each child.

⇒ DSS leaflet NI 252, *Severe Disablement Allowance.*

Attendance Allowance

In addition to the above 'incapacity benefits', there are two benefits to help with the costs of caring: Attendance Allowance and Invalid Care Allowance.

Attendance Allowance is paid to adults or children aged 2 or over, who are severely disabled, either physically or mentally, and who need close attention from a carer. The allowance is paid to you, the disabled person, not to the carer. The carer may be able to claim Invalid Care Allowance (see below). To qualify you must need 'frequent attention' with personal things such as washing, dressing, eating or going to the toilet, or you must need 'continual supervision' to avoid substantial danger to yourself or others. If you have daytime care needs only you can get £25.05 a week; if you need attention night and day the rate goes up to £37.55.

⇒ DSS leaflet NI 205, *Attendance Allowance.*

Invalid Care Allowance

If you are of working age and spend a lot of time caring for a severely disabled person, you may be able to claim Invalid Care Allowance (ICA). You don't have to be related to the disabled person, or even to live with them, but you must spend at least thirty-five hours a week caring for a person who receives Attendance Allowance. If you do this for part of the year (for example in school holidays) you may qualify for ICA during this period. Invalid Care Allowance is worth £28.20 a week, with an additional £18.85 for an adult dependant and £9.65 for each child, and is taxable.

⇒ DSS leaflet NI 212, *Invalid Care Allowance.*

Mobility Allowance

Mobility Allowance is designed to help severely disabled people become more mobile out of doors. It can be used in any way you choose: towards buying or hiring a car, taking a taxi, driving lessons, operating a wheelchair, going on holiday, etc. You do not have to give any proof of how you spend the money. It is not means-tested but, like Attendance Allowance, there is a medical test for eligibility. You need to demonstrate that your physical condition is such that you are unable or virtually unable to walk, or that the exertion required to walk would have an adverse effect on your health (for example, if you had a serious heart or lung condition). The current rate is £26.25 a week.

⇒ DSS leaflet NI 211, *Mobility Allowance.*

Orange Badge Scheme

The Orange Badge Scheme gives parking concessions to people receiving Mobility Allowance, to those using a government-supplied vehicle, to those registered as blind, and to others 'with a permanent or substantial disability which causes inability to walk or very considerable difficulty in walking'. Orange Badges are issued by local authorities: contact your local SOCIAL SERVICES DEPARTMENT.

Road Tax Exemption

If you are receiving Mobility Allowance or if passengers are getting Attendance Allowance, you can apply to your local Vehicle Licensing Centre for a 'tax exempt' disk.

For more information on help with mobility problems send for the free Department of Transport guide, *Door to Door*. Just write to Department of Transport, Door to Door Guide, FREEPOST, Ruislip, Middlesex, HA4 OBR.

There is also a comprehensive book entitled *Motoring and Mobility for Disabled People* published by RADAR 25 Mortimer Street, London W1N 8AB, 1988.

A leaflet on fare concessions for disabled people is available from railway stations.

The following organizations are also useful contacts:

– MOBILITY INFORMATION SERVICE Unit 2a, Atcham Industrial Estate, Upton Magna, Shrewsbury SY4 4UG Tel: 0743 77489
– DISABLED DRIVERS ASSOCIATION 18 Creekside, London SE8 3DZ Tel: 081-692 7141
– MOBILITY ADVICE AND VEHICLE INFORMATION SERVICE (MAVIS) Department of Transport, Crowthorne, Berkshire RG11 6AU Tel: 0344 779014

Income Support

Both Attendance Allowance and Mobility Allowance have added significance in that eligibility for one or both is also a passport to higher rates of 'disability premiums' as part of Income Support. Income Support has replaced Supplementary Benefit and is now the main means-tested benefit for people on low incomes. The system works through a series of weekly personal allowances (for example, £57.60 for a couple) with additional premiums for eligible people. For example, there is a severe disability premium of £28.20 for a single person, £56.40 for a disabled couple, and £15.40 for a disabled child. There is also a carer's premium of £10.00.

More information ⇒ DSS leaflet SB20, *A Guide to Income Support*.

Social Fund

The Social Fund provides interest-free loans for essential expenses to those on Income Support. These include maternity payments, funeral expenses and cold weather payments. There are also additional discretionary payments, including COMMUNITY CARE GRANTS. These are payments to enable disabled people to move out from institutions into community care, or to avoid going into institutional care. Grants could cover things such as removal expenses, redecoration and minor structural repairs and furniture.

To apply for a Community Care Grant ⇒ DSS form SF300.

Poll Tax

The Community Charge, commonly known as the poll tax, replaced domestic rates in Scotland in April 1989, and in England and Wales in April 1990. (Domestic rates continue in Northern Ireland.) Certain people are exempt from paying the poll tax. They include:

– people who are severely mentally impaired, and are of pensionable age or receiving Severe Disablement Allowance or Invalidity Benefit. 'Severely mentally impaired' means in a state of arrested mental development, or permanent mental impairment due to brain injury. People with Alzheimer's disease are also exempt under this category.
– people who are 'solely or mainly' patients in hospital
– people who are 'solely or mainly' resident in a nursing home, residential care home, or private hospital.

Other categories of disabled people are not exempt, but they may be entitled to a COMMUNITY CHARGE REBATE if they are on a low income. Contact your District Council offices or Citizens' Advice Bureau for advice.

Blind and partially sighted people can get information on the community charge on cassette tapes and also in Braille and Moon writing from: ROYAL NATIONAL INSTITUTE FOR THE BLIND
224 Great Portland Street, London W1N 6AA Tel: 071-388 1266.

Other Sources of Financial Help

Independent Living Fund

The Independent Living Fund is a charity which has been set up by the DSS in cooperation with the Disablement Income Group to make payments from a government-funded trust. The Fund's initial resources are £5 million and although this sum was intended to last five years, it is rapidly being used up. In order to be eligible for payments from the Independent Living Fund you must be receiving Attendance Allowance, or the Trustees must be satisfied that you are likely to get it. The Fund concentrates on giving grants to pay for domestic help and personal care.

More information from: Independent Living Fund, PO Box 183, Nottingham NG8 3RD.

Family Fund

The Family Fund is run by the Joseph Rowntree Memorial Trust, but is funded by the government. Its aim is to help families caring for a severely disabled child under 16, by giving lump sum grants for specific items which are needed in the care of the child. The kinds of thing most commonly provided are: help with washing machines; holidays for the family; clothing, bedding or footwear if the child wears these out quickly; or help with the costs of transport.

More information from: Family Fund, PO Box 50, York YO1 1UY.

Help from charities and benevolent funds

There are literally thousands of charities and benevolent funds which may be able to provide financial help, perhaps to those who are not eligible for DSS assistance. Some of these relate to particular illnesses or disabilities (see pages 310–20). Some are benevolent funds for people who have done particular jobs or have been in particular professions. Trade unions usually have welfare funds for members. And in every part of the country there are local charities, perhaps set up in the will of a local benefactor many years ago. If you fit the terms of reference (for example, if you live in a particular parish) it may be possible to tap this source of funds. Relevant funds of this kind can be difficult to trace at the right time. The best sources of advice would be your Citizens' Advice Bureau, public library or local Council for Voluntary Service (see page 28). If you have a social worker he or she should be able to advise too.

The following books are potential goldmines for sources of financial help:

Charities Digest (Family Welfare Association, 501–5 Kingsland Road, London E8 4AU. Published annually)

A Guide to Grants for Individuals in Need (London: Directory of Social Change, 1990)

Practical Help

Social services for disabled people are governed by the Chronically Sick and Disabled Persons Act 1970, and the Disabled Persons (Services, Consultation and Representation) Act 1986 (see page 94 for the latter). Under the CSDPA 1970 it is the responsibility of Social Services Departments to assess the needs of disabled people for:

– practical help in the home, such as a home help
– meals, either at home or at a local centre
– radio, television and help in using the local library
– any help needed to take advantage of educational facilities
– help with transport to these or similar activities
– adaptations or special equipment in the home
– a telephone and any special equipment necessary to use it
– holidays

In practice these services may actually be provided by a range of agencies, particularly those in the voluntary sector.

Home helps

Social Services home helps are provided in most areas. Home helps mainly provide a cleaning service in the home but they may also do washing, shopping and collect prescriptions. They are available free in some areas; in others there is a charge.

Care attendant schemes

The home help service is not designed to provide the level of home care necessary to enable disabled people to live independently at home. However, many areas now have care attendant schemes which use trained helpers to help disabled or elderly people to live in the community. Your local Social Services will be able to tell you if there is a care attendant scheme in your area. Otherwise contact ASSOCIATION OF CROSSROADS CARE ATTENDANT SCHEMES 10 Regent Place, Rugby, Warwicks CV21 2PN Tel: 0788 73653.

Incontinence services

Some areas have a laundry service attached to the home help service. In other areas it may be run by the District Health Authority. The laundry service collects soiled bedding and clothing from disabled people with incontinence problems, and returns them laundered. The local authority should also collect and dispose of soiled incontinence pads and dressings. District Health Authorities may also supply incontinence pads, drawsheets, bed linen, commodes, etc. Your DISTRICT NURSE (see page 74) should be able to advise. Many areas also have CONTINENCE NURSE ADVISERS. The Association of Continence Advisers is based at the Disabled Living Foundation (see page 116). The Disabled Living Foundation also produces *Advisory Notes on Incontinence*.

Meals on wheels

Meals on wheels are administered by Social Services Departments but are usually delivered by volunteers. You will need to check whether they can cater for any special dietary requirements you may have. There is usually a charge of upwards of 50p a meal. If you are disabled or elderly, your GP or social worker should be able to arrange a home help and/or meals on wheels for you.

Education

The Chronically Sick and Disabled Persons Act 1970 emphasizes the importance of access to educational opportunities for disabled people. There is a need for provision both for handicapped children and for further education for disabled adults. The provision of special education to children with 'special educational needs' is governed by the Education Act 1981. Under the Act it is the responsibility of local education authorities to identify children with special needs. The needs of the child must be assessed and a decision made on the best form of educational provision. Wherever possible this means placing the child in a normal school, perhaps with special classes. Some parents may prefer their child to go to a special school because they feel the child may get more attention. The decision rests with the local education authority (LEA) but they should take the parents' wishes into consideration.

The address and phone number of your LEA is in the phone book under the name of your County Council or Metropolitan Borough. The organization 81 ACTION 52 Magnaville Road, Bishops Stortford, Herts CM23 4DW Tel: 0279 503244 gives information on the workings of the 1981 Education Act and offers support to parents of children with special educational needs.

There is a variety of options for further education. Many young people with disabilities can attend colleges and universities. Educational establishments are increasingly paying attention to the access needs of disabled students. A survey published in 1987 by the National Bureau for Handicapped Students showed that in that year 55,000 disabled young people and adults benefited from further and higher education. In addition to courses open to all, some colleges also offer special courses designed to help disabled young people to live independently. There is also a number of residential colleges for disabled students, usually run by voluntary organizations. More than 100 are listed in *COPE: Compendium of Post-16 Residential Establishments* (available from Wiltshire Careers Service, Room 341, County Hall, Trowbridge BA14 8JB).

For those not wanting to go on to higher education but who want work experience, there is the Youth Training Scheme (YTS). Both the trainee and the employer may be eligible for help with special equipment and adaptations. To apply for a YTS place, contact the specialist careers officer at your LEA.

For more information on all aspects of further and higher education for disabled people contact SKILL: NATIONAL BUREAU

FOR STUDENTS WITH DISABILITIES 336 Brixton Road, London SW9 7AA Tel: 071-274 0565.

Employment

Disabled people over 16 may apply to their local Job Centre for registration under the Disabled Persons (Employment) Act 1944. A Disablement Resettlement Officer will arrange for registration following a medical certification. There are some advantages in being registered, because firms employing more than twenty staff should employ no fewer than 3 per cent registered disabled people (how rigorously this is enforced is quite another matter). Certain other facilities, in particular employment in sheltered workshops, are only available to those who are registered.

For information on employment opportunities contact the DISABLEMENT RESETTLEMENT OFFICER at your local Job Centre (in the phone book under Employment Service).

Leisure and recreation

Disabled people want the opportunity to participate fully in the leisure activities which give extra meaning to all our lives. Local authorities are empowered under the CSDPA 1970 to provide radios, televisions and social and educational activities. Many local authorities provide DOMICILIARY LIBRARY SERVICES which call regularly at the homes of disabled or housebound people. SPORTS CENTRES are increasingly providing opportunities for disabled people to participate in sporting activities, and there may be clubs specifically for people with disabilities. Ask at your local sports centre or contact BRITISH SPORTS ASSOCIATION FOR THE DISABLED 34 Osnaburgh Street, London NW1 3ND Tel: 071-383 7277.

The major barrier to the full participation of disabled people in leisure activities is insufficient ACCESS provision (doors are too narrow for wheelchairs, there are stairs instead of lifts, there are no communication facilities for hearing impaired people, etc.). RADAR have produced a series of access guides (to sports centres, arts centres, public conveniences, etc.) and also stock access guides to towns throughout the UK. Write for a publications list to RADAR 25 Mortimer Street, London W1N 8AB.

Informative fact sheets on leisure activities and sport and physical recreation are available from the DISABLED LIVING FOUNDATION. They form sections 6 and 6a of the DLF's comprehensive *Information Service Handbook*. A wide range of arts, leisure and sports clubs, from the Braille Chess Association to the Uphill Ski Club, are also listed in the *Directory for Disabled People* (see page 95).

Transport

There is no point in statutory and voluntary agencies providing services for disabled people if they are unable to take advantage of them because they do not have transport. If you are receiving Mobility Allowance (see page 103) you can use it to help you with any aspect of your transport needs. Most Social Services Departments provide transport to clubs, day centres and workshops for disabled people who are unable to use public transport. There are also travel passes which allow disabled or elderly people to use public transport free or at a reduced rate. In many parts of the country there are now Dial-a-Ride schemes, often run by voluntary organizations, which provide door-to-door transport for disabled people in specially adapted vehicles. For more information on these contact your Social Services Department, DIAL or Citizens' Advice Bureau.

Holidays and respite care

Under the CSDPA 1970, Social Services Departments are empowered to provide financial help for holidays for disabled people. Relevant charities and benevolent associations may also provide financial help (see pages 310–20) and the Family Fund (see page 107) can help with holidays for disabled children.

Some voluntary organizations for specific health problems such as Arthritis Care, the British Diabetic Association, the Multiple Sclerosis Society) have their own holiday homes, but increasingly standard holiday companies are accepting that disabled people have a right to take the same holidays as able bodied people. Many holiday guides now use the access symbol to indicate facilities for disabled people.

There are several good sources of information on holiday opportunities for disabled people:

Holiday Care Service 2 Old Bank Chambers, Station Road, Horley, Surrey RH6 9HW Tel: 0293 774535
An information service on holiday and travel facilities for disabled people, and on financial help where available.

Holidays in the British Isles: a guide for disabled people (Annual publication)

Holidays and Travel Abroad: a guide for disabled people (Annual publication)

Both available from RADAR or branches of W. H. Smith.

MENCAP Holiday Guide (1989)
From MENCAP Holiday Office, 119 Drake Street, Rochdale, Lancs OL16 1PZ

Carers need an occasional break as much as the disabled or elderly person themselves. One way to get a break is to find a holiday scheme suitable for the disabled person. Some Social Services Departments also offer RESPITE CARE SCHEMES, whereby the dependent relative can be provided with full-time care for a short period. Some voluntary organizations offer similar schemes. There is a good leaflet on respite care called *Taking a Break*, available from from Taking a Break, Newcastle upon Tyne NE85 2AQ.

Equipment and adaptations

Local authorities have a statutory responsibility to provide equipment for daily living to help disabled people in their own homes. Disabled people may need NURSING AIDS (special beds, commodes, incontinence pads, etc.). The provider of these varies from one part of the country to another; in some areas it is the health authority, in others Social Services. Your GP, district nurse, health visitor or social worker will be able to advise on availability.

Hospital consultants may prescribe any piece of equipment which they feel is essential to the patient's treatment. This might include appliances such as surgical footwear. Ear, nose and throat consultants can prescribe hearing aids which are then loaned from NHS Hearing Aid Centres. Low vision aids can be prescribed by a consultant ophthalmologist. Wheelchairs are supplied and maintained free of charge by Disablement Services Centres on receipt of an application from a doctor. GPs or consultants can ask for environmental control systems (for example, to control lights, electrical appliances) and aids to communication to be supplied.

People with disabilities may incur additional housing costs because they need to adapt their home. If you are a council tenant you can get help under the CSDPA 1970, although you may have to pay part of the cost. You should approach the housing department for details. If you own your own home or are a private tenant you need to approach your Social Services Department. Building alterations are subject to VAT but certain adaptations for disabled people (constructing ramps, provision of ground-floor toilet, etc.) are zero-rated. For more information see the *Disability Rights Handbook* or send for the booklet *Housing Grants and Allowances for Disabled People* from RADAR.

The DISABLED LIVING FOUNDATION 380–4 Harrow Road, London W9 2HU Tel: 071-289 6111 has the most comprehensive information service in Europe on aids and equipment for disabled people. A computerized database (DLF-DATA) holds details of thousands of pieces of equipment and their suppliers, and there is a demonstration centre with many items on show. You should be able to look at the print version of the database, called the *DLF Information Service Handbook*, in larger public reference libraries.

Reference libraries may also keep the *Equipment for Disabled People* series of handbooks published by Mary Marlborough Lodge, Headington, Oxford OX3 7LD. There are thirteen titles in the series including *Gardening, Parents with Disabilities, Housing and Furniture*, and *Wheelchairs*.

A useful single publication is the *Directory of Aids for Disabled and Elderly People* by Ann Darnbrough and Derek Kinrade (Cambridge: Woodhead Faulkner, 1986).

There are DISABLED LIVING CENTRES in many parts of the UK, where aids and equipment can be viewed and expert advice is available. Sometimes DLCs are situated in hospital rehabilitation departments, sometimes they are based in the community and linked to a DIAL information service. Addresses of local centres are available from the Disabled Living Foundation.

Elderly People

In the UK today there are 5 million women and 3.25 million men aged 65 or over. Elderly people make up 15 per cent of the total population, and the head of over a quarter of all households is over 65. Elderly people are major consumers of health care. Many of the sources of help described above will be relevant to elderly as well as disabled people. In fact many of the disabled people in this country are also elderly (70 per cent are aged 60 or over). However, elderly people also have some special needs and services.

Financial help

RETIREMENT PENSIONS are paid to people who have reached pension age, are considered to be retired and have paid sufficient National Insurance contributions. Pension age is 60 for women and 65 for men. Elderly people may also be eligible for disability benefits, such as Mobility Allowance and Attendance Allowance. They can also get Income Support, Housing Benefit and help from the Social Fund. For those receiving Income Support there is also help available with insulation costs, cold weather payments, etc.

For information on all aspects of financial support for elderly people, send for a copy of the annual booklet *Your Rights: a guide to money benefits for retired people*, from Age Concern, Astral House, 1268 London Road, London SW16 4EJ Tel: 081-679 8000.

⇒ DSS leaflet FB6, *Retiring? Your Pension and Other Benefits*, available from DSS offices and post offices.

Residential Care

Under Part III of the National Assistance Act 1948, local authorities have a duty to provide residential accommodation to all those who 'by reason of age, infirmity, or any other circumstances are in need of care and attention which is not otherwise available to them'. Local authorities can meet this duty either through providing places in their own homes (so-called Part III accommodation) or through sponsorship of places in the private sector. The National Health Service and Community Care Act 1990 encourages local authorities to act as purchasers of places from private and voluntary sector homes rather than necessarily providing them themselves.

The main types of local authority homes are for the elderly and for people with physical disabilities. Places in these homes are usually arranged by a social worker or GP. You and your family should visit the home to have a look at the care provided before accepting a place. Charges for local authority homes vary from one authority to another, but they are obliged to make a minimum charge of £37.50 a week. The local authority will assess your income and see how much you should pay above the minimum charge. You may be eligible for Income Support while in a home and if your 'sole or main residence' is in Part III accommodation you are exempt from the community charge or poll tax. For advice on the financial implications of going into a home, talk to a social worker, the DSS or see the *Disability Rights Handbook*.

Most elderly people want to remain in their own homes, but many will go into residential or nursing homes. Others will be able to take advantage of sheltered housing schemes. The main difference between residential and nursing homes is that the latter provide a greater degree of round-the-clock care. Almost anyone can open a RESIDENTIAL HOME, as long as they are considered a fit person by the local authority, who is responsible for registering and monitoring the home once a year. If you are considering a residential home, your Social Services Department will be able to give you a list of local homes. Look for those which belong to the Registered Residential Care Homes Association. A NURSING HOME has to be registered with the local health authority and there must be a nurse or doctor on duty twenty-four hours a day. Make sure the home belongs to the Registered Nursing Home Association.

Age Concern publishes a booklet called *A Home in a Home: a guide to residential care* and also a free factsheet, *Finding Residential and Nursing Home Accommodation*.

There are now many sheltered housing schemes and housing associations for retired people (for example, Abbeyfield Society, Hanover Housing Association, Raglan Housing Association). These schemes vary in what they offer but features typically include a resident manager or warden, a twenty-four-hour alarm system, and a residents' lounge.

For more information read the Age Concern booklet, *A Buyer's Guide to Sheltered Housing* and the *College of Health Guide to Homes for Elderly People.*

Mental Health Care

In the 1950s psychiatric patients accounted for 40 per cent of all NHS-occupied beds, with 150,000 people with mental health problems in hospital. Today the total is down to 50,000 beds (or 20 per cent of all NHS in-patients). Mental health problems are very widespread. Between 4 and 5 million people a year consult their family doctor because of conditions such as depression and anxiety. More than a quarter of a million people in the UK have been diagnosed as having schizophrenia at some point in their lives. Half a million people are thought to suffer from senile dementia.

Since the 1960s it has been the policy to care for people with mental health problems in the community, and since then about 3,000 psychiatric beds a year have been closed. Although closing the large Victorian asylums seems a laudable objective, the reality is that too many patients have been discharged to inadequate community care provision and some end up in bed and breakfast accommodation or on the street.

Financial help

People with a mental illness can take advantage of a number of the benefits for disabled people listed above. However, they may find it more difficult to prove their entitlement to Attendance Allowance, for example, than people who are physically disabled. If you are trying to claim your entitlements because of a mental health problem you should get hold of a copy of the *A–Z of Welfare Benefits for People with a Mental Illness* from MIND Mail Order, 4th Floor, 24 Stephenson Way, London NW1 2HD. MIND also publishes an excellent series of RIGHTS GUIDES ADVICE LEAFLETS on different types of mental illness and leaflets on different types of TREATMENT for mental illness. Ask for a publications list. MIND's head office at 22 Harley Street, London W1N 2ED Tel: 071-637 0741, will also put you in touch with your local MIND group.

Day care

Local authorities provide DAY CENTRES for people with mental health problems. Sometimes these centres are for specific problems such as alcoholism or drug dependency. National Health Service DAY HOSPITALS provide support and rehabilitation services, including group therapy, relaxation classes, arts and crafts.

Specialist help is available from a number of specialist professionals to people in the community with mental health problems. These include clinical psychologists, community psychiatric nurses and social workers. For more information on their work see Section 2.

Hospital care

If you are diagnosed as suffering from a mental illness you are far less likely to spend time in hospital than you would have been ten or twenty years ago, and even if you are admitted your stay will be shorter. But despite the moves to care in the community there are still good reasons why some people go into hospital. It may be that there is a need for careful observation and assessment before deciding on a course of treatment. You may feel so distressed and disturbed that hospital care is needed, or you may need constant monitoring because of a condition like anorexia nervosa. It may be that there is no one at home capable of looking after you.

The vast majority (as much as 95 per cent) of psychiatric patients are voluntary patients (or 'informal patients'). As a voluntary patient you have a right to refuse treatment and to discharge yourself, although obviously it would be sensible to discuss this with staff first. You may be admitted to one of the old-style psychiatric hospitals or to a department of psychiatry at your local district general hospital. In addition to the treatment you receive from your psychiatrist, there is likely to be a programme of activities including occupational therapy, art and music therapy and group discussions.

A small number of patients are compulsorily detained under the Mental Health Act 1983. Detained patients are not free to leave hospital when they wish and are subject to special rules regarding treatment. Applications for compulsory admission can be made by the 'nearest relative' (this may be the person who lives with, or cares for, the person) or an 'approved social worker' who has special training in mental health care. The application must be supported in writing by two doctors, one of whom must be a psychiatrist.

If you are very worried about the behaviour of someone close to you, or are afraid they will harm themselves or others, your first step should be to contact their GP. If you are unable to do this you can telephone the local Social Services Department. Most have an out-of-hours emergency service. An approved social worker is obliged to visit if requested by a nearest relative. If you are unable to contact the GP or Social Services you can take the patient to the nearest hospital accident and emergency department and ask to see the duty psychiatrist.

The main grounds for compulsory admission are that the person is suffering from a mental disorder to a degree that warrants detention for assessment or treatment, and that the person also needs to be detained in the interests of his or her own safety or the protection of others. Depending on the circumstances, the person may be detained under different sections of the Mental Health Act 1983. This is often referred to as being 'sectioned' or 'on a section'.

Discharge from hospital

At the end of the period of time stipulated in the relevant section of the Mental Health Act, patients automatically become informal patients and are free to discharge themselves, unless further steps are taken under the Act. Patients are discharged from hospital to the care of the GP, although there may be continuing outpatient appointments with the consultant psychiatrist. Nearest relatives can apply to have a patient discharged by writing to the hospital managers. Patients under Sections 2 and 3, and nearest relatives of patients under Section 3, can also apply for discharge through a Mental Health Review Tribunal. This is an independent body consisting of a lawyer, a psychiatrist (from a hospital other than the one where the patient is detained) and a lay person. Although a Mental Health Review Tribunal is not a court of law it helps to be represented by a solicitor. You can get legal aid to pay for advice and representation by a solicitor if your income is below a certain level. Contact your local Citizens' Advice Bureau, MIND or law centre for advice before you proceed.

Complaints

If you or a relative wish to complain about your treatment or care as a psychiatric in-patient or out-patient, first talk to the staff

The Mental Health Act 1983

Section 2: Patients can be detained for up to twenty-eight days for assessment, and sometimes treatment. An application can be made by an approved social worker, without the consent of the nearest relative.
Section 3: Patients can be admitted for treatment for up to six months. It can be renewed for a further six months and then for periods of a year at a time by the psychiatrist in charge of the case.
Section 4: Patients are admitted under Section 4 only in an emergency, for example if they are violent or suicidal. The admission is for a maximum of seventy-two hours to enable an assessment to be made. An application can be made by an approved social worker without the nearest relative's consent.
Section 5: This section is sometimes used to detain voluntary in-patients for up to seventy-two hours to give time for decisions to be made on their treatment.

concerned. If you are unable to sort out the problem informally, put your complaint in writing to the hospital manager or the consultant in charge of your case.

Seek advice from your Community Health Council (CHC) in framing your complaint. If you are a detained patient, or a relative of one, and are not satisfied with a complaint pursued through these normal channels, you can contact the MENTAL HEALTH ACT COMMISSION Hepburn House, Marsham Street, London SW1P 4HW Tel: 071-217 6012. This body was set up in 1983 to protect the rights of detained patients.

For further information on mental health care see the many useful publications from MIND, and the following books, available through public libraries:

Not on Your Own: the MIND guide to mental health by Sally Burningham (Harmondsworth: Penguin, 1989)
Understanding Mental Health by Angelina Gibbs (London: Consumers' Association, 1986)

Complaining about Community Care

If you are not satisfied with some aspect of the care you have received in the community, start by writing to the local office dealing with the matter. If this does not lead to a satisfactory conclusion, your course of action depends on which service you were using.

Department of Social Security

If you have a complaint about the DSS, write to the manager of the local DSS office. If you feel it is a case of maladministration (neglect, undue delay, discrimination, etc.) you can ask your MP to complain to the Parliamentary Ombudsman. The Parliamentary Ombudsman deals with complaints about central government departments, but only if these are referred to him by an MP.

Social Services

If you have a complaint about Social Services, write first to the Director of Social Services of your local authority. If you feel the complaint relates to maladministration you can complain to the Local Government Ombudsman. There is a free booklet available called *Complaints about the Council: how to complain to your local ombudsman*. It even contains a complaints form. Copies should be available from Citizens' Advice Bureaux, or direct from THE LOCAL OMBUDSMAN 21 Queen Anne's Gate, London SW1H 9BU.

Health service

Seek advice in the first instance from your Community Health Council (CHC). For further information on complaining about the health service see Section 4 (pages 165–7).

4 Going into Hospital

Staying in hospital is a surprisingly common experience. Sixty-five per cent of people in the UK have stayed at least one night in hospital, excluding hospital admissions for childbirth. This percentage varies considerably depending on where in the country you live: in the Home Counties 74 per cent of people have spent at least a night in hospital, while in hale and hearty Northern Ireland the total is only 53 per cent. Over the country as a whole, 59 per cent have been referred to a consultant. In the South-West of England the total was no fewer than 70 per cent, compared with only 43 per cent in Ireland. (The difference between consultant referrals and hospital admissions is because many people are admitted directly to hospital every year following accidents.)

In 1987 over 8 million patients passed through our hospitals as in-patients; there were over 12 million attendances at Accident and Emergency Departments, and over 10 million attendances at out-patient clinics. Over 99 per cent of babies are now born in hospital. Although more and more patients are being treated in our hospitals, there are fewer hospital beds and hospital stays are shorter. The average length of stay in 1987 was 8.5 days for medical patients, 6.5 for surgical patients and 4.5 for maternity patients (*Social Trends*, HMSO, 1990). In 1977 the average stay was 11.8 days, 8.4 days and 6.6 days respectively, while back in 1967 the stays averaged 18.6 days, 10.7 days and 8.1 days.

Getting into Hospital

Going to hospital is obviously an experience most of us go through at some stage, but how do we get admitted and what can we expect when we get there? There are only three ways in which you can attend an NHS hospital:

– through the ACCIDENT AND EMERGENCY DEPARTMENT (also known as A & E, or Casualty)
– by going to a SPECIAL CLINIC for the treatment of sexually transmitted diseases (also known as the STD CLINIC, and GENITO-URINARY MEDICINE or GUM Clinic)
– referred by a doctor – usually your GP.

Accident and Emergency

Unless there is a road accident or similar emergency, you should try contacting your GP first. Accident and Emergency Departments see thousands of patients every year who really should have gone to their GP. A & E doctors can turn away people if they do not feel they need treatment. Reasons for this might include if it is some time since the accident occurred, or if you went along with a long-term problem.

If your GP cannot visit quickly or if the accident is serious, go to the nearest Accident and Emergency Department. Remember that not all hospitals have them: in an emergency you can dial 999 and ask which A & E Department you should take someone to.

If you cannot get to the A & E Department and cannot get someone to take you, dial 999 and ask for an ambulance. An ambulance should arrive within twenty minutes. Many ambulance staff are now trained in paramedical skills. The majority of accident and emergency cases can be treated on an out-patient basis and you can go home after treatment. A & E Departments vary in the level of care they can provide. Some provide little more than first aid; others can offer extensive accident treatment. More serious injuries will call for admission as an in-patient. The department to which you are admitted will depend on the type of injuries sustained (for example, someone with head injuries may be admitted to a neurological unit).

NHS emergency charges

NHS hospitals can charge for giving emergency treatment to people involved in road accidents. If you have to pay these charges make sure you get a receipt. You may be able to claim the cost back from your car insurance company, or that of the other driver.

STD Clinics

These special clinics are designed to treat people of all ages who have genito-urinary infections (for example, gonorrhoea, syphilis, trichomoniasis or genital herpes). They are usually attached to main hospitals and give free, confidential advice and treatment. At many clinics you can turn up without an appointment. However, some prefer you to make an appointment first, so it is a good idea to telephone for details. In any case the times of clinics vary a good deal, so you could check this too.

For the address and telephone number of your nearest clinic, look under Venereal Disease or Sexually Transmitted Diseases in the phone book. Some health authorities have tape-recorded messages giving details of STD clinics. The numbers of these are listed in the phone book too. If you have difficulty finding the number your local Family Planning clinic should be able to help. The FAMILY PLANNING INFORMATION SERVICE (Tel: 071-636 7866) has lists of STD clinics around the country.

If you feel you may have been exposed to HIV (the virus which can lead to AIDS) through unprotected sexual intercourse or through sharing a needle for injecting drugs, you can visit the STD clinic for an HIV ANTIBODY TEST. This is not a test for AIDS. It will only tell you whether or not you have been infected by the virus. It cannot predict whether you will go on to develop AIDS. It can take up to three months for antibodies to develop after you have been infected with HIV. This means that you should wait for three months after the last occasion when you think you might have been infected before you have the test. See Section 5 for more details on AIDS and HIV.

The result of the test, and the fact that you have been tested, is confidential between you and the staff involved in the test. However, all life assurance companies ask searching questions about whether you have taken the test, even if the result was negative. No major life assurance company will give life assurance to someone who has the virus, and getting a mortgage may also be difficult. You should think carefully about the consequences of taking the test before making a decision.

For further advice get a copy of the Health Education Authority leaflet *AIDS: the test* from your local health promotion department. There is more information about health promotion departments on pages 298–9.

More detailed information is given in the booklet *Mortgages and Life Assurance*, available from the TERRENCE HIGGINS TRUST 52–4 Gray's Inn Road, London WC1X 8JU Tel: 071-242 1010.

Referral by your GP

For all other hospital treatment you will need a GP's referral to see a specialist. Usually the specialist is a consultant whom you will see first of all in the out-patient department at the hospital. Some consultants also see patients in smaller community hospitals or health centres.

Referral procedure

1 Your GP writes to the consultant, asking for an appointment and classifying you as routine or urgent
2 The consultant then writes to you with an appointment date for his out-patient clinic
3 You attend the consultant's out-patient clinic and the consultant decides whether admission to hospital is necessary
4 If not, you are treated as an out-patient or referred back to your GP
5 If you do need to go into hospital (perhaps for an operation) the consultant decides how urgent admission is, and puts you on his in-patient waiting list
6 After a further wait (depending on the urgency of the problem) you are admitted to hospital for treatment
7 Following treatment you are discharged from hospital and cared for by your GP There may be follow-up appointments at the consultant's out-patient clinic.

Waiting Lists and How to Beat Them

Being told you need an operation is bad enough, but then having to face months or even years before you can be admitted to hospital can make the whole thing even more depressing. It is not very cheering to read Department of Health figures which show that over 1 million people are now waiting for admission to hospital. Department of Health figures for 1990 show that 804,182 patients are waiting for in-patient treatment and 200,188 for day surgery.

More than a quarter of the in-patients have been waiting more than a year. The majority are waiting for surgery in five main specialities; general surgery, orthopaedics, gynaecology, ophthalmology, and ear, nose and throat surgery. They are waiting for operations which surgeons regard as relatively straightforward, such as hernias, varicose veins, hip replacements, hysterectomies, cataracts and tonsils. Some are waiting with life-threatening conditions. According to a speaker at the 1990 BMA consultants' meeting nearly 500 people with heart complaints die every year while on an NHS waiting list.

An examination of hospital waiting lists by health service analyst John Yates shows that there have been long waiting lists since the NHS began. For the first twenty-five years of the NHS's existence the list remained at about half a million. Since the mid-1970s it has been rising to over three-quarters of a million.

Many theories have been advanced for rising waiting lists:

- The NHS is inefficient
- The NHS is inadequately funded
- There is a national shortage of surgeons, and nurses too
- Consultants have a vested interest in long waiting lists because patients will then see them privately
- Waiting lists are made longer by industrial action
- Waiting lists act as an effective means of rationing finite resources
- Waiting lists are meaningless because many patients on them have

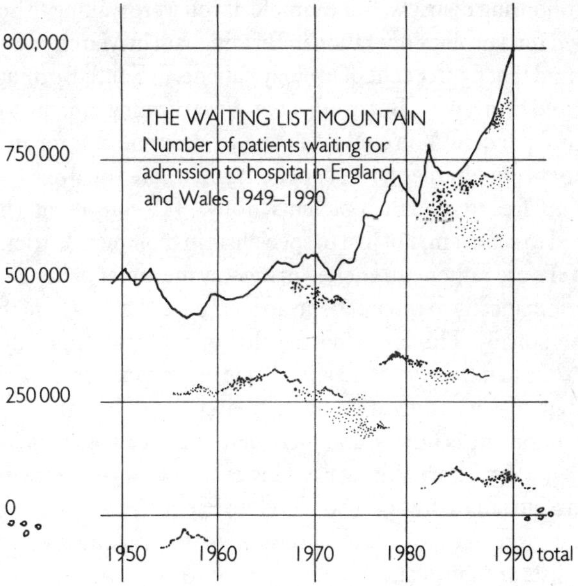

Waiting lists remain a major cause of dissatisfaction with the health service. The waiting list mountain has continued to rise in recent years. In 1990 over 800,000 people were waiting for admission to hospital (Source: Yates, J., *Why Are We Waiting?* Oxford University Press, 1987. Updated to 1990)

died, moved away or even had their operation, without being removed from the list

There may be some truth in all these theories, but they do not help the patient waiting to get into hospital. In order to be seen by a consultant as soon as possible, patients need to know how to play the waiting lists game. The key to the game is that the length of your wait may be an accident of where you live. In 1985 the size of the orthopaedic waiting list in English and Welsh District Health Authorities varied from those with fewer than 100 patients to one which had over 4,000 waiting. The variation can be enormous, even in neighbouring districts. For example, if you were waiting to be admitted for a urology operation in Birmingham in March 1989, you would find that 65 per cent of urology patients in South Birmingham had waited over a year. But in adjacent West Birmingham the total was only 8 per cent. You could wait one week or one year for an out-patient appointment, just depending on where you live.

GPs are free to send their patients to any NHS consultant who is prepared to see them, not just to specialists in their own district. Many GPs are rather entrenched in the way they refer patients. They tend automatically to refer patients to local consultants whom they know personally. This is not just the old boy network in operation. GPs do like to have first-hand knowledge of the capabilities of the consultant to whom they are sending their patients. Not all surgeons are as competent as others, and there may be a very good reason why Mr A. has a very short waiting list. However, recent government policy as laid out in the 1989 NHS White Paper, *Working for Patients*, has been to encourage GPs to 'shop around' for treatment where the waiting lists are shortest.

This idea seems to have found favour with patients too. In March 1989 the National Consumer Council commissioned MORI to carry out a survey on consumer attitudes to the health service. One of the questions was 'Would you be prepared to travel to a more distant hospital if you would be treated more quickly?' Eighty-eight per cent of respondents said that they would. The older the respondents the less likely they would be prepared to travel. In deciding whether to travel to a more distant hospital, you would have to weigh up the additional costs of travel, the fact that you might not be able to have visitors, and additional difficulties which could occur with follow-up appointments. But many people would feel that this is a reasonable price to pay for the relief of months or years of suffering and impairment.

In fact the extra travel and lack of visitors may worry people less than might be imagined. In 1989 113 patients in Crewe with long waits for varicose vein and hernia operations were given the option of travelling to the RAF hospital in Wroughton, Wilts, to have their surgery done more quickly. About half the patients accepted the 120-mile journey at the health authority's expense. For those patients travel was preferable to waiting, even with the disadvantages of the journey and lack of visitors.

Waiting list information

If you (and your GP) are to be able to exercise this choice, you need access to information. All health authorities collect information about their waiting lists and make quarterly returns to the Department of Health. Many health authorities also produce bulletins showing the waiting lists of their own consultants and distribute them to local GPs. But it is only recently that this information has been made available to the wider public, and then only in some parts of the country. Some health authorities still seem to regard this important consumer health information as confidential.

Much of the credit for opening up waiting list information for public consumption should go to the College of Health. In 1984 the College of Health published the first edition of its *Guide to Hospital Waiting Lists*. For the first time consumers could compare the waiting lists for major specialties and ask their GP to refer them to a consultant in a district with a comparatively short list.

Although the College of Health guide has broken new ground in consumer access to health service information, it does not tell the whole story. For a start, the information is broken down by District Health Authorities and not by individual hospitals or individual consultants. Even within a district waiting times can vary considerably. Second, the information is inevitably out of date as soon as the guide is published. It is based on the returns made by DHAs to the Department of Health, which are in themselves several months in arrears. By the time the information is reorganized and published by the College of Health it could reflect a situation which is two years old. Third, it only tells part of the story. The returns made

Coping with waiting lists

If you are faced with a long wait for treatment in your own district you should:

– Contact the **College of Health** St Margaret's House, 21 Old Ford Road, London E2 9PL Tel: 081-983 1225 and order a copy of the latest *Guide to Hospital Waiting Lists*

– Check the guide to see which district has the shortest waiting list, and think about how far you would be prepared to travel

– Ask your GP to consider referring you to a consultant in that district. Having got an indication of good districts to try, you could find the address and telephone numbers of individual hospitals from the annual *Hospital and Health Services Yearbook* (available in main public reference libraries). Even if you do the homework for your GP, you will still have to ask him or her to contact the consultant asking whether you can be taken on as an NHS patient

– If you feel you cannot travel elsewhere for treatment, you should consider putting your name on a **short notice** list in your own district. This means that you could take up a vacancy if someone else was unable to accept the date they were offered to come into hospital. As the hospital has very little time to fill the bed you could be telephoned and offered admission, even at a few hours' notice

by the DHAs, and reported in the College of Health guide, only cover 'in-patient waiting times', that is, the time between seeing the consultant as an out-patient and admission to hospital. In fact there are two waiting lists. You wait to see the consultant as an out-patient, and having seen him you wait to be admitted to hospital.

Few health authorities have attempted the difficult task of giving an overall picture of the two waiting periods. In Wessex, we have set up a phone-in information service on waiting lists. WESSEX WAITING LINE holds on a microcomputer information on out-patient and in-patient waiting times across the Wessex Region (Hampshire, Isle of Wight, Wiltshire and Dorset). The information has the advantage of being updated monthly and being available on a phone-in basis. The service is currently only available to GPs but an obvious future development would be much wider access. Work is now in hand to produce a desk-top version of the database which could be available within GP practices, Community Health Councils and libraries.

Despite the government's commitment to consumer choice, in future it may be only those GPs with their own practice budgets (see page 51) who have the freedom to shop around, using their buying power to send patients to those hospitals offering the shortest waiting lists or the highest-quality service. The remaining GPs will be restricted to sending patients to the hospitals with which they have a block contract for treatment, resulting in a lesser degree of choice than existed before NHS reforms.

NHS Hospitals

NHS hospitals range from 1,500-bed establishments to those with fewer than fifty patients. They may be the most up-to-date hi-tech units, or places where the fabric of the building, at least, has changed little since the eighteenth century.

All District Health Authorities have at least one DISTRICT GENERAL HOSPITAL, which offers mainly acute (short stay) services.

> Main services offered by District General Hospitals:
>
> – medical wards (adult)
> – medical wards (children)
> – surgical wards (adult)
> – surgical wards (children)
> – Accident and Emergency Department
> – maternity unit
> – out-patient clinics
> – x-ray and facilities for other tests
> – rehabilitation services (occupational therapy, physiotherapy, speech therapy, etc.)

Depending on the type of treatment, you may be treated in another kind of hospital:

– COMMUNITY OR COTTAGE HOSPITALS: local neighbourhood hospitals providing a less extensive range of facilities. Many offer day surgery, out-patient clinics and maternity services.
– GP HOSPITALS: GPs are able to treat their own patients, including performing some minor surgery. GPs may also have beds in larger general hospitals.
– DAY HOSPITALS: day surgery may be used for fairly minor

operations where the patient does not need to stay overnight. Day hospitals also provide services, such as occupational therapy, for elderly or psychiatric patients.

– CHILDREN'S HOSPITALS: centres with an environment better equipped for children's needs. Your Community Health Council will be able to tell you if there is a children's hospital in your region (or check in the *Hospitals and Health Services Yearbook*). Nowadays general hospitals have their own trained children's nurses, and recognize the importance of play and parental contact.

– REGIONAL SPECIALTIES: some specialist services such as kidney treatment, plastic surgery or neurosurgery are organized on a regional basis, and are provided at regional units. Attendance at a regional unit will probably involve you in travel to another hospital.

– MENTAL OR PSYCHIATRIC HOSPITALS: although more people with mental problems are being cared for in the community (see pages 120–4), there are still patients in large psychiatric hospitals. Many of these are elderly, mentally infirm people. District General Hospitals often have their own Departments of Psychiatry.

– MENTAL HANDICAP HOSPITALS: again, the policy nowadays is to care for mentally handicapped people in community-based homes, but there remain a number of mental handicap hospitals.

Hospital Staff

You will see so many doctors, nurses and other health staff during your hospital stay that you will begin to wonder who they all are and what they all do. Good hospitals produce booklets which are given to patients on admission, giving details of who's who and how to recognize staff by their uniform.

Doctors

You are admitted to hospital under the care of a particular CONSULTANT. He has a TEAM OF DOCTORS working with him, known as a 'FIRM'. It is extremely likely that your consultant will be a man. Of the 3,136 consultant surgeons working in operating theatres in England and Wales in 1988 only eighty-nine were women – less than 3 per cent. In comparison, 25 per cent of all hospital doctors and 20 per cent of GPs are women.

The hierarchy of a 'firm' of hospital doctors

Consultant
Senior registrar
Registrar
Senior house officer
Junior house officer

All these are qualified doctors. In teaching hospitals, and in some other hospitals, MEDICAL STUDENTS may accompany the consultant on his ward round. It is assumed that you have no objection to medical students being present when you are being examined. You are perfectly entitled to refuse permission if you would prefer them not to be present. You cannot, however, object to the presence of other doctors and nurses.

Recent guidelines issued by the Royal College of Surgeons (*Consultant Responsibility in Invasive Procedures*, 1990) have emphasized the ultimate responsibility of the consultant for every operation, even if he is not present in person. The extent to which procedures can be delegated 'must depend on the consultant's knowledge of the ability and experience of the team'.

Nurses

Nurses are either REGISTERED NURSES or ENROLLED NURSES (the latter have a shorter training). Most Registered Nurses train as RGNs (REGISTERED GENERAL NURSES) but there are also separate courses as RMNs (REGISTERED MENTAL NURSES) and RSCNs (REGISTERED SICK CHILDREN'S NURSES). Nurses now have the opportunity to take 'conversion courses' to transfer between the different parts of the Register, and from Enrolled to Registered Nurse.

The head of nursing on a particular ward is a SISTER (or CHARGE NURSE if a man). Under her there will be qualified STAFF NURSES as well as STUDENT NURSES. There will also be qualified and trainee ENROLLED NURSES. NURSING AUXILIARIES, who are not trained nurses, help with duties such as bathing and meals. NURSE MANAGERS are in charge of nursing staff on a number of wards, in a unit or a hospital. Some hospitals have introduced the concept of PRIMARY NURSING where you have your own nurse, who is particularly responsible for your care.

It is important to note that nurses work alongside doctors and do not report to them. The nursing hierarchy is quite separate from the medical hierarchy.

Other hospital staff

During your hospital stay you may also come across the following staff:

– RADIOGRAPHERS who take X-rays

– OCCUPATIONAL THERAPISTS who help patients to readjust to activities of daily living following illnesses or accidents
– PHYSIOTHERAPISTS who use techniques such as exercise and manipulation to help prevent disabling effects of illness
– SPEECH THERAPISTS who help patients who have had strokes, head injuries, etc. to recover their powers of speech. They also work with children with speech problems.
– DIETITIANS who advise on diet for patients with conditions such as diabetes, kidney and heart disease
– SOCIAL WORKERS who advise patients on entitlement to welfare benefits and services, and arrange the provision of help at home after discharge.

These professionals usually work in the community as well as in hospitals.

Your Hospital Stay

Transport to hospital

If you would have difficulty travelling to hospital (for example, because you are disabled or elderly) you may be entitled to be taken to hospital by the HOSPITAL CAR SERVICE. Your GP will be able to advise on this.

Help with PUBLIC TRANSPORT FARES is also available for those on low incomes. The social worker at the hospital will be able to advise on refunds of fares. Make sure you keep the tickets or receipts. ⇒ DSS leaflet HI I, *Your Hospital Fares*, which should be available from post offices and Social Security offices.

Visitors

Visiting times vary between hospitals, and within hospitals between wards. These used to be rigidly enforced, but things are changing. For example, essentially healthy patients such as women who have had babies may find they can have visitors at almost any time. You would also expect staff to interpret the visiting times more freely for relatives or friends of seriously ill patients. Many hospitals also have overnight accommodation for these relatives, and visitors should be able to use the hospital canteen, at a charge. If there is no overnight accommodation available the social work department should be able to suggest somewhere close to the hospital.

Meals

For many people hospital food is one of the less attractive aspects of their stay. However, increasing numbers of hospitals are now producing meals which are more appetizing for people who may have a reduced appetite. With advice from dietitians and health promotion staff, there is an increased fibre content, and better provision for vegetarian and ethnic diets. You are also likely to have a choice of meals. As this choice is usually made a day in advance, you may find yourself eating your predecessor's choice on the first day of your stay, and on the final day making the choice for your successor!

Amenity beds

Some hospitals have single rooms for patients who want more privacy. These are called amenity beds and are part of the NHS provision. You cannot book these in advance, but can ask on arrival if there are any single rooms available. If your condition merits a single room there is no charge; otherwise you will have to pay a daily fee. You may have to move out of your amenity bed if another patient needs it more than you do.

If you want to know more about going into hospital you should read the excellent *Which?* publication, *A Patient's Guide to the National Health Service* (London: Consumers' Association/Patients Association, 1983).

Children in Hospital

One out of four children has had a hospital stay by the age of 5. This can be a very distressing and difficult experience for children, who have special requirements when they are admitted to hospital. Not only are they more vulnerable emotionally and reliant on adults, but they require different equipment, techniques and skills from hospital staff. It has been Department of Health policy since the Platt Report on the Welfare of Children in Hospital in 1959 that parents should be admitted to the hospital with the child. The policy now is to:

– prevent the admission of children to hospital; in-patient stays should be as short as possible, and where possible avoided altogether
– ensure hospital facilities and routines are adapted to the needs of children

Since 1961, the National Association for the Welfare of Children in Hospital (NAWCH) has been working to raise awareness of the needs of sick children and their families. This has been done by representing children's interests in health service planning at local and national level, and promoting good services, as well as providing support to individual parents. In 1985 NAWCH published its *Charter for Children in Hospital* with the support of the British Medical Association, Royal College of Nursing, National Association of Health Authorities and many other professional and voluntary bodies.

In 1988 NAWCH published its *Quality Checklist for Caring for Children in Hospital* which translated the principles of the charter into clear standards which could be used to assess the quality of services for children in each District Health Authority. In a National Health Service which is increasingly quality-conscious, these standards are widely accepted. You may not find all elements in place in your own local hospital, but the NAWCH Charter

The NAWCH Charter

1 Children shall be admitted to hospital only if the care they require cannot be equally well provided at home or on a day basis.
2 Children in hospital shall have the right to have their parents with them at all times provided this is in the best interests of the child. Accommodation should therefore be offered to all parents, and they should be helped and encouraged to stay. In order to share in the care of their child, parents should be fully informed about ward routine and their active participation encouraged.
3 Children and their parents shall have the right to information appropriate to their age and understanding.
4 Children and their parents shall have the right to informed participation in all decisions involving their health care. Every child shall be protected from unnecessary medical treatment, and steps taken to mitigate physical and emotional distress.
5 Children shall be treated with tact and understanding and at all times their privacy shall be respected.
6 Children shall enjoy the care of appropriately trained staff, fully aware of the physical and emotional needs of each age group.
7 Children shall be able to wear their own clothes and have their own personal possessions.
8 Children shall be cared for with other children of the same age group.
9 Children shall be in an environment furnished and equipped to meet their requirements, and which conforms to recognized standards of safety and supervision.
10 Children shall have full opportunity for play, recreation and education suited to their age and condition.

provides a good shopping list for checking on the availability and quality of local services.

At the very least you should be able to stay with your child as much as possible (this is NHS policy). The hospital may provide a chair, mattress or folding bed for you to sleep on, although this may not necessarily be next to your child's bed. Most hospitals do not have strictly enforced visiting hours for parents, and you should be able to give your child his or her meals, bath, etc. Children's ward kitchens often have supplies of breakfast cereals, baked beans, etc. for children who are not partial to hospital food. If you are not able to be with your child all the time, you can tell the ward sister about any food fads, comfort habits, special words, etc. that your child has. Most hospitals allow children to wear their own clothes as much as possible, and also to bring in their own toys.

All nurses have some experience on children's (paediatric) wards, but some have specialist training as REGISTERED SICK CHILDREN'S NURSES. Some hospitals also have HOSPITAL PLAY SPECIALISTS who play with children on the wards, and may also help prepare them for admission. Hospital-based TEACHERS provide lessons for children of school age. This may be in consultation with the child's school.

If your child is going into hospital, make sure you contact NAWCH Argyle House, 29–31 Euston Road, London NW1 2SD Tel: 071-833 2041. NAWCH publish useful leaflets on subjects including:

– Coming into hospital (information on preparation, visiting, etc.)
– Your baby in special care

There is also a comic for children and a series of reading lists, books and reports.

The NAWCH head office will be able to put you in touch with your nearest local branch. Local branches can offer personal support. Twenty-four NAWCH branches also run travel funds for parents on low income who are visiting children in hospital. A list of schemes is available from NAWCH head office.

Benefits and Your Stay in Hospital

Being admitted to hospital as an in-patient, or having to attend an out-patient clinic on a regular basis, is a stressful enough experience for most people without having to worry about claiming benefits. People who are ill or disabled have a wide range of benefits available to them but because of their condition can find it especially difficult to find their way through the social security system. Furthermore, many patients are unaware of the effects of hospitalization on their receipt of benefits. Long-term residents in mental illness and handicap hospitals particularly need good advice. Yet a recent survey of 270 establishments published by the Disability Alliance (*Not a Penny to Call my Own*) showed that only one offered newly admitted patients a benefit check and advice on claiming.

Within hospital you should be able to turn to the MEDICAL SOCIAL WORK DEPARTMENT for advice. Some hospitals even have a CITIZENS' ADVICE BUREAU on site; others have branches of DIAL: Disablement Information and Advice Lines (see pages 302–5 for more information on CABs and DIALs). The best detailed source of information on benefits for hospital in-patients, out-patients and their advisers is the *Hospital Patients' Handbook* (published by the DISABILITY ALLIANCE 25 Denmark Street, London WC2 8NJ Tel: 071-240 0806, 1988). There is also invaluable information for advisers on benefits in the Disability Alliance's annual *Disability Rights Handbook*, which is updated during the year by regular bulletins. In January 1990, *Nursing Times* published a series of three articles on money rights. The first, dealing with benefits for hospital patients, appeared on 31 January 1990.

While you are in hospital you are accepted as being unable to work. If you are employed you should send a medical certificate to your employer to confirm this. The hospital will provide the certificate. If you are receiving benefits you should let the

Department of Social Security know that you are in hospital as many benefits are affected by this.

– MOBILITY ALLOWANCE, STATUTORY MATERNITY PAY and STATUTORY SICK PAY are not affected by a stay in hospital
– ATTENDANCE ALLOWANCE is lost once the disabled person has been in hospital for four weeks
– SEVERE DISABILITY PREMIUM is not affected by the loss of attendance allowance after four weeks
– INVALID CARE ALLOWANCE is lost if the person you are caring for loses their attendance allowance
– HOUSING BENEFIT, and help with housing costs from INCOME SUPPORT, is only paid where the stay in hospital is likely to be less than fifty-two weeks
– CHILD BENEFIT can be removed if your child is in hospital for twelve weeks and you are spending nothing on him or her.

There are REDUCTIONS in contributory benefits and income support for hospital in-patients after six weeks in hospital, and again after twelve weeks. Retired people will have their STATE RETIREMENT PENSION cut after six weeks in hospital, and again after a year. For details see the *Hospital Patients' Handbook*, or speak to the social worker or Citizens' Advice Bureau.

Information on the benefits and services available to sick and disabled people in the community is given in Section 3.

Consent to Treatment

Examining or treating patients without their consent is a form of assault. The only exceptions to this are:

- if a person has a notifiable disease
- if a person has been detained under the Mental Health Act 1983

In the case of operations under local or general anaesthetic, doctors and hospitals ask patients to sign a CONSENT FORM. There is a standard consent form agreed by the Department of Health, the BMA, the Medical Defence Union, and the Medical Protection Society. The form is evidence of the patient's consent to the proposed surgery, and also authorizes the surgeon to perform 'such further or alternative measures as may be necessary'. The use of standard forms is not compulsory within the NHS, and you may find different forms used in private hospitals.

Of course some patients will be admitted to hospital UNCONSCIOUS. In this case it is the usual practice to try to contact the next of kin for their consent on behalf of the patient. If delay would be dangerous, a doctor is entitled to carry out any necessary treatment or operation. However, the doctor should not give the patient more extensive treatment than is absolutely necessary to cope with the emergency.

Patients are entitled to REFUSE any form of treatment proposed, including drug treatment. Doctors should explain the risks and benefits to enable you to make that decision. If you refuse treatment, a consultant can discharge you from his care. If a Jehovah's Witness refuses to consent to a blood transfusion, then legally that treatment cannot be given.

The law requires PARENTS to give or refuse consent for a child who cannot consent for himself. If a child is in care, or a ward of court, then parents lose this right, although they may be consulted. As soon as a child is able fully to understand what is proposed (in a doctor's judgement) he or she can give consent for themselves.

Clinical trials

Patients may, sometimes unwittingly, be participating in CLINICAL TRIALS. These trials are part of medical research in which, for example, the efficacy of a drug is tested in a group of patients, with a control group of patients not receiving the drug. Press coverage of recent cases has highlighted a situation in which patients are, according to Dr Andrew Herxheimer, 'mostly passsive participants in trials, unwitting beneficiaries of the results, innocent victims of the mistakes' ('The rights of the patient in clinical research', *Lancet* 2 (8620) 1988). The position on consent for medical research varies according to whether the research is expected to benefit the patient or not. Where no benefit to the individual patient is expected, Department of Health guidelines state that 'a full explanation of the proposed procedure should be given and the patient must feel free to withdraw at any stage'. Where research is expected to benefit the patient, 'although consent should ordinarily be sought, there are sometimes circumstances in which it is inappropriate or even inhumane to explain the details and seek consent' (for example, if a person does not wish to know they have a fatal illness). Every hospital or institution where clinical trials are carried out has its own ethical committee which oversees the conduct of medical research. Patients are at liberty to refuse to take part in any clinical trial.

Informed consent

For consent to be real, it must be INFORMED. The patient must be told what operation is to be performed and why it is to be done. In signing the standard consent form the patient declares that 'the nature and purpose of the operation has been explained to me'. However, it is clear that the patient who is under physical and/or emotional stress is often unable to take in and question the information given. In turn the doctor may be poor at communicating quite technical information to a lay person.

Researchers at Ninewells Hospital, Dundee interviewed 100 patients after their operation. Although they were all aware that they had had an operation, 27 per cent did not know which organ had been operated on and 44 per cent did not understand the nature of the operation.

Under British law you must be told something about the treatment proposed, but the amount of information is decided by the doctor. This state of affairs has been supported by a number of cases in the courts.

Sidaway v. the Board of Governors of Bethlem Hospital (1985)

In this celebrated case the Law Lords ruled that the amount of information given to a patient, and the assessment of the risks worth mentioning, 'must primarily be a matter of clinical judgement'. Mrs Sidaway had a history of severe pain and, in 1974, had an operation on her neck to relieve this. The doctor, whom she described as 'a man of very, very few words', did not tell her that there was a small risk that her spinal cord might be damaged. In the event it was damaged, leaving Mrs Sidaway paralysed. The grounds for her action were that the doctor had not disclosed the risk, and that had she known of it she would not have consented to the operation.

The court found that the risk from the operation was very small (about 1 per cent) and in deciding not to mention it the doctor had acted in accordance with responsible medical opinion. There was no evidence that Mrs Sidaway had specifically asked whether her disability might get worse because of the operation. If she had done so, the doctor would have been obliged to give her the information. Deciding what information to give a patient is, according to Lord Diplock, 'as much an exercise of professional skill and judgement as any other part of the doctor's comprehensive duty of care to the individual patient'. In other words, in the UK there is no absolute right to information on your treatment.

Judgments subsequent to Sidaway (see box, left) show that the debate continues on the legal basis of informed consent. In Blyth v. Bloomsbury Area Health Authority (1985) a woman who suffered prolonged bleeding after receiving the contraceptive drug Depo-Provera received compensation because, despite questions, she was not told of the potential side-effects. In 1986 Mrs Gold won substantial damages when she became pregnant three years after she had been sterilized. The surgeon had not warned her of the possibility of failure. The judge decided (in Gold. v. Haringey Health Authority) that this was vital information which any prudent person would wish to use to enable them to make an informed decision. Both the Blyth and Gold cases suggest there are different standards of information-giving where consent is given for procedures of convenience (such as choice of contraception), compared with consent for purely medical treatment (as in Sidaway).

For more information on informed consent:

Patients' Rights: a guide for NHS patients and doctors (London: National Consumer Council, 1983) (also available as an updated summary sheet 1989, from Association of Community Health Councils for England and Wales, 30 Drayton Park, London N5 1PB)
Rights and Responsibilities of Doctors (London: BMA, 1988)
Medicine, Patients and the Law by Margaret Brazier (Harmondsworth: Penguin, 1987)
Whose Body Is It? The troubled issue of informed consent by Caroline Faulder (London: Virago, 1985)
'Bodies belong to patients', *Which way to health?* (June 1989)
Research Involving Patients (London: Royal College of Physicians, 1990)

Patient Information

Beyond the need to demonstrate informed consent, there are other good reasons for ensuring that patients are given clear information on what to expect when they come into hospital. There is a growing body of research which indicates that giving people information before admission to hospital, during their stay and on discharge can have clear benefits for the patients themselves, and for the health service. Philip Ley, Professor of Psychology at Sydney University, has been studying the effects of providing patients with information for a number of years. Recently he published the most comprehensive review of the topic, which analyses over 300 studies (*Communicating with Patients: improving communication, satisfaction and compliance*, London: Croom Helm, 1988). Ley concludes that giving patients information leads to:

– more truly informed consent
– increased patient understanding and satisfaction
– increased compliance with treatment, particularly taking medication properly
– quicker and less stressful recovery from illness and surgery

Understanding and satisfaction

Increasingly, hospitals are producing leaflets and other information materials for patients. This can help to give the hospital a user-friendly image, an important part of today's quality assurance drives. If hospitals go to the trouble of ensuring that their patients have information it is likely that this will be received positively by patients. Most surveys show that patients would like more information about services and treatment; not many patients complain about having too much information.

Provision of information to patients seems to increase patient satisfaction, but there is also evidence that it improves understanding of the illness and its treatment. Doctors at Queen's Medical Centre, Nottingham designed a patient information booklet to take home on discharge from hospital, giving details of treatment and continuing care. Patients who were given the booklet were appreciative of receiving it, and they also knew significantly more about their treatment than a control group of patients who were given no information – 86 per cent knew the names of their drugs and 85 per cent the reasons for taking them.

Other methods of putting over information seem to be popular and successful. When the day care unit at Kingston Hospital was opened, an educational cassette tape was recorded to prepare patients for hernia repair operations. Patients were lent the twenty-minute tape when they came to the out-patient clinic for the first time (most people owned a cassette player or could borrow one). Few patients listened to the tape alone: 75 per cent listened with their spouse and in 32 per cent of households other members of the family also listened. A significant minority (15 per cent) called in friends and neighbours to hear the tape! The vast majority of patients (90 per cent) were satisfied with the information given. Most of those who were not satisfied wanted more information. More importantly, 94 per cent said that the tape accurately reflected the events on the day of the operation and helped to relieve anxiety.

Patient information in audio-visual form is becoming increasingly common: 46 per cent of households in the UK now own video recorders and for many people this is a natural way of assimilating information. For example, at the Royal Devon and Exeter Hospital consultants and nursing staff have worked with a professional video company to produce a series of programmes for patients with various conditions, including kidney failure and cancer. A video programme is used within the hospital to prepare cancer patients who are going to administer their own cytotoxic drugs at home as part of Exeter's Home Oncology Project.

Making patients feel involved in the choices that are being made about their treatment can have a therapeutic effect. Research carried out in the Psychology Unit of the Royal Free Hospital in

London and broadcast on Radio 4's 'Medicine Now' programme, has demonstrated that when patients feel in control of their own treatment they do tend to recover more quickly from illness. The very act of seeking information can be an important way of coping with illness and lessening a sense of powerlessness. There is no doubt that many people with serious illnesses such as cancer and AIDS become assiduous gatherers of information, and experts in their own right.

Compliance with treatment

The term 'compliance' is not a very attractive one, and tends to suggest a state of passive acquiesence ('Doctor knows best'). *Roget's Thesaurus* offers the alternatives 'obedience, docility, pliability'. Perhaps a more acceptable term would be cooperation with treatment, but it is compliance which is used in the medical and nursing literature. In the classic study *Compliance with Therapeutic Regimens* by R. B. Haynes and D. L. Sackett (Baltimore: Johns Hopkins University Press, 1976) over 250 reasons are identified for not taking medicines properly. These range from the state of the weather to the difficulties of opening containers with safety-lock caps. Lack of information has consistently been found to be a cause of non-compliance.

In one hospital study 30 per cent of patients were wrong when questioned as to how often they took their drugs; only one in sixty knew the names of the drugs they were taking, and 75 per cent were wrong about the part of their body affected by the drug. More worrying was the fact that over half assumed they did understand their medication, and only 5 per cent asked the doctor for clarification. It is not surprising that when these patients go home from hospital and are responsible for their own medication, they make mistakes in taking their drugs. American pharmacologists Ronald Stewart and Leighton Cluff estimate that the percentage of patients making errors in self-medication range from 25–60 per cent depending on the drugs. They conclude that 'in our society better information is given when purchasing a new camera or automobile than when the patient receives a life saving antibiotic or cardiac drug'.

In the years since Stewart and Cluff made their appeal for better information on medicines, there have been many improvements. In part this has been prompted by an awareness of the huge costs of non-compliance. The US Department of Health and Human Services estimated in 1980 that non-compliance with ten common drug categories costs the United States as much as $790 million a year. The costs are made up of unnecessary repeat prescriptions, additional visits to the doctor, loss of work days and readmission to hospital (because treatment has not worked or because of unnoticed side-effects). In part improved information has been due to consumer protection legislation. Pharmacists are increasingly being seen as important sources of information and advice on medication (see Section 1). Hospitals are also recognizing that patients need to be prepared for taking medicines on their own once they are discharged from the sheltered environment of the ward. Patients in hospital wards are protected and cocooned, with few decisions to make. Then, suddenly, as the ambulance arrives to take them home, they are handed their tablets with some hasty verbal instructions. No wonder they take the tablets in the wrong way, at the wrong time of day, or neglect to finish the course. Many hospitals are now preparing patients for discharge through programmes of training in self-medication.

The need is particularly great for elderly patients who may be taking a whole cocktail of different drugs and can easily get confused. At Odstock Hospital in Salisbury, Southern General Hospital in Glasgow, and Princess Margaret Rose Orthopaedic Hospital in Edinburgh, for example, self-medication programmes for elderly patients have been in place for several years. At Burford Cottage Hospital (see page 169 below) the traditional medicine round has been discontinued. In keeping with the philosophy of maximum independence and minimum institutionalization, patients have the responsibility for taking their own drugs. Each patient has a primary nurse responsible for his or her care. The primary nurse produces an individual information guide for the patient giving details of the drug, the dose and why it is taken, and records that the patient has taken the drug at the right time. But patients learn how to tackle the packaging, read the label and understand the dosage as a preparation for taking responsibility for their own care on discharge.

Reduction of stress and anxiety

Entering hospital, particularly for surgery, is a stressful event. Patients experience fear of the unknown, fear of pain, fear of mutilation and death. Fear and anxiety is not only distressing in itself but may have profound effects on recovery. Some of the earliest work on information and stress was carried out by I. L. Janis over thirty years ago. He conducted a series of interviews with patients in hospital for surgery and made observations on their levels of anxiety before the operation and their recovery after it. He found that extreme anxiety was often followed by a poor recovery. But interestingly enough absence of any fear was almost as bad. The ideal state of mind was a realistic degree of anxiety – an informed apprehension.

Since then many studies have demonstrated the benefits of preparing patients for operations by giving them information on what to expect. A report which has been influential in the nursing profession is *Information: a prescription against pain* by Jack Hayward (London: Royal College of Nursing, 1975). Professor Hayward compared groups of patients who had received information about anaesthesia, operative techniques, sensations following the operation and exercises, with a control group of patients who did not receive information. The informed patients required fewer drugs, and those who had not had information reported more pain. In addition to experiencing less pain and consuming fewer drugs it also seems that informed patients have fewer post-operative infections and can be discharged from hospital sooner.

Mr Michael Edwards, a forward-thinking consultant surgeon at Friarage Hospital, Northallerton, has used his word-processor (Wordcraft on an Apricot F2) to create a bank of information sheets for his patients on sixty-five different operations. The sheets range from three pages of A4 for simple procedures to seven pages for the most complex (oesophagectomy). It was estimated that each leaflet contained information which would take at least twenty minutes to give verbally. The beauty of the system, called OP-FAX, is that it is easy to use the word-processor to customize the information for different patients and different doctors. Reaction from patients has been positive, with those receiving the leaflets expressing significantly more satisfaction with the information they received than those who had verbal advice alone.

It is not only operations that can give rise to considerable anxiety. Tests such as barium meals, mammographies and biopsies which hospital staff regard as routine can be frightening and undignified for many patients. Too often people are summoned for tests without any clear idea of what is going to happen to them. Will it hurt? How long will it take? Do I have to get undressed? Can I eat a meal beforehand? Will I be able to drive home afterwards? Some hospitals (although still not enough) are now producing information leaflets which accompany the letter telling you the date and time of your appointment. A particularly good series of leaflets has been produced for the Radiology Department of Morriston Hospital in West Glamorgan. Leaflets for individual tests are colour-coded to match the doors in the relevant departments. In a standard format, they are divided into three sections ('Before', 'The examination' and 'After') and include a map of the hospital site. Appointment details are printed out by computer on to the back of the leaflet, so that every patient getting an appointment automatically gets sent the leaflet.

So it has been shown time and time again that information reduces anxiety, aids drug compliance and helps speed up recovery. If you are not given adequate information about an operation or test, do ask your GP to tell you more.

Reading for further information

A Dictionary of Operations by Andrew Stanway (London: Granada, 1981)
A Patient's Guide to Operations by David Delvin (Harmondsworth: Penguin, 1981)
Thorsons' Guide to Medical Tests by Joan Trevelyan and David Dowson (Wellingborough: Thorsons, 1989

Discharge from Hospital

When you are discharged from hospital, make sure you have all the information you need about any medication you are prescribed, taking care of stitches and dressings, how soon you can go back to work, etc. You may go home with a couple of days' supply of medicine but will probably need to see your GP for a larger supply. The hospital may also give you a letter for your GP, telling him or her about the treatment you have received. This is not usually for the patient's eyes, but Dr Robert Tattersall, a consultant physician in Nottingham, has recently launched an experiment whereby he gives his patients a copy of the letters he sends to their GP. Writing the letters requires a little more thought and a little less medical jargon, but there are clear benefits in improved communication.

In 1989 the Department of Health issued a circular – HC(89)5 – to all health authorities giving guidance on good discharge procedures. The circular emphasizes the need to:

– provide families with the necessary information and reassurance about the care of the patient after discharge
– check on the day of departure that the patient is in fact fit to leave hospital
– assess any needs for special facilities in the home prior to discharge
– inform the patient's GP, community nursing service, and social services in adequate time

Many good hospitals have implemented check-lists to ensure that these procedures are carried out before the patient goes home.

Although it may not be a very good idea, you can discharge yourself at any time, even against the advice of your consultant. The only exceptions, when you can be compulsorily detained in hospital are:

– under the Mental Health Act 1983

– if you have a notifiable infectious disease
– if you are unable to look after yourself and have no one else to do so

If you do discharge yourself you will have to sign a form saying you are no longer the responsibility of the hospital. The consultant is not obliged to readmit you if your condition worsens.

Some health authorities are now introducing HOSPITAL AT HOME schemes, where patients are discharged to home care a few days after surgery. They then receive twice-daily visits from a member of the hospital team and there is close GP involvement. Patients seem to prefer being cared for at home, and the NHS benefits from shorter hospital stays and reduced waiting lists. Schemes at Peterborough Hospital and Oldchurch Hospital in Essex, as well as similar services in France, are described in *Hospital at Home: the coming revolution* available from King's Fund Centre, 126 Albert Road, London NW1 7NF.

A useful book, designed for professionals but also of value to carers, is *Going Home: a guide for helping the patient on leaving hospital* by Peter Simpson and Ruth Levitt (Edinburgh: Churchill Livingstone, 1981). Although now rather out of date in the addresses it gives, it is still a good overview.

Complaints about Hospital Treatment

Making a complaint about hospital treatment can be a difficult process to go through. You may still feel unwell and may feel very emotional about a bad experience. Health staff may seem defensive and the processes which you have to go through may seem unclear. These are the steps to take:

– If the complaint is comparatively minor it should be possible to deal with it with a minimum of fuss. Speak to the WARD SISTER. The complaint should be investigated quickly, and an explanation and apology given.

– If the complaint is more serious, or if you get nowhere with the ward sister, write to the HOSPITAL MANAGER (probably called the Unit General Manager) or the DISTRICT GENERAL MANAGER. Many health authorities now have managers in charge of quality assurance, with a specific responsibility for consumer relations. Basingstoke Health Authority, for example, has appointed Complaints Counsellors to provide a more personal service to patients, and to improve the authority's response to complaints. The project recognizes that formal complaints usually arise from a very traumatic experience. Complaining is not just a means of seeking an apology; it is an important way of reducing stress and regaining balance.

– You might also consider writing to the CHAIRMAN of the District Health Authority. He or she would certainly ask the District General Manager to look into the complaint and get the member of staff concerned to report back.

– Each District Health Authority has a COMMUNITY HEALTH COUNCIL, which acts as 'the patient's friend' in the NHS (for more information, see pages 300–1). Addresses and telephone numbers are in the phone book: look under Community Health Council. If you take your complaint to your local CHC, they will be able to advise you on the complaints procedure and may take up the case on your behalf.

– You may also find it worthwhile to contact the PATIENTS ASSOCIATION for advice. The address is: 18 Victoria Park Square, London E2 9PF Tel: 081-981 5676.
– If you are still dissatisfied then you should write to the HEALTH SERVICE COMMISSIONER Church House, Great Smith Street, London SW1P 3BW. The Commissioner (also known as the NHS Ombudsman) has a parliamentary duty to investigate complaints about issues such as poor communication or failures in services. If you do wish to complain to the Commissioner:

The complaint must be in writing
The complaint should be made within a year of the incident
You should complain to the Health Authority first to give them a chance to investigate the problem

The Community Health Council will be able to tell you more about the Health Service Commissioner, and may help you to write to him.

– If your complaint is about negligence or incompetence in the treatment you have received from a doctor, talk in the first instance to the CONSULTANT. You may find it easier to write. If there is no satisfactory outcome you can write to the REGIONAL MEDICAL OFFICER at the Regional Health Authority. If the complaint is serious, the Regional Medical Officer may arrange for a second opinion.
– If your complaint is about improper conduct by a doctor (such as abusive behaviour, drunkenness or sexual advances) you can complain to the GENERAL MEDICAL COUNCIL 44 Hallam Street, London W1N 6AE. Again, your CHC will be able to help with this.

Most complaints should be dealt with satisfactorily through these procedures. However some people do have to resort to taking LEGAL ACTION against Health Authorities. You cannot take action in the courts if you are also seeking help through the Health Service Commissioner. The action would probably be on the basis of negligence by the doctor concerned. Your Community Health

Council or Citizens' Advice Bureau should be able to give you advice on choosing a solicitor. Many solicitors offer a half-hour consultation for a fixed fee, usually £5.00. This may be enough to establish whether or not you have a case worth pursuing.

It might also be helpful to contact ACTION FOR THE VICTIMS OF MEDICAL ACCIDENTS (AVMA) Bank Chambers, 1 London Road, Forest Hill, London SE23 3TP Tel: 081-291 2793. AVMA advises victims of medical accidents on their rights and can put them in touch with solicitors experienced in medical negligence cases.

Health-promoting Hospitals

Hospitals today are becoming consumer-conscious. The watchword is quality assurance, and increasingly funds are being made available to improve communication with patients and the environments in which people are treated. The NHS White Paper, *Working for Patients* seeks to ensure that every hospital considers patients as people, by offering:

– clear information leaflets about facilities available and what patients need to know when they come into hospital
– once someone is in hospital, clear and sensitive explanations of what is happening
– quiet and pleasant waiting and other public areas

Despite these aims, there is no doubt that most hospitals are still impersonal and frightening places where patients experience a loss of dignity and control over their own lives. Some of the most important moments in people's lives are spent in hospitals. Yet in achieving a hi-tech environment for diagnosis and medical treatment many hospitals have lost sight of the possibilities which exist for healing, for the active participation of patients in their own care, and for the promotion of continuing good health once patients leave hospital. However, there are exceptional hospitals and units which are showing the way forward for patient-centred health care.

ST MARY'S HOSPITAL
Newport
Isle of Wight PO30 5TG
St Mary's in Newport, Isle of Wight is a new NHS hospital, designed for maximum energy conservation and to provide a more sympathetic environment for patients, staff and visitors. Research has shown that the environment plays an important role in determining rate of recovery, yet little has been done to improve the aesthetic quality of hospitals and to ease the trauma which people

feel when separated from their family and familiar surroundings. The site has been landscaped to include a lake with fountains, a sun garden, a children's play area and a quiet rest garden. The small wards make maximum use of natural light and look out over the hospital gardens. There is a major 'Healing Arts' project, which aims to provide visual and performing arts throughout the hospital through business sponsorship. A nautical theme is carried throughout the hospital, with sculptures, tapestries and mosaics. The X-ray Unit, usually rather an intimidating place, has become the prow of a ship. Magicians and clowns perform on the children's wards, and there is music, ballet and reminiscence therapy for longer-term elderly patients. Information for patients is also seen as crucial, and a project (The Acorn Project) is underway to examine the effectiveness of this.

BURFORD COTTAGE HOSPITAL
Burford
Oxfordshire OX6 7DV
St Mary's above shows what can be done in a District General Hospital. At the other end of the spectrum is Burford Cottage Hospital in Oxfordshire. This little hospital, with only nine beds, was threatened with closure in 1980. Then it was transformed into the grandly named Burford Nursing Development Unit, with the aim of nursing patients in partnership, involving them in planning their own health care and making their own decisions. Nurses do not wear uniforms and are called by their first names. Patients have full access to their medical records. Mealtimes are regarded as social occasions where staff, patients and visitors sit down together. Friends and relatives can visit at any time: even pets can visit.

LONDON LIGHTHOUSE
111–17 Lancaster Road
London W11 1QT
St Mary's and Burford are both NHS hospitals. There is also exciting work going on in the voluntary sector to create healthy environments. In 1986 London Lighthouse took over a derelict

school in London. The intention was to establish Britain's first major residential and support centre for people with HIV and AIDS. It was clear that people wanted an environment which was light, colourful and welcoming, functional yet domestic in style. Transforming the ugly, austere school into a place of beauty and safety was a major challenge, but it has been achieved with great style and was opened officially by Princess Margaret in November 1988. A large reception area provides a relaxed meeting place where people can chat or join in social activities. There is an information centre and café. The centre offers a range of creative and complementary therapies including writing, art, music, therapeutic massage and hypnotherapy. A twenty-four-bed unit staffed by thirty-five trained nurses provides residential care for people with AIDS. In addition there is a home support service and a network of over 200 volunteers.

PLANETREE CENTER
2040 Webster Street
San Francisco
California 94115
USA
Probably the most fully developed example in the world of a health-promoting hospital is the Planetree Center in San Francisco. The Planetree project began in 1978 as an information centre. There is a library of popular health books, a collection of press cuttings and leaflets, information on local doctors, self-help groups, etc., all accessible to the general public. Then, in 1984, Planetree took another step by persuading a local hospital (Pacific Presbyterian Medical Center) to transform one of its wards in association with Planetree. Formica, chrome and fluorescent lighting were eliminated and replaced with wood surfaces, pastel shades and soft lights. The traditional nurses' station, a barrier between patients and staff, was done away with. There is a small cosy lounge and a kitchen which patients and relatives are encouraged to use to prepare their own meals. Every patient has his or her own nurse

who coordinates care and is responsible for educating the patient and family about their condition. Visiting hours are unrestricted and relatives may stay the night if they wish.

Planetree began as an information centre, and free access to information plays a very important part in the model unit. Patients who want to know more about their condition can use the patient information library which forms part of the lounge. Information packs are provided to all patients on admission, and before discharge. Patients are not only permitted but actively encouraged to read their own medical notes, ask questions and discuss findings. As in the other centres, there is recognition of the therapeutic value of the arts. Patients' rooms are decorated with paintings on loan from local art galleries. There is an extensive library of music tapes, and Wednesday evening is movie night, when patients, relatives and staff get together to watch comedy videos.

The Planetree model unit is currently being evaluated by a team from Washington University. Early findings suggest that, compared with patients in conventional wards in the same hospital, patients who have been through the Planetree Unit have higher levels of satisfaction, can be discharged sooner, and need to be readmitted to hospital less frequently. This research should confirm that the kind of humane hospital care which patients like best is also cost-effective for the health service.

5 Making Special Choices

There are times in all our lives when we have to make very personal and difficult decisions. In terms of health care, these may literally be those of life and death – where to give birth and where to die. When coping with illness they may be decisions we have to make without the benefit of clear medical guidance, for however expert and however caring our doctors may be, medicine is not an exact science. In many areas of health care there is no absolute consensus on the effectiveness or otherwise of treatments. The ultimate decision on whether to accept medical advice rests with the patient. Doctors, rightly, tend to err on the side of caution and to recommend a minimization of risk. And their whole training and culture spurs them towards the preservation of life at all costs.

Patients often view things differently. For many people quality of life is more important than its absolute preservation. As a preference for home birth shows, the possibility of being cared for in familiar surroundings, with dignity, may be worth any additional risk in medical terms. Many people with terminal illness choose to give up the treatment which, at a cost, may prolong their lives, and opt instead to die peacefully in a hospice. Others, with a diagnosis of AIDS or cancer for example, may turn to unproven alternative therapies when they feel conventional medicine has nothing to offer them. People may choose complementary medicine practitioners or turn to private medicine, and often make these choices without advice from their GP or consultant. Indeed, it is often dissatisfaction with their current treatment which makes people turn to alternative or private health care.

These decisions which we make for ourselves cut across the neat boxes of self-care, primary care, community care and hospital care. They also form important case histories of the way health consumers behave independently of medical practitioners and some of the pitfalls they face. For these reasons they are considered separately in this section.

Having a Baby

Most of us become parents. With 2,000 births every day in the UK (788,000 for the year of 1988), pregnancy and labour are the most likely reason for healthy women to come into contact with the National Health Service. Having a baby is one of the high points of most people's lives and we have high expectations of the event. More than for most types of health care, we hope that birth can take place in surroundings which are pleasant and familiar, and that women can be treated with warmth and dignity. Of these 2,000 births a day 1,980 take place in hospital. But the birth itself occurs on only one day out of the 280 days of pregnancy. Before that there is a nine-month period of antenatal care which largely takes place in the community, using the services of the GP, community midwife and voluntary agencies. And after the birth the mother and baby return to the community, where the health visitor joins the team.

Pregnancy tests

For a reliable pregnancy test you need to wait until two weeks after the first day of a missed period (that is, about four weeks after conception). You can get pregnancy tests from:

– Your GP – this may take some time, but it is free and reliable
– Your FAMILY PLANNING CLINIC – this should be free if you use the clinic for your contraception
– CHEMISTS – chemists who do pregnancy tests usually have a sign in the window. There is a fee. You can also buy 'do-it-yourself' pregnancy tests at chemists. These have the advantage of a quick result and doing the test in private but you have to do the test very carefully to get an accurate result
– WELL WOMAN CLINICS – some Well Woman Clinics do pregnancy testing, as do some women's centres and pregnancy advisory services

This section assumes that you want to have the baby. If you decide to have an abortion, see pages 56–7 above.

Antenatal care

Throughout your pregnancy you will have regular check-ups, either at a hospital antenatal clinic or with your own GP. Where you go for your antenatal care depends on where you are going to have your baby.

– If you are going to have your baby in HOSPITAL, you will either go to the hospital antenatal clinic for all check-ups or have a system of 'shared care', where you go to your GP for most checks, with a couple of visits to the hospital.
– If you are going to have your baby in a GP UNIT, under the 'DOMINO' system, or AT HOME, you will probably go to your own doctor and midwife for all your antenatal care.

Hospital antenatal clinics have been criticized in reports over a number of years. Most women's complaints focus on the long waits (all patients may be booked in at the same time at the beginning of the clinic) and the lack of continuity of care (women rarely see the same doctor twice). Women's experiences, backed up by research, show that the most effective antenatal care is provided by the general practitioner and midwife seeing the woman regularly throughout pregnancy.

To book in for antenatal care your first step is to see your own GP. You can use this appointment to discuss the kind of delivery you want for your baby (see 'Choices in childbirth' below). The first antenatal appointment is around the eighth to twelfth week of pregnancy. Remember that if you are working you are entitled to paid time off work for antenatal appointments.

Antenatal classes

Going to antenatal classes can help to keep you fit during the pregnancy and prepare you (and your partner) for the birth itself. They are sometimes called parentcraft classes. There will probably be a number of different classes run in your area – by the hospital, in the community by midwives or health visitors, or independently by the local branch of the National Childbirth Trust (NCT). The hospital classes have the advantage of giving you the opportunity of finding out more about hospital procedures and seeing round the labour wards, but you may prefer the smaller, more informal classes run by the NCT. These often take place in the teacher's home, and place particular emphasis on managing birth without the use of drugs or other interventions. There is a charge for NCT classes (although there are usually concessions for people with low incomes), but the NHS classes are free.

You can find out about antenatal classes from your GP, midwife or health visitor. Libraries and CHCs should be able to give you the contact for your local NCT group. Or you could get this from NATIONAL CHILDBIRTH TRUST Alexandra House, Oldham Terrace, Acton, London W3 6NH Tel: 081-992 8637. Although best known for antenatal classes, NCT groups also offer continued support to mothers after the baby is born, through postnatal supporters. Many groups also keep 'experiences registers' through which people with particular problems (stillbirth, sudden infant death, children with handicaps) can be linked together for mutual support.

Choices in childbirth

In 1958, when a national survey of births in England and Wales was carried out, a third of all births took place in the home. By the time a further survey was done in 1970, only 10 per cent of births were at home, and now the total is less than 1 per cent. This compares with an average of 30 per cent in the Netherlands, with over half the babies in some rural Dutch areas being born at home. Medical opinion over the last forty years has been that all childbirth is high risk and should therefore be conducted in a place equipped to deal with any unexpected complications, with medical staff and medical technology to hand. An alternative view held by many parents, consumer groups and indeed many midwives, is that childbirth is a normal, healthy event which need not take place in a clinical environment. This position is supported by the World Health Organization in its report *Having a Baby in Europe* (Copenhagen: WHO Regional Office for Europe, 1985):

> It is not physicians, midwives, hospitals, electronic fetal monitors, or other machines or medicine that have babies – only the mother can do that. All services should reflect this fact and be planned to *assist* the woman as she carries out this profound social and biological act.

Because 99 per cent of births are in hospital, it is easy to dismiss alternatives as a minority interest of the trendy middle class. However, research suggests that as many as 15 per cent of women who have had a previous birth in hospital would prefer to have a subsequent birth at home (*Public Health* 1985), and that those who actually have babies at home are spread across the full spectrum of social class and age.

For several years now a debate has raged on the comparative safety of home and hospital deliveries. Although the mortality rate for home births seems to be high, when unplanned emergency home deliveries are excluded the mortality rate for *planned* home births is in fact better than for hospital deliveries. Research carried out by the National Perinatal Epidemiology Unit suggests that

> there is no evidence to support the claim that the safest policy is for all women to give birth in hospital. In fact there is some evidence, though not conclusive, to suggest that morbidity is higher in mothers and babies cared for in an institutional setting. For some women the iatrogenic risk associated with an institutional delivery may be greater than the benefit conferred.

Many obstetricians take the view that while birth at home is safe for women with low risks, rapid intervention is needed to save the life of mother and baby in about 5 per cent of labours in which a problem might not have been expected. Until these risks can be predicted more accurately by antenatal screening, doctors prefer hospital deliveries. Many parents feel that if no problems have come to light during antenatal check-ups, then the small risk attached to a home delivery is worth it for the opportunity to give birth in relaxed and familiar surroundings. Remember, the decision is yours.

The choice of where to give birth is not a straight choice between hospital and home. There are other options which offer some of the advantages of home birth, but with the emergency medical cover quickly to hand. Facilities and policies vary around the country, and some people may have more choices than others, but basically you can choose between birth:

– in hospital
– in a GP unit
– under the 'domino' system
– at home

BIRTH IN HOSPITAL The advantage of a hospital birth is that expertise and equipment are at hand in case they are needed. If something goes wrong (for example, if you need a Caesarean delivery) then you won't have to be moved. If there is anything wrong with the baby, life-saving equipment is immediately available. For the majority of parents and doctors this is the paramount consideration and they would think no further than a hospital birth.

However, you should still find out as much as possible about the hospital's practices so that you know what to expect. If there is more than one hospital in the area to which you could go, try to find out about the practice at each so that you can decide which will suit you best. Your doctor, health visitor or midwife should be able to advise, as should other mothers and groups like the National Childbirth Trust.

A few years ago there was an attempt to bring this sort of information together in a single consumer guide – *The New Good Birth Guide*, edited by Sheila Kitzinger (Harmondsworth: Penguin,

1983). The book used women's own experiences to give a comparative user guide to maternity units throughout the UK. It was an excellent example of using information to help consumer choice but the guide, based on experiences between 1979 and 1982, has not been revised since. Practices change a lot and it is difficult for publications to keep up to date. For example, some of the procedures described at Odstock Hospital, Salisbury were quite different even in 1982 when our first son was born there.

BIRTH IN A GP UNIT In some districts there is the option of giving birth in a GP unit. This may be a separate unit, or a part of the hospital's ordinary maternity wards. Your baby can be delivered by your community midwife, with the assistance of your GP. The birth is therefore more personal, but you have hospital facilities if you need them.

Many GP units are faced with closure as part of 'rationalization' of maternity services. The ASSOCIATION FOR GENERAL PRACTICE MATERNITY CARE (Dr Gavin Young, The Surgery, Temple Sowerby, Penrith, Cumbria CA10 1RZ) has been set up to publicize the benefits of GP/community midwife care, and to defend units threatened with closure.

BIRTH IN THE 'DOMINO' SYSTEM 'Domino' stands for Domiciliary-In-Out. The system may also be known as a 'district bed'. Under this system you receive your antenatal care from your community midwife. She gets to know you in pregnancy, accompanies you to hospital and delivers your baby. If all goes well you can go home after about six hours (or after a night's sleep if your baby is born late in the evening).

BIRTH AT HOME If you want to have your baby at home, the first thing to do is to talk to your GP early in the pregnancy. Most doctors advise against home deliveries for the first baby because it is hard to predict how the birth will go. Although it is your right to have a home birth, you should talk to your doctor about whether you have any 'risk factors' which mean that it would be inadvisable. These would include existing medical conditions such as epilepsy, diabetes, severe anaemia; previous problems in labour; or known difficulties for the baby such as breech presentation.

If your own GP is unwilling to undertake to care for you during your pregnancy and home delivery, you can register with another GP just for antenatal care, the delivery and postnatal care. You can stay with your usual doctor for the rest of your medical care. In many areas it can be very difficult to find a GP sympathetic to home births. National Childbirth Trust branches would usually have inside knowledge, and it would also be worth contacting your Community Health Council and Family Health Services Authority. A few years ago the pressure group Healthrights approached all the Family Practitioner Committees (now FHSAs) in the country and asked them for a list of GPs prepared to carry out home births. Only one (Lambeth and Southwark FPC) was willing or able to send a list. However, a number of FPCs suggested that if individuals were to contact the FPC in person they would be able to give them the information.

Another course of action is to write directly to the Director of Midwifery in your District Health Authority, telling her that you wish to have your baby at home and asking her to allocate you a community midwife. The ASSOCIATION FOR IMPROVEMENT IN THE MATERNITY SERVICES (AIMS) has produced a booklet, *Choosing a Home Birth*, which includes a sample letter. You can get the booklet from AIMS 163 Liverpool Road, London N1 0RF Tel: 071-278 5628. There is also a National Childbirth Trust booklet, *Giving Birth at Home*, available from the NCT at the address on page 178.

Further advice is available from SOCIETY TO SUPPORT HOME CONFINEMENTS Lydgate, Lydgate Lane, Wolsingham, Co. Durham DL13 3HA Tel: 0388 528044.

MIDWIVES' INFORMATION AND RESOURCE SERVICES (MIDIRS), Institute of Child Health, Bristol BS2 8BJ Tel: 0272 251791 offers an extensive information service on subscription, covering all aspects of pregnancy and childbirth. Although primarily designed for midwives, MIDIRS is also used by voluntary organizations and individuals.

If you are unable to arrange a home birth under the NHS you might consider having your baby delivered privately by an independent midwife. Contact the INDEPENDENT MIDWIVES ASSOCIATION 94 Auckland Road, London SE12 2DH Tel: 081-771 7143. For those in the London area, leading midwife Caroline Flint has set up a personalized independent home birth service called SPECIAL DELIVERY Tel: 071-498 2322.

Maternity benefits

FREE PRESCRIPTIONS There is an automatic entitlement to free prescriptions from when the pregnancy is confirmed to when the child is a year old. ⇒ DSS leaflet P11.

FREE DENTAL TREATMENT Women are entitled to free dental treatment during pregnancy and until the child is a year old. ⇒ DSS leaflet D11.

HELP WITH FARES This may be available for visits to antenatal clinics or for visiting a baby remaining in hospital after the mother's discharge, if she is receiving Income Support or Family Credit. ⇒ DSS leaflet H11.

MILK Mothers on income support automatically receive milk tokens for themselves during pregnancy and for each child under 5. The tokens can also be used to obtain formula baby milk from child health clinics. Child health clinics also give out free vitamins to mothers on Income Support during pregnancy and breastfeeding, and to their children under 5.

STATUTORY MATERNITY PAY SMP is paid by the woman's employer, providing she has worked there for six months, with no obligation for her to return to work. SMP is paid for eighteen weeks, including a core period of thirteen weeks starting six weeks before the birth. The other five weeks are flexible and can be taken before or after the core period.

MATERNITY ALLOWANCE Maternity allowance is paid to women unable to claim SMP, providing they have paid sufficient National Insurance contributions. The rate is £35.70 a week, payable for up to eighteen weeks. ⇒ DSS leaflet NI17A.

MATERNITY PAYMENTS Maternity payments from the Social Fund may be payable if the woman and her partner receive Family Credit or Income Support, and their savings do not exceed £500. Claim forms are available from DSS offices.

CHILD BENEFIT Child benefit of £7.25 a week per child is paid to all mothers with children under 16 (or under 19 if they are in full-time education). Application forms are available from DSS offices or are included in the general leaflet FB8, *Babies and Benefits*.

ONE-PARENT FAMILIES This benefit is payable to single parents bringing up a child alone. It is worth £5.60 a week for a first or only child and is usually paid with child benefit. ⇒ DSS leaflet FB27, *Bringing up Children*.

HIV Infection and AIDS

AIDS has posed the greatest challenge to doctors, scientists and government health departments for many years. It is not only research into the virus and the possibilities of a vaccine and a cure which has been challenging, but also the way in which AIDS has called into question many of the basic assumptions we have about health and medicine. Until the AIDS epidemic we had become used to the idea that communicable disease was under control in the developed world. Medical science had come up with a vaccine or a cure for the scourges of earlier generations. Now we are faced with a major public health crisis to which doctors have no answer. Instead the answer lies with people becoming better informed and taking personal responsibility for the preservation of their own health. The crucial role of information in the prevention of HIV infection was underlined in 1987 by the delivery to every home in the UK of the government leaflet *AIDS: don't die of ignorance.*

While there is evidence of a disturbing lack of knowledge and considerable prejudice amongst some health professionals, people with HIV and AIDS are often extremely well informed, highly motivated to learn more about their illness and its management. In an article in *The Independent* (21 March 1989) a GP wrote about how he acquired most of his knowledge of HIV infection and AIDS from his first AIDS patient, Clive. Clive had access via a home computer to databases held by the Gay Community Computer in San Francisco. He could also tap in to an 'electronic buddy' system using a computer bulletin board. In this way he learnt about the latest advances in retrovirus research, trials in the use of pentamidine for pneumocystis carinii, and modes of transmission of cytomegalovirus before his doctor.

The AIDS crisis has called for swift responses. In the UK, as in the USA and other countries, the most effective services (in both prevention of infection and the care of people with AIDS) have been developed by voluntary sector agencies, such as the Terrence Higgins Trust and London Lighthouse (see pages 197 and 169).

With the freedom to act quickly and if necessary in an unorthodox way, the AIDS organizations stepped in to provide practical support and information while government departments considered what to do.

AIDS is a tragedy, but within that tragedy there are very positive elements. It has led to a reappraisal of professional mystiques. There has been a recognition of the importance of ordinary people having access to the information they need to protect their own health. There has been a flowering of self-help and support agencies on an unprecedented scale over a ten-year period. And individuals and communities (particularly the gay community) have found within themselves a new capacity for caring and responsible behaviour. Thrown into sharp relief by the urgency and scale of the crisis, we have in AIDS a model of all the other developments in self-care and health consumerism of recent years.

What is AIDS?

AIDS stands for Acquired Immune Deficiency Syndrome. It is caused by a virus called HIV (Human Immunodeficiency Virus). HIV attacks a person's immune system, making it progressively less able to fight infections. When someone is infected with HIV they may remain healthy for years. They may have no outward signs or symptoms but they are still infectious to others. They may then go on to develop the characteristic signs of AIDS or AIDS-related illness (ARC). These include weight loss, persistent diarrhoea, night sweats, infections and skin blotches (Kaposi's sarcoma). Although no one has been cured of AIDS, treatment with drugs such as zidovudine (AZT) has improved life expectancy.

Being infected with HIV (HIV antibody positive) is not the same as having AIDS. Most HIV-infected people have no symptoms and there is no way of telling whether they have the virus. No one really knows how many people who are infected will go on to develop AIDS. It was once thought that only a minority of people with HIV infection would develop AIDS. It is now thought that at least half will develop AIDS within eight years of being infected. It is too early to know what the final proportion will be or how long AIDS may take to develop.

AIDS is sometimes called a mystery illness. In fact, although researchers have not yet been able to discover a vaccine or a cure, we know quite a lot about HIV. Most importantly, we know how it is transmitted. We also know that HIV is a fragile virus which cannot be passed on in everyday social contact (sharing crockery, swimming pools, lavatories, etc.). HIV can only be transmitted in the following ways:

– SEXUAL CONTACT HIV is present in semen, vaginal secretions and menstrual blood and can be passed on through sexual contact from man to woman, woman to man, or man to man. The greatest risk is unprotected penetrative sex – vaginal or anal. Oral sex also carries a risk. You can reduce the risk of HIV infection a great deal by using a condom. Make sure the brand you use carries the British Standard Kite Mark (BS3704). You can also explore with your partner ways of making love which do not involve penetration. *Safer Sex* by Peter Gordon and Louise Mitchell (London: Faber and Faber, 1988) has lots of ideas. For more information on safer sex ask your local health education/promotion department for the Health Education Authority leaflets *Your Guide to Safer Sex and the Condom* and *Safer Sex for Gay Men*.

– BLOOD HIV can also be transmitted by infected blood getting into your blood stream. Injecting drug users can become infected if they share needles or syringes ('works') with an infected person. Avoid injecting drugs, but if you have to, never share needles or syringes. Many areas now have needle exchange schemes. Your local health promotion department or drug advisory service (in the phone book) will be able to tell you if there is a scheme locally. Or contact SCODA (Standing Conference on Drug Abuse) 1–4 Hatton Place, London EC1V 8ND Tel: 071-430 2341 for details of local services and a copy of their leaflet *AIDS: how drug users can avoid it*.

– TRANSFUSIONS The virus could also be transmitted during the transfusion of contaminated blood or blood products, or through an operation. All blood donated in Europe and the USA is now tested for HIV antibodies, and blood products are treated to kill any virus which may be present. There is virtually no risk of HIV infection through medical treatment in the UK, although this is not the case in some parts of the world (see pages 252–3). Anyone who is infected with HIV, or thinks they may be, should not donate blood or sperm, or carry an organ donor card. A leaflet emphasizing this, entitled *AIDS: important information for blood donors*, is available at Blood Transfusion Services.

Since July 1985 all blood products used in Britain for the treatment of haemophilia have been heat-treated to destroy HIV. However, prior to this some contaminated blood was used and many people with haemophilia were infected. In 1987 the government set up a special fund for people with haemophilia who had been infected with HIV, called the MacFarlane Trust. The trust is administered by the HAEMOPHILIA SOCIETY 123 Westminster Bridge Road, London SE1 7HR Tel: 071-928 2020.

– MOTHER TO BABY HIV can be passed on from a mother to a baby during pregnancy, at birth or possibly by breastfeeding. Recent research has suggested that the risks of a mother infecting an unborn infant vary according to the mother's state of health. HIV-positive women with no symptoms seem to have a one in five chance of passing on the infection; mothers who have symptoms of HIV disease carry a much greater risk. For advice and support for women who are HIV-positive or have AIDS, contact POSITIVELY WOMEN 5 Sebastian Street, London EC1V 0HE Tel: 071-490 5515.

The AIDS epidemic

AIDS is a huge worldwide problem. Although the syndrome was first recognized in the USA in 1981, HIV infections were already present in four other continents. Indeed, tests on stored blood samples from a British sailor suggest cases as far back as the 1950s.

By 1990 almost 200,000 cases of AIDS from over 150 countries had been reported to the World Health Organization. However, it is likely that this is a considerable underestimate. Many cases of AIDS are not officially reported. WHO estimates that the actual cumulative total of AIDS cases worldwide is approximately 600,000, three times the official total.

As AIDS can develop several years after HIV infection these figures in fact reflect the pattern of infection up to ten years ago. A clearer picture of the current severity of the epidemic would be provided by the number of people currently infected with HIV. WHO estimates that there are now between 6 and 10 million people worldwide with HIV infection. Research and experience now suggest that most, if not all, of these people will develop AIDS over a period of about ten years. Far from declining, as some sections of the media have suggested, the global AIDS epidemic is just gaining momentum. By the year 2000 6 million people worldwide may have developed AIDS, a ten-fold increase over today.

The national distribution of HIV infection is very variable. In Europe, the USA, Canada, Australia and New Zealand spread of the virus began in the late 1970s and early 1980s, primarily amongst homosexual men and injecting drug users. In these countries infected men outnumber women nine to one. In sub-Saharan Africa and some parts of the Caribbean HIV infection is predominantly heterosexual, with some transmission from mother to baby and infection through unscreened blood and contaminated needles. In the UK there had been 3,798 cases of AIDS by the end of September 1990. Of these just over half (2,040) had died. About 80 per cent of cases are homosexual and bisexual men. Although this is still by far the largest category, the percentage increase amongst homosexual men is much less than in the early stages of the epidemic. This is largely due to the widespread adoption of safer sex by gay men in the mid-1980s. People infected through heterosexual sex account for 6 per cent and injecting drug users for 3 per cent of all UK cases. The percentages are small but it is important to note that it is here that the number of cases is increasing most rapidly. According to the Department of Health, in a few years' time over half the UK cases of AIDS could be amongst heterosexuals and injecting drug users.

Testing for HIV

There is no test for AIDS. AIDS is a group of conditions rather than a single disease. However, there is a blood test to find out whether you have been infected with HIV. The test in fact detects antibodies to HIV in the blood.

A POSITIVE test result means that you have been infected with HIV and are infectious to others. It does not tell you whether you will necessarily go on to develop AIDS.

A NEGATIVE result means that you probably are not infected. However, it cannot be regarded as a definitive result as it can take three months from the time of infection for the body to produce antibodies. To be absolutely sure you would need to be tested six months later, and during this time stick to safe sex and avoid sharing blood.

HIV antibody tests are available:

– at GENITO-URINARY MEDICINE (GUM) clinics or SEXUALLY TRANSMITTED DISEASE (STD) clinics
– through your own GP
– PRIVATE CLINICS

It is best to go to a GUM or STD clinic for the test. There are the highest standards of confidentiality and you will be able to receive counselling on the implications of taking the test before you go ahead. You need to consider whether you could cope with the stress of a positive result. You may also face practical difficulties too. Most insurance companies will refuse life assurance if they know you have taken the test – *whatever the result*. Have expert counselling before making up your mind. The Health Education Authority leaflet *AIDS: the HIV test* sets out the issues (available from local health education/promotion departments).

Depending on the clinic, it usually takes between one and three weeks to receive the result. Some clinics offer same day results but this may not allow enough time to double-check results.

There have been cases of surgeons insisting that people whom they categorize as belonging to 'high risk groups' be tested for HIV antibodies before undergoing surgery. This cannot be done without your consent and as there is unlikely to be good counselling or assurance of confidentiality you should refuse. Professional guidelines on good control of infection practice should mean that hospital staff take precautions as if *all* patients are HIV-positive. If you were refused treatment or pressurized into having the test you should contact your local Community Health Council (page 300) with a complaint.

Confidentiality

GUM or STD clinics are governed by the Venereal Disease Regulations which impose a duty of confidentiality. The clinic may request consent to pass on information to your GP and sexual contacts. GPs and other members of the primary care team also have a duty to keep information about their patients confidential, including whether they are HIV-positive. Again, the patient's consent is needed before information is passed on to anyone else. However, doctors can pass on information about whether a patient is HIV-positive or not to an insurance company or employer if they are examining the patient on the company's behalf. Under the Access to Medical Reports Act (page 71), you have a right to see the report before it is sent out.

In January 1990 a programme of ANONYMOUS TESTING for HIV was begun. In the first two years this will be restricted to STD clinics and antenatal departments. People attending these departments will be asked to give permission for an HIV antibody test to be included with other routine blood tests. The survey will then be extended to other hospital admissions. The sole use of this testing is statistical. The results will not be traceable to individuals.

Finding out about treatment

Many HIV-positive people are highly motivated to find out more about the latest research into treatment. Faced with what many regard as a death sentence, they may wish to take part in clinical trials or choose to take risks, which medical opinion would find unacceptable, by taking experimental and alternative therapies. After all, they say, what have we to lose? There is a case here for patients to have access to information services as good as those available to doctors to enable them to weigh up the risks and benefits and make choices on treatment.

A huge amount of research is going on into the development of an effective anti-HIV drug. So far only one drug is licensed for use in the UK – zidovudine (formerly known as AZT, brand name Retrovir). Zidovudine does not kill HIV but it does stop it from reproducing. This means it has to be taken continuously and it has unpleasant side-effects. Trials in the USA have shown that zidovudine decreases the severity and frequency of opportunistic infections and can prolong the life of patients. The search continues for better alternatives. In addition to zidovudine, people with AIDS may be receiving a range of treatments for illnesses and infections: antifungals for thrush, acyclovir for shingles, aerosolized pentamadine for pneumocystis carinii, etc.

Your local library, health promotion department or AIDSline may have a copy of the *National AIDS Manual* (see box, page 198). This comprehensive resource covers every aspect of living with HIV and AIDS but in particular it has detailed information on treatment issues, clinical trials, drugs and complementary therapies.

Articles on research into treatments appear in the major medical journals like the *British Medical Journal* and the *Lancet*. Probably the easiest way to find out what is being published is to read the brief summaries published in the excellent *AIDS Newsletter* published by the Bureau of Hygiene and Tropical Diseases, Keppel Street, London WC1E 7HT Tel: 071-636 8636. This should be available in most medical libraries and even in large public libraries.

The American Foundation for AIDS Research (AMFAR)

publishes a quarterly *AIDS/HIV Experimental Treatment Directory* which gives details of current experimental and complementary treatments. It costs $50 a year ($15 for single copies) from AMFAR 1515 Broadway, Suite 3601, New York NY 10036, USA. It is also available in libraries in the UK and at organizations like the Terrence Higgins Trust.

The AMFAR directory, along with the database of the Bureau of Hygiene, the full text of the AIDS articles from major medical journals and the San Francisco General Hospital *AIDS Textbook* are all available on one compact disk, as the *AIDS Compact Library*. A number of medical libraries and HIV/AIDS information services now have the facilities to search this sort of information medium, called CD-ROM (see page 285) and print out results for inquirers.

Health and community care

For people with HIV, as for all health care consumers, it is the GP who is the key to the rest of the health services available. A good GP will help anyone with HIV to get the best out of the health service and can arrange for nursing and other help at home. If you are HIV-positive and are not happy with your GP (perhaps because of his or her attitude to HIV infection or concerns over confidentiality) you should consider changing your doctor. A local support group or AIDSline should be able to recommend a sympathetic doctor. See pages 44–50 for information on choosing and changing a GP.

Someone who is ill with AIDS and living at home is entitled to the range of community health services described in Section 3. These include:

- district nursing
- occupational therapists
- home helps
- meals on wheels
- nursing aids and equipment
- social workers

In many areas there are Macmillan nurses and Marie Curie nurses (see pages 206–7) who take care of people with cancer at home. Depending on the policy of the Health District they may also be available for people with other terminal illnesses, including AIDS.

Some health authorities and local authorities have also set up HOME CARE TEAMS for AIDS, with a responsibility for coordinating hospital and community care (for example in Brighton and Bloomsbury). Some schemes are run by voluntary agencies such as London Lighthouse (see page 169). Most people with AIDS who are no longer well enough to live at home will be admitted to their local District General Hospital. Increasingly, HOSPICES are accepting people with AIDS, though not all. Some hospices are funded by cancer charities and cannot accept people with other illnesses, but this is likely to change with the need to care for increasing numbers of terminally ill people with AIDS (see pages 207–8 below for more information on terminal care).

A survey of AIDS-related deaths by the Communicable Diseases Surveillance Centre (*The AIDS Letter* No 16, December 1989) showed that 84 per cent occurred in hospital, 15 per cent at home and only 1 per cent in a hospice. The survey was done before the opening of the Mildmay AIDS Hospice in February 1988 and London Lighthouse in September 1988, but in most parts of the country the choices available to people with AIDS are still very limited. Interestingly, the CDSC survey showed that many people actually preferred to be cared for in hospital, because it provided a greater sense of security. Dying at home can seem very isolated, and people may be afraid of going into a hospice because the word has such a final ring. The services at Mildmay are designed to give people with AIDS the maximum choice (home care, respite care, rehabilitative care, convalescent care and terminal care) within an overall programme of support.

For more detailed information on health and community care, obtain a copy of *Caring for Someone with AIDS* (London: Consumers' Association, 1990). This is the most detailed and accessible guide for people with HIV and AIDS, and their carers.

Welfare benefits and financial help

There are a number of benefits which people with HIV and AIDS can be entitled to, depending on their condition (see pages 101–6 for more details of the benefits and current rates).

INCOME SUPPORT If you are incapable of work because of sickness for twenty-eight weeks or more you are entitled to the disability premium. If a child has HIV infection the parent or guardian may receive the disabled child's premium.

SOCIAL FUND A person with AIDS could be entitled to a community care grant if it enabled them to be cared for at home and not be admitted to hospital.

ATTENDANCE ALLOWANCE A number of conditions associated with AIDS may mean entitlement to Attendance Allowance (for example, changing and washing bed linen for night sweats).

MOBILITY ALLOWANCE Extreme weakness, fatigue or dizziness associated with AIDS may mean entitlement to mobility allowance.

In 1989 the Terrence Higgins Trust, the Federation of Independent Advice Centres and the National Association of Citizens' Advice Bureaux published a report, *Double Deficiency*, which expressed serious concern about the adequacy of benefit provision for people with AIDS. In particular, severe hardship was being caused by the twenty-eight-week delay before Attendance Allowance and disability premium are paid: some people have died in those twenty-eight weeks. From 1 October 1990 the provision was changed and a person with a terminal illness (a progressive disease likely to cause death within six months) can now claim Attendance Allowance immediately, without waiting for the six-month qualifying period. In order to claim under this new provision the patient's doctor has to complete claim form DS 1500. In the absence of adequate financial provision many people with AIDS have to turn to hardship funds set up by the various voluntary organizations and charities. These can help with grants or loans for special diets, clothing and bedding, household bills, holidays, etc. For information on appropriate sources contact a local AIDSline or the Terrence Higgins Trust.

Other practical issues

EMPLOYMENT People with HIV infection often face discrimination at work, both from employers and workmates. Employment laws do not specifically protect people from discrimination because of HIV. However, if you were dismissed from work just because you were HIV-positive you would probably be able to claim unfair dismissal. This is made clear in the government booklet *AIDS and Employment* sent to all employers in 1986. If an employer insisted that male employees have an HIV antibody test this could be sex discrimination. Similarly, singling out workers for testing because of their race (for example if they came from Africa) would be racial discrimination. For further advice contact your trade union, Citizens' Advice Bureau or Immunity (see page 198).

There is also a new booklet for employers, published in 1990, entitled *AIDS and the Workplace* and available from ID6, Department of Employment, Caxton House, Tothill Street, London SW1H 9NF.

HOUSING If a landlord finds out that a tenant is HIV-positive or has AIDS he or she may face eviction. The landlord may object to the person living in the property (because of misplaced fears of infection) or the tenant may have got behind with the rent because they are no longer able to work. People with HIV and AIDS have the same security from eviction as any other tenant. Again, contact your CAB or law centre for advice. There is an *AIDS and Housing Project* (16–18 Strutton Ground, London SW1P 2HP Tel: 071-222 6932) which advises housing associations and other organizations on developing good-quality accommodation for people with HIV and AIDS.

INSURANCE Most insurance companies will refuse to issue insurance for life, health, endowment or repayment mortgage to a person infected with HIV. Applicants are usually asked if they have had a blood test in connection with HIV or any other sexually transmitted disease. As with all insurance the person applying has a duty to answer all questions truthfully or the policy is invalid. Applicants also have to give the name of their GP and give consent for the company to approach him or her for a medical report (see 'Confidentiality', above). The Terrence Higgins Trust is able to give advice on applying for insurance and has produced a useful leaflet, *Mortgages and Life Assurance*.

TRAVEL ABROAD Some countries insist on tests for HIV before they will allow entry. The relevant embassy will be able to advise and there is a list of current restrictions in the *National AIDS Manual*. There are no restrictions between European Community Countries. It is the policy of the UK that neither HIV infection nor AIDS justifies refusal of entry to the UK. There may be restrictions on taking medication into or out of some countries. See the Department of Health booklet *The Traveller's Guide to Health*, and Section 6 for further information.

Information on living with HIV and AIDS

THE TERRENCE HIGGINS TRUST 52–4 Gray's Inn Road, London WC1X 8LT, is the major national source of information and advice. The THT Helpline is available on 071-242 1010, 3 pm–10 pm. The Helpline is also available on VISTEL (071-405 2463) for people who are deaf or hard of hearing. THT provides support and counselling; puts people in touch with local AIDSlines and support groups; provides up-to-date medical information and welfare advice; has a hardship fund; and can link HIV-positive people with volunteer 'buddies'. The separate Legal Line on 071-405 2381 provides help with employment problems, welfare rights, complaints about medical treatment, etc.

NATIONAL AIDS HELPLINE is available twenty-four hours a day, seven days a week, on 0800 567 123 (all 0800 numbers are free). As well as the spoken English line there is a VISTEL service for deaf people on 0800 521 361; an Asian language service on 0800 282 445; a Cantonese service on 0800 282 446 and an Arabic service on 0800 282 447.

IMMUNITY, 260a Kilburn Lane, London W10 4BE Tel: 071-968 8908, gives free legal advice on topics such as employment rights, wills, power of attorney, security from eviction, benefits and immigration. A set of thirteen leaflets is available, covering these topics, entitled *Your Rights in the AIDS Era*.

There are many other organizations and support groups for specific HIV-related issues, for example, black people, drug users, women, deaf people. It is impossible to list all these without producing another whole book about HIV. There are a number of these already (see box below).

Useful books giving practical advice on the problems of living with HIV and AIDS

Caring for Someone with AIDS (London: Consumers' Association, 1990)

Living with AIDS: a guide to survival by people with AIDS (Frontliners, 1988)

AIDS: a guide to the law (London: Terrence Higgins Trust, 1990)

The huge and comprehensive *National AIDS Manual* (NAM, PO Box 99, London SW2 1EL) is available in most CABs, public libraries and AIDSlines. It covers all aspects of HIV and AIDS: safer sex, testing, transmission and prevention, social and practical issues, treatments, and many sources of further information.

In some parts of the country health authorities and other organizations have produced local information manuals. The best known is the Wessex *HIV/AIDS Response Manual* (Help for Health, Grant Building, Southampton General Hospital, Southampton SO9 4XY, 4th edition 1990).

Cancer

Although HIV infection is a serious worldwide health problem, most people (as yet) have not been close to somebody who has died with AIDS: tragically, one day this will be so. Cancer, however, already affects us all. One in three people in the UK will develop some form of cancer during their lifetime. A quarter of all deaths are from cancer. In 1986 cancer deaths totalled 140,000. The good news is that 75,000 people with cancer recover every year, whereas fifty years ago a diagnosis of cancer was almost certainly a death sentence. The majority of children who develop cancer can now be cured.

What is cancer?

Cancer is not a single disease but a blanket term for a wide variety of diseases, all characterized by uncontrolled growth of abnormal cells. These 'malignant' cells displace or destroy the normal healthy cells of the body, and if not stopped can spread to other parts of the body. We do not yet know what causes cells to become cancerous, but scientists believe that most causes are linked to our environment and how we live.

There are almost as many types of cancer as there are parts of the body. However, the most common cancers are lung, breast, uterus, bowel and prostate. Cancers of the bladder and stomach, and leukaemias, are also relatively common. As well as there being many different cancer sites, these sites can themselves be affected by different kinds of cancer, depending on the type of tissue involved.

The relative incidence of different cancers has changed over the years and this gives important clues to the causes and what we can do about them. In the last fifty years the only cancer which has increased dramatically in both sexes is lung cancer. We are now witnessing the price of widespread smoking in the 1920s, 1930s and 1940s before the now undisputed link between tobacco and cancer was established. Two cancers have become steadily less common: stomach and uterus. No one really knows the reason for the decline in stomach cancer, but the reduction in the incidence of uterine cancer is certainly linked to improved methods for early diagnosis and early, comparatively simple surgery.

Preventing cancer

We can do a great deal as individuals and communities to prevent cancer. Epidemiological and clinical research over many years has shown that there are choices which we can make in our lifestyles which can reduce the risk of cancer. In 1989 the countries of the European Community started a Europe Against Cancer campaign and designated 1989 European Cancer Year. The aim of the campaign is to reduce the number of deaths from cancer by 15 per cent by the year 2000.

Doctors divide cancers into three groups: carcinomas, sarcomas and leukaemias.

Carcinomas are cancerous changes in the tissues which cover or line the organs of the body (e.g. the lining of the lungs or bowel)
Sarcomas are cancers which arise in connective tissues, such as bones, nerves and muscles (e.g. brain tumours)
Leukaemias are cancers of the blood and lymphatic system
You may hear doctors and nurses refer to cancers in this way, identifying the type of cancer and the site. So lung cancer may be called 'carcinoma of the bronchus'.

Scanning and diagnosis

Many forms of cancer can now be treated successfully if they are diagnosed early enough. As the European Code emphasizes, you should become sufficiently aware of your own body to notice any unexplained changes, and consult your GP about them. Breast self-examination is a good self-screening habit for women – men

The ten-point European Code Against Cancer gives the following practical lifestyle check-list:

1. Do not smoke. Smokers, stop as quickly as possible and do not smoke in the presence of others. Cigarette smoking causes a third of all cancer deaths
2. Moderate your consumption of alcoholic drinks, beers, wines or spirits
3. Avoid excessive exposure to the sun
4. Follow health and safety instructions at work concerning production, handling or use of any substance which may cause cancer (asbestos, radiation, etc.)
5. Frequently eat fresh fruit and vegetables and cereals with a high fibre content
6. Avoid becoming overweight and limit your intake of fatty foods
7. See a doctor if you notice a lump, a change in a mole or abnormal bleeding
8. See a doctor if you have persistent problems such as a persistent cough, a persistent hoarseness, a change in bowel habits, or an unexplained weight loss
9. For women, have a cervical smear regularly
10. And check your breasts regularly. If possible undergo mammography at regular intervals above the age of fifty

should remember to examine their testicles for lumps on the same regular monthly basis. Local health education/promotion departments will be able to let you have leaflets on how to do this.

Most of the symptoms of cancer are common in other conditions too – nine out of ten breast lumps are benign, for example. In many cases your doctor will be able to reassure you that there is nothing untoward to worry about. Or he or she may arrange for tests to be carried out to find out the exact nature of the problem.

You may be referred to your local hospital out-patient department for x-rays or possibly scans. There are three main types of scanner in use in the UK. A CT (COMPUTERIZED TOMOGRAPHY) scanner uses x-rays to get cross-sectional pictures of 'slices' through your body. ULTRASOUND scanners use sound waves to produce a picture of different tissues in the body, using the different 'echo' given off by abnormal growths. MAGNETIC RESONANCE IMAGING (MRI) uses a magnetic field to detect the response to radio waves passed through your body. Doctors may also use a FIBREOPTIC tube to look inside the passageways of the gut or respiratory system. If the examination reveals the presence of a tumour it will be necessary for a sample of tissue to be taken for laboratory examination. This is called a BIOPSY and involves a small operation under local or general anaesthetic.

Finding out the truth

Telling someone they have cancer is one of the most difficult tasks a doctor has to perform. Some believe in a policy of total honesty, that patients should be told the diagnosis from the beginning. Others believe that patients should be spared the full shock, and decide to conceal the diagnosis. Others are simply poor at communicating and the patient may end up finding out they have cancer from an overheard remark or a sneak look at their notes.

Of course patients vary too. Some feel they have a right to the truth from the start. Others prefer to take things more slowly. Some will never want to know. Sometimes relatives decide for themselves that the truth should be concealed from the patient. A good doctor will be able to assess the best way to communicate information about a diagnosis of cancer. But ultimately it is your body and if you want to know the truth your questions should be answered openly and honestly. Your first source of information should be your doctor, but if you feel you want to find out more for yourself you can contact one of the organizations listed below.

A growing number of research studies have shown that most patients want to be told the truth about cancer, more and more doctors are prepared to provide information, and that seeking and receiving information can be an important part of the coping process. Pat Webb, at the time Patient Education Nurse at the Royal Marsden Hospital, said in 1988:

> 'People with cancer consistently express a need for more information about their illness and what it means for them. This helps them to retain control over their own lives during the crisis they experience. Most patients want to be involved in decisions about their illness and its treatment, and they need adequate information to do this.'

Information on treatment is particularly important where there are a number of alternatives, and where there are different opinions in the medical profession as to the best course of action. Treatment for breast cancer is an example, where expert medical advice and personal choice can conflict. Many patients complain they are not consulted about treatment choices or informed sufficiently about the advantages and disadvantages of various therapies. Patients need to understand that what they receive from the doctor is not instruction but advice on treatment options. Of course this advice should be carefully considered, but ultimately decisions are taken by patients.

Cancer treatment

If you need treatment for cancer, your doctor should discuss the various treatment options with you. Sometimes there are different treatments for the same condition, such as lumpectomy, mastectomy or radiotherapy for early breast cancer. Your doctor should seek to ensure that you have sufficient information to give an informed consent to the treatment proposed (see pages 152–5). If your doctor is unwilling to give you information on the options available you can seek a second opinion. You can also refuse treatments offered. For instance, you may not want surgery or a course of drugs, particularly if you have already had extensive treatment. But do think very seriously about refusing treatment. In recent years medical techniques like radiotherapy have improved enormously and are leading to much higher rates of recovery. 'Gentler' alternative therapies may seem attractive, but do not reject orthodox treatment for cancer too hastily. Again, the organizations listed below can provide good information on treatments available.

Briefly, the main cancer treatments are:

SURGERY Wherever possible doctors try to remove the cancerous tumour, or sometimes the entire organ affected. Surgery is most commonly used for cancer of the breast, uterus, bowel, stomach and testicles and for skin cancers on the surface of the body. Some surgery (the loss of a breast or creation of a colostomy or ileostomy) can be disfiguring and lead to problems with self-image. Many hospitals now have specialist nurses, including breast care nurses and stoma care nurses, who provide expert advice and counselling.

RADIOTHERAPY Radiotherapy is generally used to treat cancers which are difficult to reach surgically, or as a combination treatment with surgery and chemotherapy. Radiotherapy is given in two ways, usually externally from a machine which directs high energy rays on to the tumour but sometimes internally by radioactive implants. Treatment is given in a hospital radiotherapy department, usually on an out-patient basis. Some people experience side-effects including nausea, tiredness and skin soreness. Medical staff should discuss the effects of treatment, and in turn it is important to report any side-effects to them.

CHEMOTHERAPY Some cancers, particularly leukaemias and lymphomas, respond best to chemotherapy – treatment with anti-cancer, or 'cytotoxic', drugs. These can be given as tablets or by injection into a muscle or vein, to out-patients and in-patients. Cytotoxic drugs often cause sickness, and sometimes mouth ulcers, loss of appetite and hair loss. But people vary enormously in the way they react. Tell the staff if you are suffering side-effects. Drugs given with chemotherapy can help to suppress sickness. BACUP and the Royal Marsden Hospital (see pages 208 and 210) have both published information on how to cope with hair loss, get rid of mouth ulcers and boost a flagging appetite.

HORMONE TREATMENT The growth of some cancers, such as breast and prostate, seems to be influenced by sex hormones. Tamoxifen has been used successfully with some women as an addition to surgery for breast cancer.

COMPLEMENTARY TREATMENTS There are now many non-medical regimes which claim to slow the development of cancer and in some cases to cure it. Sometimes these are known as 'alternative treatments' but more usually they are complementary, in that they are used in conjunction with conventional treatments. Many doctors agree that there is no reason why patients should not try these methods, provided they do no harm.

Complementary therapies have a number of positive aspects. Practitioners may have more time to spend talking to patients. For their part patients may feel more actively involved in their treatment and experience less loss of control. Some diets recommended by complementary practitioners are good healthy eating, but do discuss any dietary changes with your GP and beware of miracle cures. Learning techniques of relaxation and visualization can be very helpful in promoting a positive attitude to recovery. And there are well-proven examples of complementary therapies helping to overcome some of the side-effects of orthodox treatment, such as the use of acupressure to combat nausea.

The best-known centre offering complementary therapies for people with cancer is the BRISTOL CANCER HELP CENTRE Grove House, Cornwallis Grove, Clifton, Bristol BS8 4PG Tel: 0272 743216. There are also affiliated groups and centres in other parts of the UK (list available from the Centre).

HOME CARE SERVICES The best place for most people with cancer to be cared for is in their own home. The following is a brief guide to the people who are likely to be involved:

GENERAL PRACTITIONER who will assess the overall need for medical and nursing care and mobilize relevant help. The GP can also arrange for admission to a hospital or hospice once home care is no longer possible.
DISTRICT NURSE who will carry out practical nursing care, administering injections, bathing, catheter care, etc.
HEALTH VISITOR who is particularly likely to be involved where children are concerned, either as cancer patients themselves or as children of patients.
SOCIAL WORKER who can advise on welfare and charitable benefits, holidays, home helps, etc.

For more information on these services see pages 74–8. In addition to general community care provision, there are specialist community nursing services for people living with cancer at home.

MACMILLAN NURSES There are more than 300 Macmillan nurses working in the community alongside the primary care team. They have undergone special training in pain control, counselling and care of the dying. They do not usually provide day-to-day home nursing, but do make regular visits to monitor drug regimes, etc. and to provide emotional support. Many Macmillan nurses are attached to hospices and arrange admissions, in conjunction with the GP. Not all parts of the country have Macmillan nurses. Your GP, community nursing office or Community Health Council will be able to advise on availability in your own area. Or contact

CANCER RELIEF MACMILLAN FUND Anchor House, 15–19 Britten Street, London SW3 3TZ Tel: 071-351 7811.
MARIE CURIE NURSES Together with the local health authority, Marie Curie funds part-time community nurses who are able to give extra nursing care cover. The main demand is for night nursing to give family carers some respite. Again, ask your GP, community nursing office or CHC about the availability of the service, or contact MARIE CURIE CANCER CARE 28 Belgrave Square, London SW1X 8QG Tel: 071-235 3325.

Terminal care

Hospice care for people dying with cancer (and some other conditions like AIDS) is provided by specialist units in general hospitals, by home care teams, and in hospices themselves. Most deaths from cancer take place in hospital but about a third are at home and 10 per cent are in hospices. Where someone is cared for depends on personal and family choice, home circumstances, doctors' preferences and the progress of the disease. The best place will vary according to individual circumstances. Some people are determined to remain at home in familiar and secure surroundings. Others find security in knowing that they are receiving round the clock medical treatment and pain control within hospital. Hospice care can provide the benefits of specialist, professional support within a homely environment.

Originally a place of rest for medieval pilgrims, the term hospice now refers to a small, specialist unit caring for the dying and those with incurable illnesses. Hospices aim for a calm and peaceful environment and emphasize the involvement of the patient and relatives. They are usually run on very informal lines, with minimal restrictions on visiting. There are now more than 100 hospices in the UK, ranging from the sixty-bed St Christopher's Hospice in Sydenham to the eight-bed children's hospice in Oxford, Helen House. St Christopher's has a HOSPICE INFORMATION SERVICE (51–9 Lawrie Park Road, Sydenham, London SE26 6DZ Tel:

081-778 9252 ext 262) which holds details of hospices throughout the UK and abroad. A 1990 *Directory of Hospice Services* has been produced. Hospices in the UK have been set up largely by voluntary organizations, but the NHS supports many of them financially.

People do not just enter hospices to die. It is quite normal for people to be admitted for short periods to give relatives a break, or to monitor and control symptoms. They can then return home. Many hospices have emergency beds for patients who have to be admitted quickly, but you should not have to wait more than a week or two for admission. There is no charge for hospice care but donations are always welcomed by the voluntary organizations who often run them. In addition to residential hospices, many areas also have HOME CARE TEAMS, bringing hospice-type care to people in their own homes and using the skills of the specialist nurses described above.

UK hospices include:

Macmillan Continuing Care Units, built in the grounds of NHS hospitals with funding from Cancer Relief
Marie Curie residential nursing homes for people with cancer
Sue Ryder homes which care for disabled as well as terminally ill people
Continuing care wards for the incurably ill in NHS hospitals

Finding information about cancer

By far the most comprehensive source of information for the general public on cancer is the Cancer Information Service run by BACUP (British Association of Cancer United Patients), 121–3 Charterhouse Street, London EC1M 6AA Tel: 071-608 1661 (within London) and 0800 181 199 (freephone line for callers outside London). BACUP was established in 1985 by Dr Vicky Clement-Jones, a doctor who came to realize the lack of information experienced by many people with cancer when she became a patient herself. BACUP's information service is run by trained and experienced cancer nurses who answer over 100 inquiries a day, mainly over the telephone (analysis of the first 30,000 inquiries showed that 80 per cent of inquirers were women). The nurses are able to give information on screening facilities, treatments, local support groups, sources of financial help, home nursing services and hospices. A newspaper, *BACUP News*, is published three times a year and gives the latest information on research and developments in treatment and care. An excellent series of booklets is also available giving practical advice on coping with individual cancers. There is a one-to-one counselling service for those able to visit the BACUP offices in London.

A complementary national information service is provided by CANCERLINK 46 Pentonville Road, London N1 9HF Tel: 071-833 2451. Cancerlink also provides an excellent information service

Public libraries should have available a number of books on cancer for lay people. Titles to look out for are:

Cancer: a guide for patients and their families by Chris and Sue Williams (Chichester: Wiley, 1986)

Cancer: your questions answered by Charles Dobree (London: Ebury Press, 1988)

Living with Cancer by Jenny Bryan and Joanna Lyall (Harmondsworth: Penguin, 1987)

Guide to Cancer by Pat Young (Edinburgh: Churchill Livingstone, 1986)

by telephone and letter. There is also a newsletter and a series of booklets on topics such as caring for a sick person at home. In addition Cancerlink specializes in support for local cancer self-help groups, providing training and assistance for 300 groups throughout the UK. Cancerlink's annual *Directory of Cancer Support and Self-help Groups* gives details of support organizations nationwide for specific problems such as mastectomy, colostomy and laryngectomy.

The Patient Education Group at the ROYAL MARSDEN HOSPITAL is responsible for another series of information booklets and leaflets. Currently there are sixteen titles covering individual cancers, treatments such as radiotherapy and chemotherapy, and tips on overcoming eating difficulties. The booklets are distributed by Haigh and Hochland Ltd, The Precinct Centre, Oxford Road, Manchester M13 9QA.

Complementary Therapies

Large numbers of people in the UK choose complementary therapies as a routine form of health care. A national opinion poll carried out in 1984 found that 10 per cent of the population 'believed strongly' in complementary medicine. By 1985 the number had increased to 13 per cent, and the same percentage replied that they had actually used non-orthodox medicines at some time. A survey of Consumers' Association members published in *Which?* (October 1986) seemed to confirm this level of use. One in seven members had used some form of alternative or complementary medicine during the previous twelve months. Consumers' Association (CA) members are probably not typical of society as a whole, but it would be a reasonable estimate that one in ten of the population are contacting complementary practitioners.

There are many different kinds of complementary therapies: the authoritative *Handbook of Complementary Medicine* (see below) describes seventy therapies, ranging from rolfing to medical dowsing. The most common types of practitioner consulted by CA members were:

osteopaths	42 per cent
homoeopaths	26 per cent
acupuncturists	23 per cent
chiropractors	22 per cent
herbalists	11 per cent

The most common problem was pain or a joint disorder (71 per cent). This major reason for seeking complementary medicine was confirmed by a survey carried out in 1984 at the Centre for the Study of Complementary Medicine in Southampton. Here almost half the patients were seeking relief from back pain, arthritis, etc. Other common problems were allergies, skin problems and 'general malaise'. There was a high level of satisfaction shown by the CA survey: 82 per cent of respondents claimed to have been cured or improved; 74 per cent said they would definitely use this form of medicine again. In the Southampton survey 60 per cent of patients felt much better after eight weeks' treatment.

Why people choose complementary medicine

Eighty per cent of the CA members who chose to use complementary medicine had already consulted their GP. Most of these said they were dissatisfied with the conventional medical treatment they had received, largely because it had failed to solve a long-term intractable problem like chronic pain or stress. So it seems that most people regard this kind of treatment as *complementary*, to be used alongside orthodox medicine (for those things that orthodox medicine is not very good at treating) rather than as a totally *alternative* system.

There is no doubt that the popularity of complementary medicine is a reflection of a general crisis of confidence in orthodox scientific medicine. There is an awareness of the limitations of scientific medicine in dealing with many of the illnesses of modern society. Not only that, but modern technical medicine harms as well as cures. One in ten hospital patients suffer a hospital-acquired infection. Thirty per cent of all hospital patients suffer unwanted side-effects from drugs. The Director General of the World Health Organization, Halfden Mahler, summed up the problem in 1977:

> Most of the world's medical schools prepare doctors, not to take care of the health of the people but instead for a medical practice that is blind to anything but disease and the technology for dealing with it; a technology involving astronomical and ever increasing prices directed towards fewer and fewer people. The medical empire and its closely related aggressive industry of diagnostic and therapeutic weapons sometimes appears more of a threat than a contribution to health . . . the very attempt to diagnose and treat one ill may produce another, be it through side-effects or iatrogenesis.

In choosing complementary therapies people are looking for a gentler form of treatment, free from side-effects. They are also looking for a system of medicine which treats the whole person rather than the disease (the 'holistic' approach to health). The complementary practitioner usually spends considerably longer talking to the patient than an NHS GP could ever hope to do. The aim is to build up a picture of the patient's personality and lifestyle in order to find out why this person developed this illness in this particular way. This personalized treatment (two patients with similar symptoms could be treated in very different ways) and the time spent allowing the patient to talk about their problems are certainly among the attractions of complementary medicine.

What doctors think of complementary medicine

Although what we now call complementary therapies have been practised for centuries, the profile was raised considerably when HRH Prince Charles was elected chairman of the British Medical Association in 1983. He immediately exhorted doctors to re-examine the basic assumptions of scientific medicine and be more open-minded about alternatives. In his words:

> The whole imposing edifice of modern medicine, for all its breathtaking success, is like the celebrated tower of Pisa, slightly off balance. It seems to me that account has to be taken of those long-neglected complementary methods of medicine which in the right hands can bring considerable relief, if not hope, to an increasing number of people.

Partly in response to their chairman's criticism, the BMA launched a celebrated inquiry into complementary medicine (Board of Science and Education, *Alternative Therapies*, London: BMA, 1986). The report was critical of complementary therapies as being unscientific, although it did acknowledge the value of some therapies. These were: homoeopathy as a safe placebo; hypnotherapy for psychological problems, acupuncture for pain relief; and osteopathy and chiropractic for spinal problems. The BMA argued that complementary medicine should be subject to the same rigorous clinical trials as scientific medicine. Complementary practitioners argue that the techniques of scientific medicine are not appropriate for evaluation of alternative therapies. The RESEARCH COUNCIL FOR COMPLEMENTARY MEDICINE (for address see box, page 220), has been established to develop more appropriate research methods.

The BMA report was obviously out of step with public opinion. Studies also suggest that it may not have been representative of the views of doctors. A survey of Avon GPs, carried out by the Centre for the Study of Complementary Medicine in Southampton, showed a surprisingly high interest in complementary medicine. Thirty-eight per cent of the GPs had received some training in complementary medicine and a further 15 per cent wished to have training. Seventy-six per cent had referred patients for complementary treatments over the past year, and 59 per cent thought the treatments were useful. An earlier survey of 100 GP trainees found that eighteen were using at least one complementary method and seventy wanted to train in one. Twenty-two had been treated by a complementary therapist themselves and it tended to be those doctors who were more positive. In contrast to the BMA report, only 16 per cent of Oxfordshire GPs questioned in 1986 regarded complementary medicine as unscientific.

Legislation and complementary medicine

Under the 1968 Medicines Act all new medicines are required to be safe and effective before they can qualify for a licence. Medicines already on the market are gradually being reviewed and the Committee on the Safety of Medicines is now reviewing the safety and effectiveness of herbal remedies; homoeopathic remedies are next on the list. Herbalists and homoeopaths are concerned that the review procedures for assessing the effectiveness of ordinary remedies are not appropriate for alternative medications and that the review may lead to a reduction in the availability of herbal and homoeopathic preparations.

Another concern arises from the possible application of European legislation after 1992. In some European countries (including France and Belgium) it is illegal to practise complementary medicine unless you are qualified as a medical doctor. This has not put a stop to non-medical complementary medicine but has simply led to a widespread 'underground' practice, making it harder than ever for people to find proficient practitioners. In Italy, 'natural medicine' is very popular but complementary practitioners are more restricted than their British counterparts. They are obliged to refer all new patients to an orthodox doctor for an initial consultation. The European Commission has agreed to postpone proposals for single legislation on complementary practitioners for the time being, but therapists in the UK are worried that harmonization of qualifications could lead to a doctors-only profession, so reducing consumer choice.

How to get complementary medicine

Only a very limited amount of complementary medicine is available on the NHS. Some GPs are trained in one or more complementary therapies themselves (this could be a factor in choosing your GP). Others employ complementary practitioners within the health centre or surgery. If you are lucky enough to have this option you can get free treatment within the practice. Homoeopathy is the only form of complementary medicine which is generally available on the NHS. There are several homoeopathic hospitals which take NHS referrals from GPs. Beyond this the use of complementary therapies within hospitals depends very much on the interests and attitudes of the medical and nursing staff. There are pockets of good practice. At Charing Cross Hospital, London, consultant cardiologist Dr Peter Nixon offers a range of alternative therapies including massage, relaxation, osteopathy, dance therapy and hypnotherapy. At St Mary's Hospital, Isle of Wight (see page 168) nurses on one of the wards use aromatherapy to relax patients in the evenings.

As surveys have shown, many GPs do refer patients to complementary practitioners (three-quarters of the Avon GPs had done so). So a good starting-point is to ask your GP's opinion of a particular therapy and whether he or she knows of a practitioner. If there is any possibility of treatment under the NHS you will have to be referred by your GP. If your GP is unsympathetic or you want to do some homework on your own, you need to know how to find out more about the different therapies and their practitioners. There are two problems when making choices in complementary medicine. One is that most people have only a hazy idea of what a particular therapy involves. The second is being certain that you choose a skilled and reputable practitioner.

Most people choose a particular therapist on the basis of a personal recommendation from a relative or friend (seven out of ten people in the CA survey did this). But anybody can set themselves up as a practitioner of complementary medicine, even if they have had no training at all. So that you know that you are choosing a trained practitioner make sure that you select someone who is registered with the appropriate professional body. The check-list below describes briefly the most widely used complementary therapies, and gives the name and address of the professional body for each. Before you decide to try a particular therapy, write to the relevant organization asking for more details and for a list of qualified practitioners in your area.

Acupuncture

Acupuncture is an ancient Chinese art, dating back to long before Christ. It is based on the principle that in all diseases, physical and mental, there are tender areas on the surface of the body which disappear when the illness is cured. The skilled practitioner will look for signs of illness in the patient's appearance, particularly the tongue and pulse, and identify the appropriate acupuncture point.

There are about 1,000 acupuncture points in all, joined by imaginary lines on the body's surface called meridians. The meridians control twelve major organs of the body; heart, stomach, liver, kidney, etc. Once the problem is identified, the therapist inserts needles at acupuncture points along the appropriate meridian. The needles remain in place for anything from a few seconds to half an hour. They may be manipulated or an electric current passed through them. Needles are only inserted a few millimetres and patients report feeling no pain. In the associated technique of SHIATSU (acupressure) finger pressure is applied to the acupuncture points. MOXIBUSTION involves burning a herb, moxa (artemisia japonica) over the same points. Acupuncture seems to work by stimulating the release of natural pain-killers called endorphins, and its use is now widely accepted for pain-related problems.

NOTE: In 1988 a 17-year-old boy became infected with HIV in Paris, probably as a result of acupuncture with contaminated needles. These has also been an outbreak of Hepatitis B associated with acupuncture. It is now more important than ever to use a practitioner who has the highest standards of hygiene. Ensure that all equipment is sterilized (or, even better, see that once-only, disposable needles are used) to avoid any risk of transmission of HIV or other communicable diseases. The Department of Health has produced a leaflet *AIDS: guidelines for acupuncturists* which sets out the precautions acupuncturists should take (available by telephoning 0800 555 777).

Organizations for acupuncture

British Medical Acupuncture Society 67–9 Chancery Lane, London WC2A 1AF maintains a register of members who are also medically qualified. They will send you a list in return for an SAE but you need to be referred to a practitioner by your GP.

British Acupuncture Association 22 Hockley Road, Rayleigh, Essex SS6 8EB Tel: 0268 742534, has members who are not qualified in orthodox medicine

Chiropractic and osteopathy

Both these therapies are based on the theory that the spine has a profound effect on overall well-being. Ancient Egyptian manuscripts have descriptions of similar manipulative techniques, but these therapies have undergone a revival since the late nineteenth century. Both are based on manipulation of the spine and joints. Chiropractors mainly use short sudden thrusts for direct manipulation, while osteopaths combine this technique with soft tissue massage. When examining the patient, chiropractors and osteopaths would study posture, take a full personal history and often use x-rays to provide additional diagnostic information. Manipulative techniques have been found particularly useful for back and joint pain. A newer technique is cranial osteopathy, whereby the bones of the skull are manipulated. There has been some success in treating migraine and, more controversially, behaviour problems in children. Osteopathy is one of the more accepted parts of the medical scene. About 10 per cent of the 800 qualified practitioners in the UK are medically qualified. In the USA osteopathy is widely used with 7,000 osteopaths, qualified after a rigorous seven-year training. Chiropractic is probably the most widely recognized alternative medical profession worldwide, with 25,000 practitioners in the USA alone. However, in the UK it is osteopathy which is more commonly used.

Organizations for chiropractic and osteopathy

British Chiropractors' Association 5 First Avenue, Chelmsford, Essex CM1 1RX Tel: 0245 353078

General Council and Register of Osteopaths 1–4 Suffolk Street, London SW1Y 4HG Tel: 071-839 2060

Organizations for homoeopathy

British Homoeopathic Association 27a Devonshire Street, London W1N 1RJ Tel: 071-935 2163, maintains a register of medically qualified homoeopaths

Society of Homoeopaths 47a Canada Grove, Bognor Regis, West Sussex PO21 1OW Tel: 0243 860678, can provide a list of non-medically qualified homoeopaths

Homoeopathy

Homoeopathy is based on two main principles, developed by the nineteenth-century physician Samuel Hahnemann. The first is the hypothesis that like can cure like. The second is the principle of the minimum dose having the greatest effect. Homoeopathy is based on the belief that the body can cope with most illnesses itself through its immune system. The symptoms of an illness are an important part of the body's efforts to throw off the disease and should not be suppressed. Instead, a minute dose of a substance which produces similar symptoms is given to promote the healing process by effectively encouraging the symptoms for a short while. The initial consultation usually takes an hour or more and involves a detailed discussion of the patient's history, preferences and lifestyle. The homoeopath then selects a remedy from a list of about 3,000. The remedy is selected closely to match the particular patient; two people with superficially identical symptoms may be given a completely different remedy. Many local pharmacists stock homoeopathic medicines, as do health food shops. They are even more widely available in Europe where homoeopathic pharmacies are commonplace. As the doses are so tiny, homoeopathic remedies have no side-effects and some experimental self-medication is worth a try (although of course you miss out on the detailed initial consultation and your choice of remedy is a shot in the dark). GPs can write a prescription for a homoeopathic remedy or refer you for treatment to a homoeopath under the NHS.

Many people have found homoeopathy successful for the relief of chronic conditions such as allergies, skin conditions, digestive problems and joint pain. A homoeopath would not attempt to deal with mechanical problems such as musculo-skeletal injuries, with infectious diseases or cancer.

Finding more information on complementary medicine

Institute for Complementary Medicine
21 Portland Place, London W1N 3AF Tel: 071-636 9543, provides an information service on a wide range of complementary therapies.
British Holistic Medical Association 179 Gloucester Place, London NW1 6DX Tel: 071-262 5299, is a professional body for medically qualified practitioners which holds workshops and conferences and publishes a journal.
Council for Complementary and Alternative Medicine Suite 1, 19a Cavendish Square, London W1M 9AD Tel: 071-409 1440, is an umbrella group representing the interests of complementary medicine nationally. This is also the address for the **Research Council for Complementary Medicine**.
The most comprehensive guide to complementary medicine is *The Handbook of Complementary Medicine* by Stephen Fulder (Oxford University Press, 2nd edition, 1988). This provides a detailed discussion of all the important therapies with lists of further reading, a directory of 250 organizations and educational bodies, and a survey of legislation, research, historical and political issues.

Other useful guides include *Alternative Medicine* by Andrew Stanway (Harmondsworth: Penguin, 1982) and the series of Penguin books on different therapies: acupuncture, aromatherapy, chiropractic, herbal medicine, homoeopathy, hypnotherapy, osteopathy and spiritual healing. A similar series has been published by Macdonald Optima.

Private Treatment

If you can afford it, and particularly if you are faced with a long wait for NHS treatment, you might consider seeing a doctor privately. In Britain there are about 200 private acute hospitals and there are around 3,000 pay beds in NHS hospitals. Around 400,000 operations are carried out in the private sector (15 per cent of non-emergency surgery in the UK).

There are a number of reasons for considering private medical care, but there are also a number of pitfalls.

QUALIFICATIONS The NHS only employs people holding recognized qualifications in medicine, physiotherapy, psychology, etc. In private medicine there is not this safeguard. If a GP refers you to a private practitioner you can be confident about their status, but if you choose a practitioner yourself you need to be careful to check their qualifications.

MAJOR MEDICAL AND RELATED QUALIFICATIONS

AAPSW	Associate of the Association of Psychiatric Social Workers
A.B.Ps.S.	Associate of the British Psychological Society
AFOM	Associate of the Faculty of Occupational Medicine
B.Ch.	Bachelor of Surgery
B.Ch.D.	Bachelor of Dental Surgery
BDS	Bachelor of Dental Surgery
BM	Bachelor of Medicine
Ch.B.	Bachelor of Surgery
DA	Diploma in Anaesthesia
DCCH	Diploma in Child and Community Health
DCH	Diploma in Child Health
DCP	Diploma in Clinical Pathology
DIH	Diploma in Industrial Health
DMR	Diploma in Radiology
DO	Diploma in Ophthalmology
D.Obst.R.C.O.G.	Diploma in Obstetrics, Royal College of Obstetricians and Gynaecologists
F.B.Ps.S.	Fellow of the British Psychological Society

F.Ch.S.	Fellow of the Society of Chiropodists
FCST	Fellow of the College of Speech Therapists
FDS	Fellow in Dental Surgery
FFARCS	Fellow of the Faculty of Anaesthetists, Royal College of Surgeons of England
FFCM	Fellow of the Faculty of Community Medicine
F.F.Hom.	Fellow of the Faculty of Homoeopathy
FFOM	Fellow of the Faculty of Occupational Medicine
FHA	Fellow of the Institute of Health Service Administrators
FPS	Fellow of the Pharmaceutical Society
FRCGP	Fellow of the Royal College of General Practitioners
FRCN	Fellow of the Royal College of Nursing
FRCOG	Fellow of the Royal College of Obstretricians and Gynaecologists
FRCP	Fellow of the Royal College of Physicians of London
F.R.C.Path.	Fellow of the Royal College of Pathologists
FRCP (Ed. *or* Edin.)	Fellow of the Royal College of Physicians, Edinburgh
FRCP (Glasg.)	Fellow of the Royal College of Physicians and Surgeons of Glasgow
FRCPI	Fellow of the Royal College of Physicians of Ireland
F.R.C.Psych.	Fellow of the Royal College of Psychiatrists
FRCR	Fellow of the Royal College of Radiologists
FRCS	Fellow of the Royal College of Surgeons of England
FRCS (Ed. *or* Edin.)	Fellow of the Royal College of Surgeons of Edinburgh
FRCS (Glasg.)	Fellow of the Royal College of Physicians and Surgeons of Glasgow
FRCS (Irel.)	Fellow of the Royal College of Surgeons in Ireland
FRS	Fellow of the Royal Society
MB	Bachelor of Medicine
MB BS	Bachelor of Medicine and Bachelor of Surgery
MC	Master of Surgery
M.Ch.	Master of Surgery
M.Ch.D.	Master of Dental Surgery
M.Chir.	Master of Surgery
M.Ch.S.	Member of the Society of Chiropodists
MD	Doctor of Medicine
MFCM	Member of the Faculty of Community Medicine
M.F.Hom.	Member of the Faculty of Homoeopathy
MFOM	Member of the Faculty of Occupational Medicine
M.Psy.Med.	Master of Psychological Medicine
MRCGP	Member of the Royal College of General Practitioners
MRCOG	Member of the Royal College of Obstetricians and Gynaecologists
MRCP	Member of the Royal College of Physicians of London
M.R.C.Path.	Member of the Royal College of Pathologists

MRCP (Ed. *or* Edin.)	Member of the Royal College of Physicians, Edinburgh
MRCP (Glasg.)	Member of the Royal College of Physicians and Surgeons of Glasgow
MRCPI	Member of the Royal College of Physicians of Ireland
M.R.C.Psych.	Member of the Royal College of Psychiatrists
MRCR	Member of the Royal College of Radiologists
MRCS	Member of the Royal College of Surgeons of England
MRCS (Ed. *or* Edin.)	Member of the Royal College of Surgeons of Edinburgh
MRCS (Irel.)	Member of the Royal College of Surgeons in Ireland
ND	Doctor of Nursing
PD	Doctor of Pharmacy
RCNT	Registered Clinical Nurse Teacher
RGN	Registered General Nurse
RHV	Registered Health Visitor
RM	Registered Midwife
RMN	Registered Mental Nurse
RN	Registered Nurse
RNMH	Registered Nurse for the Mentally Handicapped
RNT	Registered Nurse Tutor
RSCN	Registered Sick Children's Nurse
SCM	State Certified Midwife
SEN	State Enrolled Nurse
SRN	State Registered Nurse
SRP	State Registered Physiotherapist

COMPLAINTS It is much more difficult to pursue a complaint against a private practitioner than against an NHS professional. Private treatment is given on the basis of a contract, and it may be necessary to prove a breach of this contract. However, you could take up a complaint with the General Medical Council which is concerned with the conduct of all doctors, whether in the NHS or in private practice.

QUALITY OF CARE Private does not always mean better. Private hospitals and nursing homes often do not have the facilities of an NHS hospital. They may not have intensive care units, there may not be specialist staff (such as an anaesthetist) on call, and you will have to wait for the consultant himself to be called before any treatment can be given. Although personal attention from the consultant is one of the advantages of private health care, this can seem less attractive if you are faced with an unpleasant delay. Consultants in private practice do not have 'firms' of junior doctors to carry out treatment on their behalf.

CARE PROVIDED In general the private health care covered by provident associations such as British United Provident Association (BUPA) and Private Patients Plan (PPP) does not include:

- normal pregnancy and childbirth
- long-term disability or mental illness
- routine dental treatment
- complementary therapies
- cosmetic surgery

You should compare policies very carefully to see exactly what is covered. A policy which provided for the same level of comprehensive care as the NHS would have to be very expensive indeed.

For a useful review of private medical insurance policies, what they cover and which are good buys look at 'Private medical insurance', *Which?* (April 1990).

Advantages of private hospital treatment

Despite these considerations, you still might feel that private treatment is worthwhile for you. You should get:

- a room to yourself, perhaps with telephone and television
- a choice of admission date
- visiting at any reasonable hour
- a choice of consultant, who will perform the operation himself
- a shorter wait for non-urgent conditions such as varicose veins, hip replacements and hernias (but if this is your main concern check whether you could be seen more quickly at another hospital under the NHS, see page 138)

Finding a private consultant

Most consultants will ask for a GP's letter even if you are consulting privately, so the right place to start looking for a private consultant is your GP. If you are claiming the cost through a scheme like BUPA or PPP, a GP referral is essential. Your GP should know of LOCAL CONSULTANTS with a private practice. Most of these work mainly for the NHS and see patients privately as well.

If you want to see a consultant elsewhere, or if you are looking for help with a less common problem, it can be more difficult to identify a good private practitioner, particularly as doctors are not allowed to advertise. One way to trace an expert is to check the professional literature. It is a reasonable assumption that an expert in a particular field will have written articles in medical journals on the subject. If you can get your local medical library (see page 290) to carry out a LITERATURE SEARCH on the subject, perhaps using one of the computerized indexes to the medical literature, you can then use the *Medical Register* of all medical practitioners to check the addresses of experts. Your GP will probably be interested in the results of your search.

MEDICAL ADVISORY SERVICE 10 Barley Mow Passage, London W4 4PH Tel: 081-994 9874 provides information on private health care (as well as NHS and voluntary resources).

COSMETIC SURGERY has a particular potential for abuse if a patient is exploited by an unscrupulous practitioner. Many people also have unrealistic expectations of what cosmetic surgery can do for them. If you are considering cosmetic surgery you would find it useful to look at *Cosmetic Surgery: a consumer guide* by Denise Winn (London: Optima, 1989). This book gives advice on finding a reputable surgeon and answers questions on the risks and benefits.

6 Using Health Services Abroad

We are increasingly likely to make use of health care services overseas. Each year British holiday-makers take 15 million trips abroad. More and more people go abroad on business trips, and this is certain to increase with the introduction of the Single European Market at the end of 1992. The harmonization of qualifications and the removal of barriers to employment will mean that more British people will seek work in other countries of the European Community, and at the same time Europeans will come to the UK in growing numbers.

The Single European Market has a number of implications for health care. Demand for labour in the more affluent parts of the Community is likely to encourage an inflow of migrant workers from the poorer parts of Europe. Research has shown that migrants who move from one society to another are particularly prone to physical and psychological health problems. There is also concern that the removal of national fiscal barriers such as VAT and excise duty on alcohol and tobacco will lead to increased consumption in the UK, with detrimental effects on health. And there is a growing awareness of Europe-wide health problems, including drug abuse, AIDS and an ageing population (6 per cent of the population of the European Community are over 75).

This increasingly European, and worldwide, outlook leads to a number of new information needs. UK citizens need information on health care systems, services and entitlements in other countries. Citizens of those countries, in return, need information on health care in the UK. This information should be made available in European Community languages, as well as in those of minority British communities. There will also be an increasing need for health promotion initiatives which address the needs of new groups of immigrant workers in the UK.

Entitlement to Health Care in the European Community

Free or reduced cost medical treatment is available in other European countries if you are suddenly taken ill or have an accident during your visit. Only emergency treatment under the state health care system is covered. Before you go abroad in Europe, make sure you obtain a copy of the Department of Health booklet, *The Traveller's Guide to Health*. This gives details of entitlements to health care abroad, vaccination requirements, etc. Copies are available from doctors' surgeries, post offices, travel agents, etc. or by phoning 0800 555 777 any time, free of charge. The information is also updated on Prestel, page 50063.

To get medical care in most European countries you will need a form E111. You can get this form at any post office. An E111 only covers temporary stays. If you are going to work in another EC country for more than twelve months, or to work for a foreign employer, the E111 is not appropriate as you should be insured under the social security legislation of the country of your employment. The DSS OVERSEAS BRANCH Longbenton, Newcastle upon Tyne, NE98 1YX can advise.

E111 is for emergency treatment. It will not cover you for free or reduced cost medical treatment if you are going to another EC country *specifically* for medical or maternity care. If this is the case you should still complete the form E111, but attach a letter explaining why you need to make this visit specifically for treatment. Then ask your NHS consultant for a letter recommending that you seek treatment in another EC country and giving details of the treatment. He should also give evidence either that the treatment is available under the NHS but cannot be provided within the time normally necessary, or that your case is exceptional – and why. Ask your consultant to send this to DEPARTMENT OF HEALTH INTERNATIONAL RELATIONS DIVISION Hannibal House, Elephant and Castle, London SE1 6TE. You will only be issued with the appropriate certificate (E112) if your NHS consultant recommends the treatment; if it is available under the other country's health insurance scheme; and you are entitled to a form E111. Without it you will have to meet the costs of any treatment you receive.

Remember that form E111 is for use only in countries that are members of the EC. For non-European Community countries see pages 237–45.

You should also take out travel insurance when you travel to the EC or elsewhere, which will cover you for longer-term health care as well as other mishaps. This is available from travel agents, banks and insurance companies.

Overleaf Entitlements to treatment in countries of the European Community (Source: *The Traveller's Guide to Health*, DHSS booklet)

EUROPEAN COMMUNITY COUNTRIES

Country	Documents needed to get medical treatment	What is normally free
Belgium	E111	
Denmark (excluding Faroe Islands	UK passport (E111 needed if not UK or Danish national).	Hospital treatment arranged by a doctor. In an emergency ask the hospital authorities to arrange free treatment. Medical treatment given by a doctor registered with the Danish Public Health Service. Get a receipt if charged.
France	E111	
German Federal Republic (West Germany)	E111 (to be exchanged for German health certificate).	Dental treatment. Medical treatment.
Gibraltar	UK passport (E111 needed only if not UK or Gibraltar national).	Hospital treatment in public wards of St Bernard's Hospital. Treatment at Casemates Health Centre.

What you pay charges for	Other information
Hospital treatment. Prescribed medicines. Other medical and dental treatment. Ambulance travel.	About 75% of charges are refunded by Belgian Sickness Insurance Fund (Caisse Auxiliaire D'Assurance Maladie-Invalidité or Hulpkaas Voor Ziekte-en Invaliditeits Verzekering). Full details issued with E111.
Dental treatment given by a dentist registered with the Danish Public Health Service. Get a receipt for any charges. Some prescribed medicines available at reduced cost by showing passport to chemist. Otherwise get a receipt.	Before you leave Denmark apply to the Kommunsens Social-og Sundhedsforvaltning with receipts. Medical costs, part of dental costs and part of costs of prescribed medicines will be refunded. Get details from the National Social Security Office (Sikringsstyrelsen) Æbelogade 1, Post box 2566, 2100 Copenhagen.
Hospital treatment. Dental treatment. Other medical care. Prescribed medicines.	70–80% of charges are refunded by local Sickness Insurance Office (Caisse Primaires D'Assurance-Maladie). Full details issued with E111.
Prescribed medicines. Hospital treatment. Ambulance travel.	Full details issued with E111.
Medical treatment elsewhere. Prescribed medicines. Dental treatment. But on weekdays in normal working hours extractions are obtainable at St Bernard's Hospital for a nominal charge.	*Information:* Casemates Health Centre or Medical and Health Department, St Bernard's Hospital.

Country	Documents needed to get medical treatment	What is normally free
Greece	E111 (to be exchanged for Greek certificate).	Medical treatment.
Irish Republic	No documents needed. (You may be asked to complete a simple statement and provide proof of your UK residence, e.g. NHS medical card.)	All medical and dental treatment. Local Health Board will arrange for a consultation with a public health service doctor or dentist. Hospital treatment arranged by a doctor in public ward of health service hospital. Prescribed medicines.
Italy	E111 (to be exchanged for Italian health certificate).	Medical treatment.
Luxembourg	E111 (to be exchanged for Luxembourg health certificate).	
Netherlands (Holland)	E111	Hospital treatment. Other medical treatment.
Portugal (including the Azores and Madeira)	UK passport. Other EC nationals will need form E111 to be exchanged for a medical care booklet.	In-patient treatment in the general ward of an official hospital.

What you pay charges for	Other information
Hospital treatment. Presribed medicines. (There are often long waits for treatment in the public health service.)	Although costs may be partly refunded by the Greek Social Insurance Foundation (ΙΔΡΥΜΑ ΚΟΙΝΩΝΙΚΩΝ ΑΣØΑΛΙΣΕΩΝ) travel insurance cover for private medical treatment is strongly recommended. Full details issued with E111.
	Information: From the Health Board of the area in which you are staying. Make it clear to the doctor, dentist or hospital authorities that you wish to be treated under the European Community's social security regulations.
Prescribed medicines. Most hospital treatment. Dental treatment. Specialist examinations. X-rays, laboratory tests, physiotherapy.	Full details issued with E111.
Hospital treatment. Dental treatment. Other medical treatment. Prescribed medicines. Ambulance travel.	Partial refund of charges by Luxembourg Sickness Insurance Office (Caisse National D'Assurance Maladie Des Ouvriers). Full details issued with E111.
Dental treatment. Prescribed medicines.	Full details issued with E111.
Medical treatment from a doctor working in the state scheme health centre (Centro de Saudé). Prescribed medicines. Dental treatment.	Make it clear to the doctor or hospital authorities that you wish to be treated under the European Community social security arrangements.

Country	Documents needed to get medical treatment	What is normally free
Spain (including the Balearic and Canary Islands)	E111	Medical treatment given by a State scheme doctor or hospital.

What you pay charges for	Other information
Prescribed medicines. Dental treatment.	In most holiday resorts, only a limited service is available under the Spanish scheme. You must make sure that you seek treatment from a doctor at the local State Health Centre (Ambulatorio or Consultorio), or a doctor who treats State Health Service patients, or a state hospital. You should take your E111 and a photocopy to the Health Centre or hospital. Doctors in private clinics will not accept form E111. If you have to pay the costs they will rarely, if ever, be refunded. Private medical insurance is strongly recommended.

Getting Treatment in Non-European Community Countries

The UK has reciprocal health agreements with a number of countries outside the European Community. These cover the provision of emergency medical treatment at reduced cost, or in some cases free of charge. You will normally need to produce your UK passport, and in some countries your NHS medical card as well. Remember that the range of medical care outside European Community countries may be less than that provided by the British NHS, and the costs of treatment may not be fully covered by reciprocal agreements. Make sure you have adequate personal health insurance before you go abroad. Policies should cover the cost of flying the sick person home, as well as the costs of local treatment. Medical insurance for a two-week holiday in Europe is likely to cost £15–20 per person.

See also the list of countries where vaccinations are required or recommended on pages 247–51.

Overleaf Entitlements to health care in non-European Community countries (Source: *Traveller's Guide to Health*, DHSS booklet)

COUNTRIES OUTSIDE THE EUROPEAN COMMUNITY

Country	Documents needed to get medical treatment	What is normally free
Anguilla	Proof of UK residence (e.g. NHS medical card or UK driving licence).	Minor emergency treatment.
Australia	Proof of UK residence (e.g. UK passport or NHS medical card) and temporary entry permit.	Hospital treatment.
Austria	UK passport.	In-patient treatment in public wards of public hospitals.
British Virgin Islands	Proof of UK residence (e.g. NHS medical card or UK driving licence).	Hospital and other medical treatment for persons aged 70 and over and school-age children.
Bulgaria	UK passport and NHS medical card.	Hospital treatment. Other medical and dental treatment.
Channel Islands – staying less than three months	Proof of UK residence (e.g. driving licence or NHS medical card).	*Guernsey/Alderney* Hospital treatment. Emergency dental treatment. Other medical care. Ambulance travel (Guernsey).

What you pay charges for	Other information
Hospital in-patient and out-patient treatment. Hospital accommodation. Dental treatment. Prescribed medicines. Ambulance travel.	Family doctor-type treatment is available at out-patient clinics. A charge is made.
Treatment at some doctors' surgeries. Prescribed medicines. Ambulance travel.	You will need to enrol at a local Medicare office but this can be done after you get treatment. Some doctors' charges may be partially refunded by the Medicare scheme. Claim at the local office before you leave.
Prescribed medicines. All other medical services including treatment at a hospital out-patient department or doctor's surgery. Private treatment or accommodation in a public hospital. Ambulance travel.	If you are an Austrian national resident in the UK, you will need to show your Austrian passport and UK NHS medical card.
Other visitors are charged for all services at rates applicable to residents.	
Prescribed medicines.	
Some prescribed medicines.	No out-patient department at Guernsey General Hospital.

Country	Documents needed to get medical treatment	What is normally free
		Jersey Hospital in-patient and out-patient treatment. Ambulance travel.
		Sark Medical treatment.
Czechoslovakia	UK passport.	Hospital treatment. Other medical care.
Falkland Islands	Proof of UK residence (e.g. medical card or UK driving licence).	Hospital treatment. Dental treatment. Other medical treatment. Prescribed medicines. Ambulance travel.
Finland	UK passport.	Consultation at health centre.
German Democratic Republic (East Germany)	UK passport.	Hospital treatment. Dental care. Prescribed medicines.
Hong Kong	NHS medical card and valid passport.	Emergency treatment at certain hospitals/clinics.*
Hungary	UK passport.	Treatment in hospital, polyclinic or at a doctor's surgery.
Iceland	UK passport (or NHS medical card if not a UK national).	Hospital in-patient treatment. Emergency dental treatment for children aged 6–15.
Isle of Man	No documents needed.	Treatment as for UK National Health Service.

What you pay charges for	Other information
Treatment at a doctor's surgery. Dental care. Prescribed medicines.	Free treatment at a family doctor-type clinic is available most weekday mornings at the General Hospital.
	Hospital treatment provided in Guernsey.
Prescribed medicines.	
Hospital treatment. Dental treatment. Ambulance travel. Prescribed medicines.	Some charges may be partially refunded by Finnish Sickness Insurance Institution. Claim at the local office before leaving.
Cost of treatment for road accident injuries (the authorities apply direct to vehicle's insurer).	Insurance cover essential if you are driving.
Small charges are levied for all other services and treatment.	*List available from DH IR(H) A, Hannibal House, Elephant and Castle, London SE1 6TE.
Dental & Ophthalmic treatment. Prescribed medicines (flat-rate charge).	
Hospital out-patient treatment. Medical treatment. Prescribed medicines. Other dental treatment. Ambulance travel.	
Dental treatment. Prescribed medicines.	

Country	Documents needed to get medical treatment	What is normally free
Malta – up to 30 days' stay	UK passport.	Immediately necessary medical treatment in a Government hospital, area health centre (polyclinic) or district dispensary.
Montserrat	Proof of UK residence (e.g. NHS medical card or UK driving licence).	Treatment at Government institutions for persons aged over 65 and under 16. Dental treatment for school-age children.
New Zealand	UK passport.	In-patient treatment in public hospitals. Dental treatment (person under 19). Some prescribed medicines.
Norway	UK passport.	Hospital in-patient treatment. Ambulance travel.
Poland	NHS medical card.	Hospital treatment. Some dental treatment. Other medical treatment.
Romania	UK passport and NHS medical card or driving licence.	Hospital treatment. Some dental treatment. Other medical treatment.
St Helena	Proof of UK residence (e.g. UK passport or NHS medical card).	Hospital treatment in out-patient clinics during normal clinic times.

What you pay charges for	Other information
Non-Government hospital dispensary or polyclinic treatment. Treatment at a private doctor's surgery. Prescribed medicines.	
Hospital in-patient and out-patient treatment. Hospital accommodation. Most prescribed medicines. Dental treatment. Ambulance travel.	Family doctor-type treatment is available at Government clinics and the hospital casualty department. A charge is made.
Other treatment at hospitals. Treatment at a doctor's surgery. Some medicines.	Ask hospital or doctor if a refund is due. If not, claim at the local health office. Cash benefits from New Zealand Department of Health reduce charges
Other hospital treatment. Treatment at a doctor's surgery. Dental treatment (except extractions). Prescribed medicines.	Some charges may be partially refunded by Norwegian social insurance scheme. Obtain receipt for payment and claim at social insurance office of district where treatment obtained before you leave Norway.
Doctor's visit (e.g. to your hotel). 30% of cost of prescribed medicines from a public pharmacy.	
Medicines supplied by public pharmacy.	
Hospital in-patient treatment. Dental treatment. Prescribed medicines. Ambulance travel.	Family doctor-type treatment is available at the hospital out-patient clinic.

Country	Documents needed to get medical treatment	What is normally free
Sweden	UK passport.	Hospital in-patient treatment, including medicines. Dental treatment for children.
Turks and Caicos Islands	Proof of UK residence (e.g. NHS medical card or UK driving licence).	All treatment to those under 16 and over 65. *On Grand Turk Island:* Dental treatment (at dental clinic). Prescribed medicines. Ambulance travel. *On Outer Islands:* Medical treatment at Government clinics. Prescribed medicines.
USSR (Russia)	UK passport.	Hospital treatment. Some dental treatment. Other medical treatment.
Yugoslavia	UK passport.	Hospital treatment. Some dental treatment. Other medical treatment.

What you pay charges for	Other information
Hospital out-patient treatment. Other medical treatment. Prescribed medicines (except for certain chronic conditions). Ambulance travel.	Travelling expenses to hospital may be partially refunded.
On Grand Turk Island: Hospital in-patient treatment. Other medical treatment at the Town clinic.	*On Outer Islands:* No hospital services available on the outer islands.
Prescribed medicines.	
Prescribed medicines.	If you are Yugoslav national resident in the UK, you will need to show your Yugoslav passport and a certificate of UK social security insurance, obtainable from DSS Overseas Branch, Newcastle upon Tyne, NE98 1YX. If you are not a UK/Yugoslav national but are the dependant of someone who is, you should also apply for a certificate.

Vaccinations for Travel Abroad

Before making a foreign trip you need to check what vaccinations are recommended. The only COMPULSORY vaccinations are those against yellow fever and cholera for people intending to enter countries where there are current outbreaks of the diseases (mainly Central Africa). Here immunization protects the individual and also helps to prevent the diseases spreading. However, vaccination against diseases such as typhoid, malaria and polio are commonly recommended for travellers to countries off the main tourist routes.

This alphabetical list (pages 247–51) shows for each country:

r = Vaccinations or tablets recommended for protection against disease.

E = Vaccinations which are an essential requirement for entry to the country concerned and for which you will require a certificate.

For Cholera only:

r = Cholera vaccination recommended to give improved protection against the disease especially for those who may not be able to avoid the risk of contaminated food or water.

★ = These countries consider vaccination essential for those who have visited or passed through any zone where cholera is present. A vaccination certificate (valid for six months) should be held. In the presence of a cholera epidemic, more countries may insist on a certificate.

For Yellow Fever only, the following symbols apply:

r = Vaccination recommended for protection against the disease, but note that pregnant women and infants under nine months should not normally be vaccinated and therefore should not be exposed to the disease.

E1 = Vaccination essential except for infants under one year (but note the above).

E2 = Vaccination essential except for infants under one year and except for travellers arriving from non-infected areas and staying for less than two weeks. The UK is a non-infected area, but if travelling via equatorial Africa or South America, seek medical advice.

★ = Vaccination essential if the traveller arrives from an infected country – i.e. where yellow fever is present. This will not apply if your journey is direct from the UK.

YOUR HEALTH PROTECTION CHECKLIST

Country	Malaria	Cholera	Typhoid	Polio	Yellow Fever
Afghanistan	r	r	r	r	★
Albania					★
Algeria	r		r	r	★
Angola	r	r	r	r	★r
Antigua/Barbuda					★
Argentina	r		r	r	
Australia					★
Austria					
Azores					★
Bahamas			r	r	★
Bahrain		r	r	r	★
Bali	r	r	r	r	★
Bangladesh	r	r	r	r	★
Barbados			r	r	★
Belgium					
Belize	r		r	r	★
Benin	r	r	r	r	EI
Bermuda					
Bhutan	r	r	r	r	★
Bolivia	r		r	r	★r
Botswana	r	r	r	r	
Brazil	r		r	r	★r
Brunei		r	r	r	★
Bulgaria					
Burkina Faso	r	r	r	r	EI
Burma	r	r	r	r	★
Burundi	r	r	r	r	★
Cameroon	r	r	r	r	EI
Canada					
Canary Islands					
Cape Verde Islands	r		r	r	★
Cayman Islands				r	
Central African Republic	r	r	r	r	EI
Chad	r	r	r	r	EI
Chile			r	r	
China	r		r	r	★
Colombia	r		r	r	r
Comoros	r		r	r	

Country	Malaria	Cholera	Typhoid	Polio	Yellow Fever
Congo	r	r	r	r	EI
Cook Islands			r	r	
Corfu					★
Corsica					
Costa Rica	r		r	r	
Crete					★
Cuba			r	r	
Cyprus					
Czechoslovakia					
Denmark					
Djibouti	r	r	r	r	★
Dominica			r	r	★
Dominican Republic	r		r	r	
Ecuador	r		r	r	★
Egypt	r	r	r	r	★
El Salvador	r		r	r	★
Equatorial Guinea	r	r	r	r	★r
Ethiopia	r	r	r	r	★r
Falkland Islands			r	r	
Fiji			r	r	★
Finland					
France					
Gabon	r	r	r	r	EI
Gambia	r	r	r	r	EI
German Dem. Rep. (East) } German Fed. Rep. (West) }					
Ghana	r	r	r	r	EI
Gibraltar					
Greece					★
Greenland					
Grenada			r	r	★
Guam			r	r	★
Guatemala	r		r	r	★
Guiana, French	r		r	r	EI
Guinea	r	r	r	r	★r
Guinea Bissau	r	r	r	r	★r
Guyana	r		r	r	★r
Haiti	r		r	r	★
Honduras	r		r	r	★
Hong Kong			r	r	
Hungary					
Iceland					

Country	Malaria	Cholera	Typhoid	Polio	Yellow Fever
India	r	r	r	r	★
Indonesia	r	r	r	r	★
Iran	r		r	r	★
Iraq	r	r	r	r	★
Irish Republic					
Israel			r	r	
Italy					
Ivory Coast	r	r	r	r	E1
Jamaica			r	r	★
Japan			r	r	
Jordan		r	r	r	
Kampuchea	r	r	r	r	★
Kenya	r	r	r	r	★r
Kiribati			r	r	★
Korea (North) } Korea (South) }		r	r	r	
Kuwait		r	r	r	
Laos (Lao)	r	r	r	r	★
Lebanon		r	r	r	★
Lesotho		★r	r	r	★
Liberia	r	r	r	r	E1
Libya	r	r	r	r	★
Luxembourg					
Madagascar	r	r	r	r	★
Madeira					★
Malawi	r	r	r	r	★
Malaysia	r	r	r	r	★
Maldives	r	r	r	r	★
Mali	r	r	r	r	E1
Malta					★
Mauritania	r	r	r	r	E2r
Mauritius	r		r		★
Mexico	r		r	r	★
Monaco					
Mongolia			r	r	
Montserrat			r	r	★
Morocco	r	r	r	r	
Mozambique	r	r	r	r	★
Namibia	r	r	r	r	★r
Nauru			r	r	★
Nepal	r	r	r	r	★
Netherlands					

Country	Malaria	Cholera	Typhoid	Polio	Yellow Fever
Netherlands, Antilles			r	r	★
New Caledonia			r	r	★
New Zealand					
Nicaragua	r		r	r	★
Niger	r	r	r	r	E1
Nigeria	r	r	r	r	★r
Niue			r	r	★
Norway					
Oman	r	r	r	r	★
Pakistan	r	★r	r	r	★
Panama	r		r	r	E1
Papua New Guinea	r	r	r	r	★
Paraguay	r		r	r	★
Peru	r		r	r	★r
Philippines	r	r	r	r	★
Pitcairn Island		★	r	r	★
Poland					
Polynesia, French (Tahiti)			r	r	★
Portugal					★
Puerto Rico			r	r	
Qatar		r	r	r	★
Reunion Islands			r		★
Romania					
Rwanda	r	r	r	r	E1
Saint Helena			r	r	
Saint Lucia			r	r	★
Saint Vincent and Grenadines			r	r	★
Samoa			r	r	★
Sao Tome and Principe	r	r	r	r	E2
Sardinia					
Saudi Arabia	r	r	r	r	★
Senegal	r	r	r	r	E1
Seychelles			r	r	
Sierra Leone	r	r	r	r	★r
Singapore		r	r	r	★
Solomon Islands	r		r	r	★
Somalia	r	★r	r	r	★r
South Africa	r	r	r	r	★
Spain					
Sri Lanka	r	r	r	r	★
Sudan	r	★r	r	r	★r
Surinam	r		r	r	★

Country	Malaria	Cholera	Typhoid	Polio	Yellow Fever
Swaziland	r	r	r	r	★
Sweden					
Switzerland					
Syria	r	r	r	r	★
Tahiti			r	r	★
Taiwan		r	r	r	★
Tanzania	r	r	r	r	★r
Thailand	r	r	r	r	★
Togo	r	r	r	r	EI
Trinidad and Tobago			r	r	★
Tunisia		r	r	r	★
Turkey	r	r	r	r	
Tuvalu			r	r	★
Uganda	r	r	r	r	★r
United Arab Emirates	r	r	r	r	★
USA					
USSR					
Uruguay			r	r	
Vanuatu	r		r	r	
Venezuela	r		r	r	
Vietnam	r	r	r	r	★
Virgin Islands			r	r	
West Indies Associated States			r	r	★
French West Indies			r	r	★
Yemen Arab Rep. (North) Yemen Dem. Rep. (South)	r	r	r	r	★
Yugoslavia					
Zaire	r	r	r	r	★r
Zambia	r	r	r	r	★r
Zimbabwe	r	r	r	r	★

This list is correct at the time and date of printing. Changes are notified on PRESTEL page 50063.

Ask your GP at least two months before departure to arrange for the appropriate vaccinations to be carried out. Some take time to become effective and cannot be given at the same time as other vaccinations. Some are available free under the NHS; for others your GP may make a charge. Some hospital infectious disease units run immunization clinics, as do the private health insurance organizations, British Airways and Thomas Cook.

Self-Care Abroad

Medical kits

You should always take a small first aid kit with you when travelling abroad. This should at least contain adhesive dressings, antiseptic cream, water sterilization tablets, insect repellent and an electrolyte mixture (such as Diarolyte or Rehidrat) for diarrhoea. If you need more specific medication, check whether there are any restrictions on bringing this into the country you are visiting. Even medicines which are available over the counter in the UK may be subject to controls in other countries. The relevant embassy or national tourist office will be able to advise.

The worldwide AIDS epidemic has made people wary of medical treatment in some parts of the world. If you are travelling to a country where the safety of syringes, needles, sutures, etc. cannot be assured, you may feel it worthwhile to take an emergency medical kit containing sterile supplies of these items with you. Kits and personal health advice are available at a cost from MEDICAL ADVISORY SERVICE FOR TRAVELLERS ABROAD (MASTA) at the London School of Hygiene and Tropical Medicine, Keppel Street, London WC1E 7HD Tel: 071-636 8636. The free Department of Health booklet, *The Traveller's Guide to Health*, lists other suppliers.

Protecting your health abroad

The Department of Health advises some simple measures you can take to avoid the risks of ill health when travelling abroad.

- Unless you know drinking water is safe, use bottled water or sterilize it by boiling or using sterilization tablets
- Be careful with some foods – raw vegetables, salads and unpeeled fruit; shellfish; ice cream and ice cubes, underdone meat and fish
- Always wash your hands before eating or handling food
- Take care in the sun – use protective creams, wear a sun hat and drink plenty of fluids
- Do not touch animals which may carry rabies – dogs, cats, monkeys, foxes
- Use insect repellent creams and in wooded areas cover arms and legs to help prevent insect bites.

- Avoid the risk of HIV infection and AIDS:

– If you have sex with someone other than your regular partner use a condom. Take a supply with you if you think they may be difficult to obtain locally
– Never share needles to inject drugs
– Avoid skin piercing (tattooing, acupuncture, etc.) unless you are sure the equipment is sterile
– Try to avoid needing medical and dental treatment involving surgery, blood transfusions or injections in countries where there is a risk of HIV infections through these means. In some countries blood transfusions are not screened for the presence of HIV. Consider taking a sterile medical kit with you (available from MASTA)

Holiday health guides

There are several good publications giving practical advice on health care while travelling abroad:

Well Away: a health guide for travellers (London: British Medical Journal, 1988)

How to Stay Healthy Abroad by R. Dawood (Oxford University Press, 1989)

The Tropical Traveller by J. Hatt (London: Pan, 1982)

Preservation of Personal Health in Warm Climates (London: Ross Institute of Tropical Hygiene, 1980)

Vaccination Certificate Requirements and Health Advice for International Travel (Geneva: World Health Organization, annual, available from HMSO booksellers)

Disability and Other Health Problems

If you have a disability or existing health problem you may need special help and advice when travelling abroad. The best source of information is the ROYAL ASSOCIATION FOR DISABILITY AND REHABILITATION (RADAR) 25 Mortimer Street, London W1N 8AB Tel: 071-637 5400. RADAR's book *Holidays and Travel Abroad: a guide for disabled people* (from W. H. Smith or direct from RADAR) gives invaluable information on accessible hotels, specialist tour operators, insurance companies who offer policies which do not exclude pre-existing medical conditions, disability organizations in other countries, and so on.

HOLIDAY CARE SERVICE 2 Old Bank Chambers, Station Road, Horley, Surrey RH6 9HW Tel: 0293 774535, provides an information service on all aspects of holidays and travel for people with special needs: disabled people, the elderly, one-parent families, etc.

Many European countries operate schemes of parking concessions for disabled people. There are usually reciprocal arrangements whereby holders of UK ORANGE BADGES (see page 103) are entitled to take advantage of the concessions by displaying the badge. Details of arrangements in each country are given in a leaflet, *Reciprocal Parking Arrangements for Disabled and Blind People in Europe*, available from Department of Transport, Room C10/13A, 2 Marsham Street, London SW1P 3EB.

Organizations for Disability and Other Health Problems

If you have a health problem and are visiting another country, particularly for a longer stay, you may find it useful to make contact with the relevant national organization. The national office of most UK self-help organizations should be able to give you details of equivalent organizations in other countries. Here are the addresses of some of the major organizations in Western Europe, Australia, New Zealand, Canada and the USA:

Disabled people

EUROPE

Allgemeine Unfallversicherungsansstalt
Adalbert Stifter-Strasse 65
A-1200 Vienna
AUSTRIA

Fonds National de Reclassement Social des Handicapés
Rue de Meiboom 14
B-1000 Brussels
BELGIUM

Rehabilitation International Denmark
7 Borgervaenget
DK-2100 Copenhagen 0
DENMARK

Comité National Français de Liaison pour la Réadaption des Handicapés
30–32 Quai de la Loire
75019 Paris
FRANCE

Deutsche Vereinigung für die Rehabilitation Behinderter
Friedrich-Ebert-Anlage 9
6900 Heidelberg 1
GERMANY

National Institution for Rehabilitation of the Disabled (EIAA)
9 Stassi
GR 13122 Nea Liossia
GREECE

National Rehabilitation Board
24–5 Clyde Road
Ballsbridge
Dublin 4
IRELAND

Associazione Italiana per l'Assistenza agli Spastici
Via Cipro 4/H
00136 Rome
ITALY

Dutch Council of the Disabled
Postbus 169
3500 AD Utrecht
NETHERLANDS

Norges Handikapforbund
PO Box 9217, Vaterland
N-0134 Oslo 1
NORWAY

Secretariado Nacional de Reabilitacão
Av. Conde Valbom 63
1000 Lisbon
PORTUGAL

Federación ECOM
Balmes 311 ent 2
Barcelona 08006
SPAIN

Swedish Central Committee for Rehabilitation
Box 303
S-161 26 Bromma
SWEDEN

Schweizerische Arbeitsgemeinschaft für Korperbehinderte
Feldeggstrasse 71
Postfach 129
CH-8032 Zurich
SWITZERLAND

AUSTRALIA AND NEW ZEALAND

Australian Council on Disability (ACROD)
PO Box 60
Curtin
ACT 2605
AUSTRALIA

Disabled Persons' Assembly
PO Box 27–186
63 Hanky Street
Wellington
NEW ZEALAND

NORTH AMERICA

Canadian Rehabilitation Council for the Disabled
Suite 2110, 1 Yonge Street
Toronto
Ontario M5E 1E5
CANADA

Clearinghouse on the Handicapped
Sweitzer Building, Room 3132
330 Cancer Street SW
Washington, DC 20202
USA

Mental handicap

EUROPE

Association Nationale d'Aide aux Handicapés Mentaux
13 rue Forestière
1050 Brussels
BELGIUM

Landsforeningen Evnesvages
Spaniensgade 15
2300 Copenhagen S
DENMARK

Union Nationale des Associations de Parents d'Enfants Inadaptés
15 rue Coysevox
75018 Paris
FRANCE

Lebenshilfe
Raiffeisenstrasse 18, Postfach 80
D-3550 Marburg-Cappel
GERMANY

National Association for the Mentally Handicapped of Ireland
5 Fitzwilliam Place
Dublin 2
IRELAND

Associazione Nazionale Famiglie de Fanciulli e Adulti Subnormali
Via E. Gianturco
Rome 00196
ITALY

Stichtung Federatie van Ouderverenigingen
Stadhouderslaan 43
3583 JC Utrecht
NETHERLANDS

Associaco Portuguesa de Pais e Amigos do Cidadao Deficiente Mental
Pc. de Londres, N 9-40 esq
1200 Lisbon
PORTUGAL

Confederación Española de Federaciónes y Asociaciónes pro Personas Deficientes Mentales
General Perón 32 1
28020 Madrid
SPAIN

AUSTRALIA AND NEW ZEALAND

National Council on Intellectual Disability
GPO Box 647
Canberra
ACT 2601
AUSTRALIA

New Zealand Society for the Intellectually Handicapped
National Office
Private Bag
Wellington
NEW ZEALAND

NORTH AMERICA

Canadian Association for Community Living
Kinsmen Building
4700 Keele Street
Downsview
Ontario M3J 1P3
CANADA

Clearinghouse on the Handicapped
Sweitzer Building, Room 3132
330 Cancer Street, SW
Washington, DC 20202
USA

Down's Syndrome Association, Inc.
PO Box 620847
Littleton
Colorado 80162
USA

Mental health and illness

EUROPE

Nationale Vereniging Voor Geestlijke Gezoondheidszorg
VZW Kortrijksesteenweg 369
Gent 9000
BELGIUM

Danish Society for Mental Health
Raadmandsgade 43
2200 Copenhagen N
DENMARK

Lacroix d'Or Française
10 rue des Messagaries
Paris 75015
FRANCE

Dachverband Psychosozialer Hilsvereinigungen ev
Thomas Mann Strasse 49a
Bonn 1D-5300
GERMANY

Panhellenic Union of Mental Hygiene
16 Akadimias Street
Athens 134
GREECE

Mental Health Association of Ireland
6 Adelaide Street
Dun Laoghaire
Dublin Co.
IRELAND

Nederlandse Vereniging voor Ambulante Geestelijke Gezondheidszorg
Postbus 8400
Utrecht 3503 RK
NETHERLANDS

Mental Barnehjelp
Arbiensgate 1
Oslo 2
NORWAY

Liga Portuguesa de Higiene Mental
Largodo Andaluz 15–7 esq
Lisbon
PORTUGAL

Svenska Foreningen for Psykisk Hals
Box 45246
Stockholm S-104 30
SWEDEN

AUSTRALIA AND NEW ZEALAND

Australian National Association for Mental Health
1 Cookson Street
Camberwell
Victoria 3124
AUSTRALIA

Mental Health Foundation of New Zealand
PO Box 37-438
Parnell
Auckland
NEW ZEALAND

NORTH AMERICA

Canadian Mental Health Association
2160 Yonge Street, 3rd Floor
Toronto
Ontario M4S 2Z3
CANADA

National Mental Health Association
1021 Prince Street
Alexandria
VA 22314
USA

Children in hospital

EUROPE

Vereniging Kind en Ziekenhuis
Brieversweg 121
8310 Bruges
BELGIUM

NOBAB
Carolinevej 25
2900 Hellerup
DENMARK

APACHE
63 Bde Pierre Brosolette
92160 Antony
FRANCE

Kind im Krankenhaus
Vor dem Kirchforst 1
6204 Taunusstein
GERMANY

Associazione per il Bambino in Ospedale
Via della Commenda 9
20122 Milan
ITALY

Kind en Ziekenhuis
Werengouw 23
1024 Amsterdam
NETHERLANDS

NOBAB
Bohusgaten 13
11667 Stockholm
SWEDEN

Verein Kind und Krankenhaus
Jerisberghof/Ferenbalm
3208 Gurbu
SWITZERLAND

AUSTRALIA AND NEW ZEALAND

Australian Association for the Welfare of Children in Hospital
158 Hawkesbury Road
Westmead
NSW 2145
AUSTRALIA

Children in Hospital Liaison Group
PO Box 10199
Balmoral
Auckland 5
NEW ZEALAND

NORTH AMERICA

Children in Hospital Inc
31 Wilshire Park
Needham
Massachusetts 02192
USA

Women's health

EUROPE

Centre for Research on European Women
38 Rue Stevin
1040 Brussels
BELGIUM

ISIS
Via San Saba 5
Rome 00153
ITALY

Women's Global Network on Reproductive Rights
Nieuwe Zijds Voorburgwal 32
1012 RZ Amsterdam
NETHERLANDS

La Mujer Feminista
Apartado de Correos 311
Madrid
SPAIN

AUSTRALIA AND NEW ZEALAND

Women's Health Information Resource
653 Nicholson Street
PO Box 187
North Carlton 3054
Victoria
AUSTRALIA

NORTH AMERICA

National Women's Health Network
1325 G Street NW
Washington, DC 20005
USA

Cancer

EUROPE

Osterreichische Krebsinformationdienst
Spitalgasse 11
A-1090 Vienna
AUSTRIA

Association Contre le Cancer
Place du Samedi 13
1000 Brussels
BELGIUM

Danish Cancer Society
35 Rosenvaengets Hovedvej
DK 2100 Copenhagen
DENMARK

Ligue Nationale Française Contre le Cancer
1 Avenue Stephen Pichon
F-75013 Paris
FRANCE

Deutsche Krebshilfe
Thomas Mann Strasse 40
D-5300 Bonn 1
GERMANY

Hellenic Cancer Society
6 George Street
Kanigos Square
106-77 Athens
GREECE

Irish Cancer Society
5 Northumberland Road
Dublin 4
IRELAND

Institute Nationale per la Ricerco sul Cancero
Viale Benedetto XV no. 10
16132 Genoa
ITALY

Netherlands Cancer Foundation
8 Sophialaan
1075 BR Amsterdam
NETHERLANDS

Norwegian Cancer Society
Fritj Nansens vei 12
0369 Oslo 3
NORWAY

Liga Portuguesa a Contra o Cancro
Rua Prof. Lima Basto
1000 Lisbon
PORTUGAL

Asociación Española Contra el Cancer
Hospital Clinic I Provincial de Barcelona
Villaroeal 170
0836 Barcelona
SPAIN

Onkologistk Centrum
Karolinska Sjukhuset
Box 60500
10401 Stockholm
SWEDEN

AUSTRALIA AND NEW ZEALAND

Australian Cancer Society
Box 4708
Sydney
NSW 2001
AUSTRALIA

Cancer Society of New Zealand
PO Box 1724
Auckland
NEW ZEALAND

NORTH AMERICA

Canadian Cancer Society
Suite 1001
130 Bloor Street West
Toronto
Ontario M5S 2VS
CANADA

American Cancer Society
4 East 35th Street
New York
NY 10001
USA

AIDS

EUROPE

Ostereichische AIDS-Hilfe
Wickenburggasse 14
A-1080 Vienna
AUSTRIA

ASBL
Rue Duquesnoy 45
B-1000 Brussels
BELGIUM

National AIDS Helpline
Knabrostraede 3
1210 Copenhagen K
DENMARK

AIDS Action Alliance
13 Christchurch Place
Dublin 8
IRELAND

AIDS Fédération Nationale
BP 169
75463 Paris
Cedex 10
FRANCE

Deutsche AIDS Hilfe
Nestorstrasse 8–9
D-1000 Berlin 31
GERMANY

National Centre for AIDS
Avenue Alexandros 196
Athens 115 21
GREECE

Centro Operativo AIDS
Istituto Superiore di Sanita
Viale Regina Elena 299
00161 Rome
ITALY

National AIDS Helpline
Bureau NCAB
Polderweg 92
1093 KP Amsterdam
NETHERLANDS

Landsforeningen mot AIDS
Miljoetaten
St lauspl. 5
0165 Oslo 1
NORWAY

Comité Ciudadano anti-SIDA
Calle Sandoval 7
28010 Madrid
SPAIN

Riksforbundet for Sexuellt Likagerattigande
Box 350
101 24 Stockholm
SWEDEN

AIDS-Hilfe Schweiz
Turbinenstrasse 10
8005 Zurich
SWITZERLAND

AUSTRALIA AND NEW ZEALAND

ACON–AIDS Council of New South Wales
PO Box 350
Darlinghurst
NSW 2010
AUSTRALIA

New Zealand AIDS Foundation
PO Box 6663
Wellesley Street
Auckland
NEW ZEALAND

NORTH AMERICA

ACT–AIDS Committee of Toronto
PO Box 55
Station F
Toronto M4Y 2L4
CANADA

National AIDS Network
2083 M Street NW
Suite 800
Washington, DC 20036
USA

San Francisco AIDS Foundation
333 Valencia Street
4th Floor
San Francisco
CA 94103
USA

Gay Men's Health Crisis
129 West 20th Street
New York
NY 10011
USA

Visual handicap

EUROPE

Ostereichische Blindenverband
Mariehilfer Gurtel 4
Vienna 1060
AUSTRIA

CBPAM
Centre International Rogier 7
Rue A Bertulot 21
Bureau 201
Bte 4
1210 Brussels
BELGIUM

Dansk Blindesamfund
Thoravej 35
DK-2400 Copenhagen NV
DENMARK

Fédération des Aveugles de France
58 Avenue Bosquet
75007 Paris
FRANCE

Deutsche Blindenstudienanstalt eV
D-3550 Marburg 1
Am Schlag 8
PO Box 1160
GERMANY

Lighthouse for the Blind of Greece
17 Athinas Street
Kallithea
17673 Athens
GREECE

National Council for the Blind of Ireland
P. U. Doyle House
Whitworth Road
Drumcondra
Dublin 9
IRELAND

Unione Italiana Ciechi
Via Borgognona 38
00187 Rome
ITALY

VNBW
Bilstraat 102
3572 Utrecht
NETHERLANDS

Norges Blindeforbund
PO Box 5900
Sporveisgata 10
Oslo 3
NORWAY

League of the Blind
Rue de Santa Marta 46–2
1100 Lisbon
PORTUGAL

Organización Nacional de Ciegos de Espana
Jose Ortega y Gasset 18
28006 Madrid
SPAIN

Union Centrale Suisse pour le Bien des Aveugles
Schutzengasse 4
9001 St Gallen
SWITZERLAND

AUSTRALIA AND NEW ZEALAND

Australian National Council of and for the Blind
PO Box 60
Curtin
ACT 2605
AUSTRALIA

Royal New Zealand Foundation for the Blind
545 Parnell Road
Private Bag
Newmarket
Auckland 1
NEW ZEALAND

NORTH AMERICA

Canadian National Institute for the Blind
1931 Bayview Avenue
Toronto
Ontario
M4G 4C8
CANADA

National Association for the Visually Handicapped
22 West 21st Street
New York
NY 10010
USA

Library and Information Services Abroad

In addition to the specialized sources of information listed above there are also generalist library, advice and information services. Their ability to provide good health information for consumers varies considerably from country to country, and within countries. It is fair to say that most countries, with the exception of the USA, have less well-developed health information services than we have in the UK.

Within Europe the provision of health-related information to the public still has links with the radical and alternative movements of the late 1960s. In GERMANY, in particular, the characteristic organization is the health shop or clearing-house. Provision of information is an important activity but so is the provision of practical support to local self-help and community groups through the provision of meeting rooms, training, printing facilities, and so on. For example, in Hamburg there is a clearing-house called KISS (Kontakt und Informationsstelle für Selbsthilfegruppen) which deals with inquiries on self-help groups from professionals and the general public. A national self-help clearing-house along the same lines has since been established (Deutsche Arbeitsgemeinschaft Selbsthilfegruppen, Albrecht-Achilles Strasse 65, D-1000, Berlin).

Libraries in Europe have not tended to provide much health information, although public libraries in Scandinavia often have good collections of general community information. A notable exception can be found in FRANCE at the Médiathèque of the Cité des Sciences et de l'Industrie, 30 avenue Corentin Cariou, 75019 Paris. The Cité is a huge, multi-media exhibition centre designed to popularize the sciences to the French public. Part of the complex is the Médiathèque, a library open to the general public containing books, magazines, videos and interactive computer programs. The health section of this library must be the largest collection of medical literature fully open to the public anywhere in the world. People can use the library for reference purposes at no charge; borrowing rights are available for 250 francs a year. Twenty thousand books are available and 500 journal and magazine titles. This means the public have free access to professional medical literature as well as publications for health consumers like the magazine *l'Impatient*.

The high-tech approach is emphasized by the availability of the Médiathèque catalogue via the Minitel terminals which many French households now have. Figures for 1990 show that there are over 5 million Minitel terminals in France, nine out of ten of all the videotex terminals installed worldwide (see page 285). Minitel terminals can also be used to tap into a wide variety of medical databases, making the French public, in theory at least, some of the best-informed health consumers. There is little evidence that many of them take advantage of this resource, and the problem for most parents is that Minitel is instead used as an expensive method for children to access computer games.

The European country which bears the greatest similarity to the UK in its approach to health information for the public is probably the NETHERLANDS. There are health education departments similar to our own in many Dutch towns. The Dutch Health Education Centre (Centrum Dienstverlening, Da Costakade 45,

PO Box 5104, 3502 JC, Utrecht) has an extensive library with a lot of information in English. Many Dutch hospitals have their own patient education programmes and there are patient participation groups in general practice.

In SWEDEN a 1983 law, Halso och Sjukvardsnamnden, places a responsibility on local health authorities to make information available to patients and the general public. Most now have information departments which produce leaflets for consumers and assist self-help groups with their own publications. A *Patient Information Katalog* is published by Spri (the Swedish Institute for Health and Social Welfare Planning), Box 27310, 10254, Stockholm, listing these publications as well as those from pharmaceutical companies. As described on page 22, the Swedish directory of medicines for patients, *Patient-FASS*, is widely available in libraries, bookshops and chemists. In towns like Gothenburg and Stockholm there are well-established telephone information services for the public (Sjukvardsupplysningen) staffed by nurses employed by the health authority.

Formal information services are much less extensive in Southern Europe, probably because of the continuing importance of the family and the Church as networks of social support. However, self-help support centres are beginning to be set up in SPAIN (particularly in Barcelona). In ITALY the opportunity presented by the building of a new public library next to the hospital in Antenella, Chianti is leading to the establishment of the first patient information centre in the country.

In AUSTRALIA there is a growing movement towards making hospitals more health-promoting places. The best health information centre for the public is Healthlink at Westmead Hospital, Old Windsor Road, Westmead, New South Wales 2145. Patients can buy books from a bookstore or take away leaflets and photocopies. Information is available in languages other than English, including Greek, Turkish, Polish and Croatian. An excellent booklet called *A Guide to Consumer Health Information* has been produced, which lists helpful books and support organizations from throughout Australia.

The CANADIAN government (Health and Welfare Canada, Turney's Pasture, Ottawa KIA 1B5) has also adopted a very positive approach to health promotion and support for self-help groups and community participation. A number of regional self-help clearing-houses have been set up with support from Health and Welfare. Medical libraries, in particular the Health Sciences Library at McMaster University, Hamilton, Ontario, have increasingly become involved in providing information to patients as well as staff.

Not surprisingly it is in the USA, with its very demanding health consumers, that information services on health are most extensive. American consumers have access to literally hundreds of health information hotlines and toll-free numbers. Some are run by government agencies such as the National Institutes of Health in Washington, DC. Some are run by non-governmental agencies such as the AIDS organizations. Others are part of the Tel-Med system of taped health information (like Healthcall, etc. in the UK, see page 280) which is available throughout the USA. There is a People's Medical Society (462 Walnut Street, Allentown, PA 18102) which aims to help health consumers to choose the highest-quality health care at the lowest prices. The Society has produced a series of Health Action Kits which give consumers guidelines and detailed check-lists to help them in evaluating nursing homes or physicians. There are thousands of self-help organizations for almost every complaint under the sun. The New Jersey Self-help Clearing-house, St Clare's-Riverside Medical Center, Pocono Road, Denville, New Jersey 07834 has produced a *Self-help Sourcebook* listing many of these. The New Jersey clearing-house is also leading the way with electronic self-help networks – disabled, housebound or isolated people who are able to 'meet' one another via computer links.

Since the Kaiser Permanente Medical Center in Oakland, California opened the first information and resource centre for patients in 1969, many more have followed suit. Now many American hospitals are moving in the direction of the University of

Minnesota Hospital, which has a high-tech Patient Learning Centre with video tapes, computer programmes, human mannequins, pumps, needles, etc. for practising self-care skills. The original centre at Kaiser Permanente is now a 'health media collection' with computerized personal health risk appraisal programs, a health store selling self-care aids such as blood pressure monitors, and an extensive programme of classes. The most recent programme included instruction in testing and self-management for diabetes and hypertension; self-care courses for patients with arthritis, back pain, colostomies, and headache; workshops on assertiveness and 'no fault parenting'; preparation for childbirth and Lamaze relaxation classes.

Most surgical procedures at Kaiser Permanente are preceded by a pre-operative instruction class for patients. For example, attendance at a vasectomy class is compulsory for all men considering a vasectomy (and their partners if they wish). Attendance is assured because the operation consent form is only completed after an explanation of the operation, after-care and any possible side-effects. This means that the surgeon can demonstrate informed consent and litigation is less likely. Patients joining a Health Maintenance Organization (HMO) like Kaiser Permanente pay a regular premium in return for treatment received (or their employer pays). HMOs therefore have an interest in reducing unnecessary 'utilization of service' (readmission to hospital, etc.) and invest far more resources in patient education and health information than would a British hospital.

If you are visiting the USA and want to know about the health information resources available, ask your library to get hold of a copy of the comprehensive *Consumer Health Information Sourcebook* by Alan Rees and Catherine Hoffman (Phoenix: Oryx Press, 1990).

7 Finding Health Information

We all seek information about our health. This may range from the trivial act of asking a trusted friend what you should do about a sore throat, to more important things like finding a good nursing home or how to complain about poor treatment.

Previous chapters in this book have shown that there is both a need for information and a huge number of information sources – if only you know where to look. This chapter tells you the best places to go for information and how to find out more.

It is interesting to note that, according to surveys carried out in 1970 and 1985, most health advice comes from relatives and friends; an increasing amount from books, TV, radio, magazines and newspapers; and the community pharmacist is being seen as a more important source of health advice.

The place to start looking will of course depend on the type of information and advice you need. But most information sources will give you leads to other sources. If you need advice urgently and do not want to consult your doctor then a helpline might be a good starting place.

	No. (%) of respondents	
	1985 (*n*= 500)	1970 (*n*= 1000)
Friend	259 (*51.8*)	(*49.8*)
Spouse		
Husband	132 (*26.4*)	(*25.3*)
Wife	85 (*17.0*)	(*19.3*)
Total	217 (*43.4*)	(*46.6*)
Other relative		
Mother	97 (*19.4*)	(*17.6*)
Daughter	29 (*5.8*)	(*5.1*)
Sister	22 (*4.4*)	(*5.1*)
Father	17 (*3.4*)	(*2.7*)
Others	55 (*11.0*)	(*4.6*)
Total	220 (*44.0*)	(*35.1*)
Chemist	82 (*16.4*)	(*10.8*)
Nurse		
Casual advice	68 (*13.6*)	(*10.2*)
Professional advice	20 (*4.0*)	(5.2)
Impersonal source		
Home doctor books	42 (*8.4*)	(*4.2*)
Television	29 (*5.8*)	(*1.9*)
Women's magazines	20 (*4.0*)	(*4.4*)
Newspapers	15 (*3.0*)	(*2.6*)
Other magazines incl. comics	8 (*1.6*)	(*0.9*)
Radio	2 (*0.4*)	(*0.2*)
Other	1 (*0.2*)	(*1.2*)
Total	117 (*23.4*)	(*16.2*)
No advice received	59 (*11.8*)	(*12.2*)

n = total number of respondents.

Sources of lay advice on health topics. Informal sources such as friends and family remain the most important. In the years between 1970 and 1985 television has become a more important source of health information, more people own home doctor books and more seek advice from the chemist (Source: *Journal of Royal College of General Practitioners, December 1986*)

The Media

The most pervasive sources of health information are the press and broadcasting media. We are bombarded daily with messages from newspapers, magazines, television and radio. Health and illness loom large not only in medical programmes and features themselves but also in advertisements and as an important part of the storyline in soap operas (Shula's infertility and Brian's epilepsy in 'The Archers', Nancy's ovarian cancer in 'Thirtysomething'). Soap operas have great potential for putting over sound health information in an accessible way, as well as influencing popular attitudes. Unfortunately the messages are not always positive. A study at Portsmouth Polytechnic found that 'EastEnders' (and to a lesser extent other British soaps) portrayed smoking and high alcohol consumption as a common and acceptable feature of life. However, the inclusion of Sandy, a character is a wheelchair, in 'Crossroads' during the 1970s is thought to have considerably changed attitudes towards disability in the run-up to International Year of Disabled People in 1981. In 1983 a child with Down's Syndrome was introduced into the 'Crossroads' story, and Nina Weill became the first handicapped child to appear in a TV soap. The Health Education Authority is now contributing £150,000 towards the cost of a 'medical soap opera' broadcast on the local CWR radio station in Warwickshire.

Television and radio

The Volunteer Centre has a Media Project which produces a DIRECTORY OF SOCIAL ACTION PROGRAMMES on national and local television and radio (29 Lower King's Road, Berkhamsted, Herts HP4 2AB Tel: 0442 873311). The latest issue lists 23 programmes or features on disability, 8 for the blind, 17 for the deaf and hard of hearing, 12 for the elderly, 28 in the field of health information generally (including radio doctors), and a further 74 general advice shows which sometimes have a health content. The regular health programmes on television include:

'Miriam Stoppard's Health and Beauty Show' (Yorkshire TV)
'Help!' (Thames TV)
'See Hear!' (BBC 1, for deaf and hard of hearing)
'Link' (Central TV, for disabled people)
'Same Difference' (Channel 4, for disabled people)

In addition, the popular science programmes such as 'Horizon' often feature health topics, and there are television programmes associated with Open University courses like Health and Disease. On satellite TV, Miriam Stoppard holds 'consultations' from the Milton Keynes Health Matters information centre (see page 295), broadcast as 'Morning Surgery' on BSB.

On national radio there is:

'Medicine Now' (Radio 4, a magazine programme on new treatments, research, etc.)
'Does he Take Sugar?' (Radio 4, practical information and features for disabled people)
'In Touch' (Radio 4, similar news and facts for visually handicapped people)

Newspapers and magazines

The 'quality' newspapers all have their regular health pages (the *Guardian* on Fridays and the *Independent* on Tuesdays are good sources). Of course health stories abound throughout the press, whether as news items or features. The preponderance of health scare stories in the Sunday papers is popularly regarded as one of the reasons for busy surgeries and helplines on Monday mornings. Popular magazines with large circulations may have much greater influence on the attitudes and behaviour of their readers than any government publicity campaign. According to the *British Journal of Sexual Medicine* (April 1989), there has recently been a change in the tone of erotic encounters described in men's magazines like *Mayfair* and *Men Only*. With a growing awareness of the risks of HIV infection and AIDS, more of these fantasies are described within the context of relationships, and condoms are often mentioned. Indeed putting on a condom may be described as part of the fun of the sexual encounter. This unconventional form of health education can be influential in promoting more responsible sexual behaviour amongst young men.

Free COMIC BOOKS and comic strips have been used in the UK, USA, Australia and Holland to educate young people about drugs, sex and AIDS. The best-known examples in the UK, Merseyside's *Willy Whizz* and Manchester's *Smack in the Eye*, have been commended by some as putting over punchy information in the idiom and language of the intended audience, but criticized by others as over-explicit. Similarly in the USA, a graphically illustrated comic book designed by Gay Men's Health Crisis (GMHC) in New York to demonstrate safe sex practices for gay men was condemned by right-wing Senator Jesse Helms as obscene. However, an evaluation of GMHC's sexually explicit, erotic videos found that compared with lectures or unexplicit literature, the videos were very effective in motivating change to lower-risk sexual activities.

Of all the health-related items in newspapers and magazines, the one with the greatest potential for health education is probably the PROBLEM PAGE. The 'agony columns' of women's magazines and popular newspapers are read avidly by millions, and have been for many years. Even Sherlock Holmes confessed he read 'nothing but the criminal news and the agony column. The latter is always instructive', while the agony aunt has been immortalized in literature as Nathaniel West's Miss Lonelyhearts. In 1979, problem page columnist Claire Rayner estimated that she personally received 40,000 letters a year. By 1983 the total had risen to 50,000 a year.

Claire Rayner feels that the letters she receives are an indictment of communication in the NHS.

More distressing are those who write to say the doctor has diagnosed diabetes, cholecystitis, spastic colon, or whatever, and has told them to follow a particular diet and will I please provide the diet. That even a few doctors can be so offhand about their information-giving that patients feel the need to approach a newspaper or magazine for such information speaks volumes about the quality of care they are providing.

Writing in *New Statesman and Society*, agony aunt Melanie McFadyean writes of the 12,000 letters a year she receives on the teenage magazine *Just Seventeen*. With this many letters, she says, there is no need to make them up. Most are about boyfriends, love and sex, but what they are really about is 'a national crisis in self-confidence, the desire of individuals for power over their own lives'.

In addition to general magazines which carry regular health features (the Consumers' Association magazine, *Which?*, has an article on a health topic in almost every issue, for example) there are also several popular magazines devoted entirely to health issues.

Popular health magazines

Which Way to Health? (bimonthly. Consumers' Association, 2 Marylebone Road, London NW1 4DX)
Here's Health (monthly. Emap, Victory House, Leicester Place, London WC2H 7BP)
Practical Health (quarterly. South Bank Publishing, Kings Reach Tower, Stamford Street, London SE1 9LS)

Larger public libraries should keep copies of the *British Medical Journal*, *Lancet* and *Nursing Times* (all weekly). This will enable you to check the full text of many of the medical items which are reported (not always very accurately) in the daily newspapers. There are also many magazines, newsletters, etc. produced by individual self-help groups (see pages 310–20).

It is also worth asking whether your local library takes *Popular Medical Index* (Mede Publications, 77 Norton Road, Letchworth, SG6 1AD). This index lists health articles from magazines like *Woman's Realm* through to medical journals like the *Lancet*, and is indispensable if you are trying to trace information on a particular medical topic.

Helplines

Over the past ten years there has been a rapid growth in telephone helplines. There are now over 250 in the UK. Some have been set up to support television and radio programmes, others on a more permanent basis to offer counselling on, for example, AIDS, drug abuse and incest (Childline grew from a BBC discussion programme on child abuse). They range from large national networks like the Samaritans (the first helpline, founded in 1953) to local helplines run by someone working alone from their own home. In 1990 the first telephone interpreting service, called Language Line, was set up by the London Hospital.

Helplines provide factual information and points of contact for further advice. They act as a 'listening ear', helping to alleviate loneliness and isolation. They can offer in-depth, specialist advice to which people can gain access with minimum fuss and maximum confidentiality. They can also make their organizers a lot of money. Many helplines operate on 0808 or 0839 numbers, costing 38p a minute peak time and 25p a minute cheap rate – more than a long distance phone call. Helplines are obliged to make this clear in their advertising. Make sure you know how much it is going to cost you before you call one: 0800 numbers are free.

Some helplines give you the opportunity to talk to a counsellor personally, but many nowadays operate by playing a pre-recorded tape (usually of about three minutes' duration) down the telephone. This idea was pioneered in the USA by Tel-Med, starting in the 1970s. By 1986 there were 170 Tel-Med centres in forty-eight states. When the College of Health was founded in the UK in 1983, one of the first services it offered was a British version of Tel-Med called Healthline. The first three services were in Exeter, Gloucester and London. The two main differences between the charitable Healthline and today's commercial services like Healthcall were that Healthline was free (the cost of an ordinary phone call without an 0898 premium), and that Healthline worked by the caller personally asking an operator to play the tape. Although having an operator offered the possibility of additional advice-giving, some callers found it embarrassing to ask for tapes on intimate topics. And once Healthcall was launched, Healthline did not have the resources to match the commercial service's massive promotion.

Helpline numbers allowing callers to speak personally with a counsellor

Samaritans local numbers in all phone books
(for lonely, depressed and suicidal people, or those just needing help)
Rape Crisis Lines local numbers in phonebooks, or from 071-837 1600
(for women who have been raped or sexually abused)
Women's Aid local numbers in phone books or from 0272 420611
(for victims of domestic violence)
Childline 0800 1111
(for children needing contact and support outside the family, particularly in cases of child abuse)
National AIDS Helpline 0800 567 123
(for anyone worried about HIV and AIDS – there are local AIDSlines in most towns)
BACUP (British Association of Cancer United Patients) 0800 181 199
(information and advice on cancer from experienced cancer nurses)
Medical Advisory Service 081-994 9874
(health information from volunteer nurses)
Motor Neurone Disease Phoneline 0800 626262
Cerebral Palsy Helpline 0800 626216
Cot Death Helpline 071-235 1721

Helpline numbers offering tape-based services

Healthcall 0808 600 600 (and separate numbers for individual tapes)
BUPA Medicall 0839 100 100 (and separate numbers for individual tapes)
Parents Advice Line 0898 333 002 (and separate numbers for individual tapes)
Self-Help Line 0898 777 444 (and separate numbers for individual tapes) (largely on personal and emotional problems)
Healthline Although the national Healthline at the College of Health is no longer functioning, there are local Healthlines in some parts of the country, including Exeter, Gloucester and Croydon. Your District Health Authority's health promotion department (see page 298) will have information about any local services

British Telecom's otherwise laudable intention to introduce itemized telephone bills has caused great concern amongst organizations running telephone helplines. In future bills will list both the cost of calls and the number dialled. For the literally millions of people who call helplines every year this will mean a breach of confidentiality which could deny them information which is vital to their health and well-being. Because of the highly personal nature of the subjects on which advice is sought, many people would be unwilling to disclose their contact with helplines to their immediate family. In many cases, maintaining confidentiality from other members of the household is an essential part of the service (for example Women's Aid helplines for victims of domestic violence, or incest and child abuse lines). The guarantee of anonymity is crucial to the whole Samaritans approach. In July 1989 a number of voluntary organizations produced a report on the threat to helplines called *Breach of Confidence* (published by the National Council for Voluntary Organizations, 26 Bedford Square, London WC1B 3HU). The report urges British Telecom to suppress the numbers of telephone helplines on itemized phone bills so that the cost of these calls is submerged in the un-itemized part of the bill for calls of less than ten units. As helplines contribute millions of pounds to British Telecom every year it seems the least they can do.

Computerized Information Services

The use of computers for patient interviewing and collecting information to aid diagnosis is now a well-established procedure in many areas. For example, at St James Hospital, Leeds a computerized questionnaire was introduced several years ago for routine antenatal interviewing. When questioned, 70 per cent of women liked the computer interviews. Women from ethnic minority groups, in particular, appreciated the unlimited time they had to answer questions. In Glasgow a computer interviewing system for people with dyspepsia (called GLADYS) has been in use for over a decade. In the USA there are now a number of self-diagnosis computer packages, such as the Family Care Software available for Apple and IBM PCs.

Once patients are used to computers there are obvious applications for providing databases of consumer health information. A survey in Glasgow showed that the computer systems most familiar to people are cash point dispensers, and a project is now under way to provide health information via robust 'hole in the wall' terminals. The first 'HEALTHPOINT' terminal was installed in a general practice waiting area, giving user-friendly access to information on health promotion, self-help groups, local health services, etc. The system is being put into other sites, and it is proposed to link it with a project in Townhead Health Centre in Glasgow which gives patients on-line access to their own medical records.

Viewdata

Since 1978 the British public has had access to health information through VIEWDATA SYSTEMS like British Telecom's Prestel. The pages on Prestel are compiled and maintained by a wide range of information providers such as British Rail and British Airways. Users can go into the system using a personal computer or adapted

TV set, via the telephone line. At first Prestel seemed full of promise, particularly for disabled or housebound people. You could do your shopping from home, at the same time as checking on train times or welfare benefit entitlements or share prices. In fact Prestel has failed to live up to the early expectations. People have not found in particularly easy or effective to search, the information on it can be found elsewhere, and the costs are not seen as worthwhile for home use.

The story in France has been very different. Here the telephone directory database was put up on a viewdata system and all subscribers given a MINITEL terminal. With information that everybody wanted to use forming the backbone of the system, and a huge network of users, it was well worth a wide range of information providers putting information on to Minitel. There are now many interesting health applications. For example, the catalogue of the major health library at the Cité des Sciences et de l'Industrie in Paris is available to the general public via Minitel.

In addition to Prestel, a number of smaller public viewdata services exist around the country. Many local authorities have set up systems, holding information about local services on a central computer, and making it available through viewdata terminals in public places such as libraries and leisure centres. A good example is the Berkshire County Council viewdata system, BVS. In Hackney an enterprising GP, Dr Chris Dobbing, set up his own viewdata system called HEALTHDATA. Topics include management of minor illness, health promotion information and lists of local GPs, hospitals, etc.

CD-ROM

In the past most extensive health information systems have been accessed 'on-line', via telephone links to host computers. Most medical libraries search on-line medical databases every day of the week. But a new technological revolution could spell the end of expensive on-line access to databases (and even the end of librarians). CD-ROM discs look exactly like the discs you put in your compact disc music centre, but instead of storing sound they are used to store vast amounts of data. Around 600 megabytes of information can be stored on a single disc (the equivalent of 250,000 pages of information.) The CD is read by a special CD-ROM drive attached to a personal computer. A wide variety of publications and databases are now available on CD-ROM (the complete multi-volume *Oxford English Dictionary* for example) and the market is expanding rapidly.

The attraction for health care consumers is that not only can whole libraries of health information be available at their fingertips, but CD-ROM systems can also be made very simple to use. And with no telephone connection charges mounting up you can spend as long as you like browsing until you find what you are looking for. Already the US company Information Access has brought out a CD-ROM health care consumer guide called the *Health Reference Center.* On a single compact disc, you get a shelf of reference books (a guide to medical tests, a reference book on medicines, a medical dictionary, a home medical encyclopaedia), a database of self-help groups and hotlines, summaries of hundreds of illnesses, and the full text of hundreds of articles from health magazines. At the moment products like the Health Reference Center are priced so that only large libraries can afford them, but with the technology becoming cheaper every day CD-ROM could be the most significant development yet in opening up access to health information for consumers.

Libraries

Until consumers have real access to databases of health information in their own homes, most people will need to visit libraries if they are to search for detailed information about their own health.

Public libraries

The best place to start is your own local PUBLIC LIBRARY. Although libraries do not reach all sections of the community equally well, for many people the public library is the most natural place to seek information. In a survey carried out by Salisbury Health Promotion Service, the local public library was seen as the most important source of health information after professional medical advice. The people most likely to use the library were 30–40-year-olds. Contrary to some people's expectations there was little demand for literature to enable self-diagnosis. The most popular topics were diet, relaxation and alternative medicine. While the younger people were largely interested in 'wellness' topics there was an increased tendency as people got older to seek information on coping with illness (*Reading Your Way to Health*, Salisbury Health Promotion Centre, 1990).

Public libraries are listed in the phone book under 'Libraries'. They are run by the County or Borough Council, and funded by the community charge, so most lending and reference services are free. You may have to pay for some additional services such as reservations for books which are out on loan, interlibrary loan requests, record libraries or computer literature searches. The INTERLIBRARY LOAN SERVICE is one of the most useful for health care consumers. Because all libraries are linked through interlibrary loan networks and have access to the vast stock of books and journals in the British Library Document Supply Centre (one of the largest collections in the world), your public library can offer far more than the materials on its own shelves. In theory at least, you can ask your public library to obtain for you a copy of any book or article published anywhere in the world.

If you are going to request a publication on interlibrary loan you need to understand the system of REFERENCES to books and articles. The most common system is that used in this book.

FOR BOOKS Naisbitt, J., *Megatrends: ten new directions for transforming our lives* (New York: Warner, 1982)
means that the book *Megatrends* by John Naisbitt was published in New York by Warner Publications in 1982.

FOR JOURNAL ARTICLES Rayner, C. Reality and expectation of the British National Health Service consumer, *Journal of Advanced Nursing* 1979; 4: 69–77 means that Claire Rayner's article appeared in volume 4 of *Journal of Advanced Nursing* in 1979 on pages 69–77.

The author named in a reference may be the first author of a multi-author work. Sometimes volume numbers are followed by part number, for example 4(3). You may also see journal titles abbreviated, for example *J. Adv. Nurs.* There are standard abbreviations for medical journals which a librarian will be able to decipher.

Within its own stock, a reasonably sized library should have in its reference collection copies of medical dictionaries, directories such as the *Hospitals and Health Services Yearbook*, the *Medical Register* or *Medical Directory*, drug reference books like *Martindale's Pharmacopoeia*, and general health works like *Gray's Anatomy* and the *BMA Complete Family Health Encyclopaedia.* Also in the reference library you would expect to find local community information, including the Family Health Services Authority lists of GPs, opticians, dentists and pharmacists, and lists or databases of local organizations and self-help groups. There should also be loan copies of popular medical books and some health magazines.

Most public libraries arrange their books according to the Dewey Classification system. The main 'classes' for health topics, to help you find the subjects you want on the shelves, are listed opposite.

PSYCHOLOGY

150	Psychology
153	Intelligence
154	Subconscious
158	Applied psychology

SOCIAL SCIENCES

361	Social problems and social welfare
362.1	Physical illness
362.2	Mental and emotional illnesses
362.3	Mental retardation
362.4	Problems of and services to people with physical handicap
362.5	Poverty
363	Other social problems and services
363.9	Population problems (e.g. birth control, sterilization)
364	Criminology

MEDICINE

610	Medicine
611	Human physiology
612	Human and personal hygiene
613.2	Dietetics
613.6	Special topics (e.g. industrial hygiene, travel hygiene, accident survival)
613.7	Physical fitness (including sleep, rest, exercise, yoga)
613.8	Addictions (alcohol, drugs, tobacco)
614	Public health
614.4	Incidence and control of disease
615	Pharmacology and therapeutics
615.7	Pharmacodynamics (physiological and therapeutic action of drugs)
615.9	Poisons and poisoning
616	Diseases (general)
616.02	First aid
616.08	Psychosomatic medicine
616.1	Diseases of the cardiovascular system
616.2	Diseases of the respiratory system
616.3	Diseases of the digestive system
616.4	Diseases of the blood, lymph and glandular system
616.5	Diseases of the skin, hair, nails
616.7	Diseases of the musculo-skeletal system
616.8	Diseases of nervous system and psychiatric disorders
616.85	Neuroses and personality disorders
616.86	Addictions and intoxication
616.89	Psychiatric illness including schizophrenia, paranoia
616.9	Communicable and non-communicable diseases
616.95	Venereal diseases
616.97	Allergies
616.99	Cancer
617	Surgery
617.6	Dentistry
617.7	Ophthalmology
617.8	Otology and audiology
618	Gynaecology and obstetrics
618.1	Gynaecology
618.2	Obstretrics
618.3	Complications of pregnancy
618.4	Childbirth
618.5	Complicated childbirth
618.7	Puerperal diseases
618.8	Obstetric surgery (including caesarean)
618.92	Paediatrics
618.97	Geriatrics
619	Experimental medicine

For more information on using libraries to gather health information, see *The Consumers' Guide to Health Information* (London: College of Health, 1986).

Medical libraries

You might think the best place to go for medical information is a medical library, and indeed there is a celebrated article in the *Journal of the American Medical Association* (1977; 237: 2627–9) which describes how a patient did use a medical library to diagnose her own lead poisoning, after twenty-two physicians had failed to do so. In an article which reads like a detective story she describes how she scoured the medical library of UCLA until 'finally I came across a book called *Toxicology of Industrial Metals*. In it were described the toxic effects of metal poisoning on factory workers and the descriptions of some of the illnesses fitted my own like a glove.' She was gradually being poisoned by a dietary supplement prescribed by her doctor. An editorial in the same issue of the journal praised 'her extraordinary feat of self diagnosis which will serve as a reminder of how much one can learn from a patient'.

However, as things are at the moment, few medical libraries are ready to open their doors to the public. In some places it has taken twenty years for medical libraries to admit nurses, so perhaps this is not surprising. Many medical librarians themselves feel very positively about providing access to consumers; this is a regular item of discussion at library conferences, and the professional journal *Health Libraries Review* has a regular 'Patient information' column. But librarians are often bound by the rules of their institution and, no matter how sympathetic the librarian, the collection of literature they manage is likely to be geared to the needs of people studying scientific medicine rather than to those of health consumers.

If you are a member of a self-help group, for example, you are an expert in your own right and may have a real need for access to the latest medical literature in your particular subject area. There is no reason why you should not approach your local medical library and ask whether you can use it for reference purposes. There should be a medical library or multidisciplinary health care library in your local District General Hospital. The most likely location is in the postgraduate medical education centre, perhaps with another library in the school of nursing. There are major medical libraries in the London teaching hospitals such as Charing Cross and St George's, as well as in the provincial medical schools like Southampton and Nottingham.

You may actually have a right of access to your nearest medical library. The Public Libraries and Museums Act of 1964 requires all local authorities to provide a comprehensive free library service to the local community. This legislation does not cover medical libraries but many have obligations under the Library Licence discount scheme operated by the Publishers' Association. In order to qualify for this discount (and many university and NHS libraries have it) the library must declare that it is open to the public and not just to its staff or members. The library should display a sign stating that there is free access to the library (for reference purposes; they are not obliged to lend books).

Health Information Services

In recent years a new kind of library and information service has developed in the health field. Combining the public library virtues of free and welcoming access for consumers with the medical library's expertise and specialist stock, these centres are usually called health information services or consumer health information services. The first services were established in Stevenage (Health Information Service) and Southampton (Help for Health) in the late 1970s. There are now over twenty in various stages of development and in various settings. Some form part of existing public library services (as in West Sussex) or medical libraries (as in Tunbridge Wells and Rotherham). Others are in hospitals (Frenchay Hospital, Bristol) or health centres (Nottingham). Others have been set up as separate services in shop front premises (like Health Matters in Milton Keynes and the Sunderland Health Information shop), as mobiles (like the Hertfordshire Women's Health Information Mobile) or as nationwide phone-in services (like Health Search Scotland).

Information provided by health information services

- details of national and local self-help groups (almost all health information services subscribe to the Helpbox database, see page 27)
- collections of popular health books, in some cases for loan
- leaflets from self-help groups, the Health Education Authority, etc. to take away
- self-help magazines
- details of local health and social services
- staff qualified in information work or health promotion

The following are examples of health information services in a variety of settings:

Health Information Service

Lister Hospital
Coreys Mill Lane
Stevenage
Herts SG1 4AB Tel: 0438 314333, ext 520

The Health Information Service (HIS) arose out of librarian Sally Knight's personal involvement in health information, and in particular her compilation of the *Popular Medical Index*, an index to health-related articles in the general press and to popular medical books (see page 279). In 1982 Hertfordshire County Library provided additional funding to employ a member of staff specifically to support Sally in the development of the HIS, and more recently an HIS Development Officer was appointed to develop new services, in particular in GP practices. The core of the HIS information centre at the Lister Hospital is a collection of some 3,000 subject files made up largely of cuttings from medical and popular journals. There is also a library of popular medical books and the Helpbox database is taken on subscription from Help for Health. HIS has always received its largest proportion of inquiries directly from the public and total inquiries per month now average 300. Many inquiries result from HIS acting as a back-up service to the local telephone information service, NHS Direct.

Help for Health

Grant Building
Southampton General Hospital
Southampton SO9 4XY Tel: 0703 779091

Help for Health was established in 1979, following a British Library research study. Originally funded by Wessex Regional Health

Authority, Help for Health is now an independent charity. Although based in a District General Hospital, most inquiries come from members of the public and health professionals in the community, from throughout Wessex and beyond. Over 900 inquiries are answered each month. The largest number of these come directly from the public, either from people seeking information about their own health and illness, or acting as carers on the part of others. The leading professional users are health visitors, but there is also extensive use by ward nursing staff, district nurses, general practitioners, social workers and health promotion officers.

Help for Health has undoubtedly the largest collection of consumer health literature in the UK, including a lending library of several thousand books, subject files of leaflets and articles, and subscriptions to 150 self-help periodicals. The most important resource is the Helpbox database of self-help groups and publications. The database includes details of self-help groups, pressure groups, community projects, etc., on a national level (1,000 groups), as well as details of several thousand self-help publications. The database is provided free of charge to health promotion departments, libraries, etc. within Wessex, and on a subscription basis to authorities elsewhere. In addition to its information service on self-help, Help for Health also runs services for the Wessex Regional Health Authority, including Wessex Waiting Line (see page 139) and the Region's HIV/AIDS information service.

Healthpoint

Poole Central Library
Dolphin Centre
Poole
Dorset BH15 1QE Tel: 0202 675377

Healthpoint Dorset is housed in the central public reference library in Poole, Dorset. In keeping with current emphasis on cooperative planning and funding of consumer health information service, Healthpoint has received financial support from the national Office of Arts and Libraries (OAL), Dorset County Library, local health authorities, and commercial sponsorship largely from a pharmaceutical company. Healthpoint opened in February 1989 and has resources comprising two staff, a collection of books, magazines, articles and newsletters, and the Help for Health database, Helpbox. Leaflets form another important element of the collection, and users of the centre can help themselves to a wide range. Healthpoint is located in a separate room at the main entrance to the lending library; all visitors to the library pass Healthpoint, but they can use the health information collection without having to enter the main library. On average 200 people a month make inquiries to the staff and a similar number browse in the centre without making a specific inquiry. Healthpoint is also an important county resource for branch libraries throughout Dorset. Branch libraries either contact Healthpoint directly with inquiries or give Healthpoint details direct to the inquirer.

Health Matters

795 Avebury Boulevard
Central Milton Keynes MK9 3NW Tel: 0908 677200

Health Matters was set up as part of the development of community resources in the new city of Milton Keynes. Information on health matters was seen to be a particular need and in 1989 the most comprehensive health information 'shop' in the UK was opened (although Health Matters had already been operating for fourteen months in temporary premises). Health Matters is a cooperative venture, receiving funding from Buckinghamshire County Library, local Health Authorities, the Community Health Council and Milton Keynes Development Corporation. The shop itself is in a covered shopping mall, close to a major food supermarket. The front is completely glazed and the visitor looks in to see a library of 500 books, leaflets and current journals. There is an attractive display area, and a children's corner with books and toys. Health Matters has developed its own user-friendly version of Helpbox. Staffing consists of one full-time librarian, some CHC staffing and a team of volunteers. In addition to the information service, Health Matters offers space to self-help groups for events and talks. As an integral part of the local voluntary sector, Health Matters also participates in a wide range of community events, health fairs, etc.

Patient and Family Information Centre

Frenchay District Hospital
Bristol BS16 1LE Tel: 0272 701212

While information services like Health Matters are firmly based in the community, the Patient and Family Health Information Centre is closely linked to the Frenchay Hospital out-patients department. With its location next to the department, many referrals come through out-patients. There are also particularly close links with the specialist nurses in the hospital and the accommodation is shared with the diabetes specialist nurse who runs an advice and teaching service for patients. The Centre opened in 1988 with funding largely from voluntary contributions. It now deals with approximately 150 inquiries a month, from both the public and health professionals. Women inquirers outnumber men by three to one. In addition to the inquiry work, the Centre provides a meeting room for hospital-based patient education programmes in diabetes, coronary rehabilitation and breast care following surgery. The meeting room is also used by local self-help groups. Linked with the opening of the Centre, a survey of patients and visitors to Frenchay Hospital in 1988 indicated a significant need for information. Although people would most readily turn to their GP for advice, there was a demand for written material of the kind provided by the Patient and Family Information Centre.

These services are described in more detail in a series of articles in *Health Libraries Review* in 1989 and 1990.

For overviews of consumer health information services in the UK, see:

The Health Information Handbook by Robert Gann (Aldershot: Gower, 1986)
Informing Health Consumers by Elaine Kempson (London: British Library/College of Health, 1987)

Health Promotion Services

Each District Health Authority has its own health promotion department, with a responsibility for promotion of good health and prevention of illness in the local community. Originally called health education departments, most have now taken the name 'health promotion' to emphasize a wider brief within the context of public health, that of enabling people to increase control over their own lives and thereby to improve their health. Increasingly, health promotion departments are adopting a wide variety of approaches, including sophisticated marketing techniques and 'community development' work with local self-help groups.

Health promotion officers come from a variety of backgrounds, with nursing and teaching probably still predominating. Within a district health promotion department, under the District Health

You can contact your health promotion department for:

- health education literature, particularly leaflets on topics such as smoking, diet, alcohol, HIV/AIDS. Material from the Health Education Authority should be available, as well as locally produced leaflets and publications from some voluntary groups.
- information on local self-help groups, community health projects, etc.
- advice on, and participation in, health fairs, media events, etc.
- training for smoke-stop groups, etc.
- speakers on health topics for local meetings
- advice and sometimes technical assistance in producing your own publications

Promotion Manager, you would probably find health promotion officers with specific responsibilities: for schools and young people, liaison with local industry, ethnic groups, perhaps for elderly people and almost certainly for prevention of HIV infection. Health promotion departments are found in a variety of settings: health centres and clinics, hospitals, health shops, etc. Look in the phone book under Health Promotion or Health Education.

In addition to local activity carried out by district departments there is also health promotion activity at national level, through the Health Education/Promotion Authorities. These run national campaigns (the most visible being the Health Education Authority's AIDS campaign), produce national resources such as leaflets and videos, carry out research and advise the government and the Department of Health on health promotion issues. One of the largest and most successful nationwide health promotion initiatives of recent years has been Heartbeat Wales. Heartbeat Wales began with the largest health survey ever conducted (30,000 people), and now uses a wide range of approaches involving education in schools, the involvement of industry and agriculture, community and mass media activities, and further market research.

National organizations with a responsibility for health promotion in the UK

Health Education Authority Hamilton House, Mabledon Place, London WC1H 9TX Tel: 071-383 3833

Health Promotion Authority for Wales Brunel House, Fitzalan Road, Cardiff CF2 1EB Tel: 0222 472472

Scottish Health Education Group Woodburn House, Canaan Lane, Edinburgh EH10 4SG Tel: 031-452 8589

Northern Ireland Health Promotion Unit The Beeches, 23 Hampton Park, Belfast BT7 3JN Tel: 0232 644811

Community Health Councils

Each District Health Authority also has its own Community Health Council (called Local Health Councils in Scotland). Community Health Councils (CHCs) were set up as part of the major reorganization of the NHS in 1974 and were charged with the duty of representing the local community's interest in the health service. The Community Health Council itself is made up of twelve lay members with a chairperson and a paid secretary/administrator. CHC members are supposed to represent the local community, but it is fair to say that there is an over-representation of middle-class, middle-aged or retired people, with working-class people and the young under-represented. Working-class young mothers are perhaps the least likely people to be CHC members, yet they make some of the greatest use of the NHS as consumers.

CHCs vary a lot in their everyday activities but there are functions which are common to all:

Community Health Council functions

- taking up complaints (see page 165)
- visiting NHS premises
- consultation on the planning and development of local health services
- provision of information on local services
- monitoring the quality of local services, through consumer surveys, etc.

Right The Patients' Charter, issued by the Association for Community Health Councils in 1987. Although the Charter has no 'official' standing, it is an important check-list of good practice

The government insists that CHCs will still have an important role in the new, post-*Working for Patients* NHS. There are still some areas where that role remains uncertain, in particular visiting and consultation rights with respect to self-governing hospitals. CHCs survive on paltry funding for the job they are asked to do, and the fact that they are funded by the very body they are supposed to monitor has led to accusations that they are lapdogs rather than watchdogs. But they remain an important ally for the health care consumer: find out where they are and use them.

Look in the phone book under Community Health Council. A good summary of the role of CHCs is given in *Representing the Consumer: Community Health Councils, fifteen years on*, published by the ASSOCIATION OF COMMUNITY HEALTH COUNCILS OF ENGLAND AND WALES 30 Drayton Park, London N5 1PB Tel: 071-609 8405. In 1987 the Association issued a Patients' Charter.

PATIENTS' CHARTER
Guidelines for Good Practice

All persons have a right to:

1 health services, appropriate to their needs, regardless of financial means or where they live and without delay
2 be treated with reasonable skill, care and consideration
3 written information about health services, including hospitals, community and General Practitioner services
4 register with a General Practitioner with ease and to be able to change without adverse consequences
5 be informed about all aspects of their condition and proposed care (including the alternatives available), unless they express a wish to the contrary
6 accept or refuse treatment (including diagnostic procedures), without affecting the standard of alternative care given
7 a second opinion
8 the support of a relative or friend at any time
9 advocacy and interpreting services
10 choose whether to participate or not in research trials and be free to withdraw at any time without affecting the standard of alternative care given
11 only be discharged from hospital after adequate arrangements have been made for their continuing care
12 privacy for all consultations
13 be treated at all times with respect for their dignity, personal needs and religious and philosophical beliefs
14 confidentiality of all records relating to their care
15 have access to their own health care records
16 make a complaint and have it investigated thoroughly, speedily and impartially and be informed of the result
17 an independent investigation into all serious medical or other mishaps whilst in NHS care, whether or not a complaint is made, and, where appropriate, adequate redress

Advice Services: CAB and DIAL

Citizens' Advice Bureau (CAB)

The Citizens' Advice Bureau service was set up in 1939 to meet the flood of queries from the public about wartime rationing, conscription, evacuation, etc. Today there are over 900 CABs, answering 2 million inquiries a year. The cornerstone of the CAB service is a huge body of volunteers (numbering 23,000). These voluntary advice workers undergo a basic training course and continuous in-service training, which covers information handling and interviewing skills. Volunteers handle the bulk of inquiry work. There are only about 2,000 paid staff and these tend to be more common in inner city areas because of the amount of work there and the difficulties in finding volunteers. Although the running costs of a CAB are largely met by local authority grants, the service is entirely independent.

The most common inquiries received by CABs relate to social welfare, consumer issues, debt and housing. Although specific health-related inquiries do not form a large proportion of the total, as a generalist advice service the CAB is still a key information source. It is the generalist nature of the service that is its strength in that problems relating to housing, employment, income, etc. which may be a cause or consequence of ill-health can be dealt with within the same service. The inquirer can be referred to a more specialist agency when the need arises, and some CABs have their own specialist advice sessions provided by solicitors, debt counsellors, etc.

Each CAB is independent but there is a national office, the NATIONAL ASSOCIATION OF CITIZENS' ADVICE BUREAUX 115–23 Pentonville Road, London N1 9LZ Tel: 071-833 2181, which provides a comprehensive and detailed information support service to local bureaux. Each month all CABs are sent a package containing details of new legislation, regulations, organizations, etc. This information pack ensures a consistency of advice-giving which is augmented by local information provided by the local CAB itself. You can find the address and telephone number of your nearest CAB in the phone book under Citizens' Advice Bureaux. Larger bureaux are likely to be open during office hours with perhaps some evening and weekend sessions. At the other extreme CABs may take their services to the local community with one morning a week in the village hall or community centre. Check the opening times before you make a journey.

Over twenty CABs are now operating within hospitals, providing independent, confidential advice to patients and staff alike. At any one time there are several thousand people in hospital. Some are rushed in as emergency cases, leaving bills unpaid, rent in arrears, families in financial hardship. Others, particularly those in psychiatric hospitals, may have been institutionalized for many years and are now facing the daunting prospect of a return to the community. A CAB within the hospital can provide someone to turn to for people who have nowhere else to go with these worries.

CAB advice work in hospitals reflects the resources available. Funding comes from a variety of diverse sources such as local authorities, health authorities, charitable and trust funds. The CAB presence varies from one session a week to full services with paid staff. With more resources CABs are able to offer regular ward visits, training for hospital staff in welfare benefit work, and the CAB Information System on microfilm. The National Association of Citizens' Advice Bureaux (NACAB) can provide a list of CABs currently operating hospital advice services. A special report, 'All part of the cure: CAB on the wards', appeared in *Citizens' Advice Bureau News* in autumn 1987.

Among hospitals with a CAB service are:

STOKE MANDEVILLE HOSPITAL Aylesbury CAB operates an advice centre in the main corridor of the hospital one full day a week. As the National Spinal Unit, Stoke Mandeville attracts patients from all over the UK, many of them admitted as emergencies leaving problems at home to be sorted out.

HOPE HOSPITAL, SALFORD The CAB here is open four days a week and has a manager and seven volunteers. In 1987, 1,800 inquiries were answered, the majority centring on benefit and debt problems caused by ill health and reduced income.

TOOTING BEC HOSPITAL This was one of the first advice centres to open in a psychiatric hospital, and has been offering a full-time service since 1983. The hospital is scheduled for closure and a major area of work is helping long-stay patients to adjust to the prospect of life outside.

SPRINGFIELD HOSPITAL, WANDSWORTH Each of the hospital advice services mentioned above has developed through the CAB service. The Advice and Law Centre at Springfield Hospital in Wandsworth, South London, is different in that it is a sub-office of Wandsworth Law Centre. It provides the 900-bed psychiatric hospital with the on-site services of a solicitor and an advice worker who give free advice to patients, and, to a limited extent, to staff and relatives. The service is autonomous within the hospital and is subject to solicitors' rules of confidentiality and procedure.

Disablement Information and Advice Lines (DIAL)

The first DIAL began in a cloakroom in a residential centre for disabled people in Alfreton, Derbyshire. In the mid-1970s there was a growing feeling that although existing services could provide accurate information, what they so often lacked was a direct experience of disability. DIAL Derbyshire was set up to provide a CAB-type information service, but run by disabled people for disabled people. The idea took off and soon DIALs were opening in Newcastle, Rugby, Liverpool, Norwich and Portsmouth. Before long it became apparent that they needed an umbrella body, rather like NACAB, through which they could assist each other to provide a more effective service. In 1977 a head office was established in Derbyshire called DIAL-UK.

DIALs are autonomous, self-governing and largely self-financing. There is a variety of staffing arrangements and some have paid workers, but most advisers are disabled volunteers. Most DIALs maintain close contact with libraries, CABs, social services, law centres, etc. and may involve them in their training programmes. The largest category of inquiry reaching DIALs (about one-third) relates to welfare rights. DIALs will often accompany a disabled person to a tribunal, or attend at their home if they are being assessed for Attendance Allowance, Mobility Allowance or equipment and adaptations. There are also frequent inquiries on housing, holidays, car adaptations, travel, leisure, etc.

There are now over fifty DIALs in the UK in a variety of locations, including day centres and disabled living centres. If you have a local DIAL the address and telephone number should be in the phone book under DIAL. Otherwise you can find out where the nearest DIAL is from DIAL-UK 117 High Street, Clay Cross, Derbyshire S45 9DZ Tel: 0246 250055. Some DIALs now hold information and advice sessions in hospitals, recognizing the enormous information needs which exist when a newly disabled person is discharged form the sheltered environment of the hospital to the care of untrained relatives. For example, one of the most go-ahead DIALs, DIAL Hampshire, has set up an information and advice centre at Queen Alexandra Hospital, Portsmouth. Patients can receive detailed face-to-face advice from someone with personal experience of disability, and this is backed up with a starter pack of appropriate leaflets and information sheets.

8 Self-Help Resources

There is no shortage of information, advice and support for health care consumers. The difficulty is rather one of identifying the right resources at the right time.

This section covers some of the main health problems and health information needs. It then gives the address of the main organization to contact for further information. Most organizations of this kind produce leaflets and a magazine or newsletter. They should have a publications list for more substantial publications for which there is a charge. Always enclose a stamped addressed envelope when you write to voluntary organizations such as these.

This is not a comprehensive list of self-help groups. There are several thousand groups for patients, and to list them all would require a whole publication. There are already good directories of organizations available and these are listed on page 27.

The resource guide then goes on to list, where relevant, one or two books written for lay people which provide more detailed information on individual topics. These books should be available through your public library or bookshop.

If you can't find the book you want ask your bookshop to order it for you. All good bookshops provide this service for their customers.

As well as using the information from leaflets and books for your own needs, it will help you to get more information from the medical profession by asking the right questions. Most doctors are pleased to have well-informed active patients.

AIDS

TERRENCE HIGGINS TRUST
52–4 Gray's Inn Road
London WC1N 8LT
Tel: 071-242 1010

Yelding, D., *Caring for Someone with AIDS* (London: Consumers' Association, 1990)

Alcohol

ALCOHOL CONCERN
305 Gray's Inn Road
London WC1X 8QF
Tel: 071-833 3471

Maryon Davis, A., *PSST: a really useful guide to alcohol* (London: Pan, 1989)

Allergy

ACTION AGAINST ALLERGY
Greyhound House,
23/24 George Street
Richmond
Surrey TW9 1JY

Davies, R. M., *Allergy: the facts* (Oxford Medical Publications, 1989)

Alzheimer's disease/ Dementia

ALZHEIMER'S DISEASE SOCIETY
158/160 Balham High Road
London SW12 9BN
Tel: 081-675 6557

Wattis, Dr P., *Confusion in Old Age* (London: BMA Family Doctor Publications, 1988)

Anorexia nervosa

EATING DISORDERS ASSOCIATION
Sackville Place
44/48 Magdalen Street
Norwich
Norfolk, NR3 1JE
Tel: 0603 621414

Palmer, R. L., *Anorexia Nervosa: a guide for sufferers and their families* (Harmondsworth: Penguin, 1988)

Arthritis

ARTHRITIS CARE
5 Grosvenor Crescent
London SW1X 7ER
Tel: 071-235 0902

Dieppe, P. A., *Arthritis* (London: BMA Family Doctor Publications, 1988)

Asthma

NATIONAL ASTHMA CAMPAIGN
300 Upper Street
London N1 2XX
Tel: 071-226 2260

Donaldson, John, *Living with Asthma and Hayfever* (Harmondsworth: Penguin, 1989)

Autism

NATIONAL AUTISTIC SOCIETY
276 Willesden Lane
London NW2 5RB
Tel: 081-451 1114

Everard, P., *Involuntary Strangers* (London: John Clare, 1980)

Back pain

NATIONAL BACK PAIN ASSOCIATION
31/33 Park Road
Teddington
Middx. TW11 0AB
Tel: 081-977 5474

Consumers' Association, *Understanding Back Trouble* (London: Consumers' Association, 1988)

Bed wetting

ENURESIS RESOURCE AND INFORMATION CENTRE
65 St Michael's Hill
Bristol
Avon BS2 8DZ
Tel: 0272 264920

Welford, H., *Toilet Training and Bedwetting: a practical guide for today's parents* (Wellingborough: Thorsons, 1987)

Bereavement

CRUSE–BEREAVEMENT CARE
Cruse House
126 Sheen Road
Richmond
Surrey TW9 1UR
Tel: 081-940 4818/9407

Horn S., *Coping with Bereavement: coming to terms with a sense of loss* (Wellingborough: Thorsons, 1989)

Blindness

ROYAL NATIONAL INSTITUTE FOR THE BLIND
224/228 Great Portland Street
London W1N 6AA
Tel: 071-388 1266

Ford, M., *In Touch: BBC Radio 4 guide to services for people with a visual handicap* (London: BBC Publications, 1989)

Breast cancer

BREAST CARE AND MASTECTOMY ASSOCIATION
26 Harrison Street
London WC1H 8JG
Tel: 071-837 0908

Baum, M., *Breast Cancer: the facts* (2nd edn, Oxford University Press, 1988)

Cancer

BACUP: BRITISH ASSOCIATION OF CANCER UNITED PATIENTS
121/3 Charterhouse Street
London EC1M 6AA
Tel: 071-608 1785 and Freephone 0800 181 199

Williams, C. and S., *Cancer: a guide for patients and their families* (Chichester: John Wiley, 1986)

Cerebral palsy

SPASTICS SOCIETY
12 Park Crescent
London W1N 4EQ
Tel: 071-636 5020/0800 626216

Russell, P., *The Wheelchair Child* (3rd edn. London: Souvenir Press, 1989)

Childbirth

NATIONAL CHILDBIRTH TRUST
Alexandra House
Oldham Terrace
London W3 6NH
Tel: 081-992 8637

Balaskas, J., *The Encyclopedia of Pregnancy and Birth* (London: Macdonald Orbis, 1989)

Children in hospital

NATIONAL ASSOCIATION FOR THE WELFARE OF CHILDREN IN HOSPITAL
Argyle House
29/31 Euston Road
London NW1 2SD
Tel: 071-833 2041

Cleft lip and palate

CLEFT LIP AND PALATE ASSOCIATION
1 Eastwood Gardens
Kenton
Newcastle upon Tyne
Tyne and Wear NE3 3DQ
Tel: 091 285 9396

Coeliac disease

COELIAC SOCIETY OF THE UNITED KINGDOM
PO Box 220
High Wycombe
Bucks HP11 2HY
Tel: 0494 37278

Greer, R., *Gluten-free Cooking* (Wellingborough: Thorsons, 1989)

Colitis and Crohn's disease

NATIONAL ASSOCIATION FOR COLITIS AND CROHN'S DISEASE
98a London Road
St Albans
Herts AL1 1NX
Tel: 0727 44296

Brooke, B., *The Troubled Gut: the causes and consequences of diarrhoea* (Oxford University Press, OUP, 1986)

Colostomy

BRITISH COLOSTOMY ASSOCIATION
15 Station Road
Reading
Berks RE1 1LE
Tel: 0734 391537

Deafness

ROYAL NATIONAL INSTITUTE FOR THE DEAF
105 Gower Street
London WC1E 6AH
Tel: 071-387 8044

Freeland, Andrew, *Deafness: the facts* (Oxford Paperbacks, 1989)

Depression

DEPRESSIVES ASSOCIATED
PO Box 5
Castletown, Portland
Dorset DT5 1BQ

Romanis, R., *Depression* (London: Faber and Faber, 1987)

Diabetes

BRITISH DIABETIC ASSOCIATION
10 Queen Anne Street
London W1M 9LD
Tel: 071-323 1531

Leslie, R. G., *Diabetes* (London: BMA Family Doctor Publications, 1989)

Digestive disorders

BRITISH DIGESTIVE FOUNDATION
3 St Andrew's Place
London NW1 4LB
Tel: 071-486 0341

Nicol, R., *Coping Successfully with Your Irritable Bowel* (London: Sheldon Press, 1989)

Down's syndrome

DOWN'S SYNDROME ASSOCIATION
153–5 Mitcham Road
London SW17 9PG
Tel: 081–682 4001

Cunningham, C., *Down's Syndrome: an introduction for parents* (London: Souvenir Press, 1988)
Selikowitz, M., *Down's Syndrome: the facts* (Oxford University Press, 1990)

Drug misuse

STANDING CONFERENCE ON DRUG ABUSE
1–4 Hatton Place
Hatton Garden
London EC1N 8ND
Tel: 071-430 2341 or Freephone Drug Problems

Dixon, A., *Dealing with Drugs: helping the problem drug taker* (London: BBC Publications, 1987)
Tyler, A., *Street Drugs: the facts explained, the myths exploded* (London: New English Library, 1988)

Dyslexia

BRITISH DYSLEXIA ASSOCIATION
98 London Road
Reading RG1 5AU
Tel: 0734 668271/2

Hornsby, B., *Overcoming Dyslexia: a straightforward guide for families and teachers* (London: Martin Dunitz, 1984)

Eczema

NATIONAL ECZEMA SOCIETY
Tavistock House East
Tavistock Square
London WC1H 9SR
Tel: 071-388 4097

Atherton, D. J., *Your Child with Eczema: a guide for parents* (London: Heinemann, 1984)

Epilepsy

BRITISH EPILEPSY ASSOCIATION
Anstey House
40 Hanover Square
Leeds LE3 1BE
Tel: 0532 439393/0345 089599

Chadwick, D., *Living with Epilepsy* (London: Macdonald Optima, 1987)
Oxley, J. and Smith, J., *The Epilepsy Reference Book* (London: Faber and Faber, 1991)

Eye problems

OPTICAL INFORMATION COUNCIL
57A Old Woking Road
West Byfleet
Surrey KT14 6LS
Tel: 0932 353 283

Glasspool, M., *Your Eyes* (London: BMA Family Doctor Publications, 1989)

Family planning

FAMILY PLANNING ASSOCIATION
Margaret Pyke House
27–35 Mortimer Street
London W1N 7RJ
Tel: 071-636 7866

Bromwich, P. D., *Contraception: the facts* (2nd edn, Oxford University Press, 1990)

Fertility problems

NATIONAL ASSOCIATION FOR THE CHILDLESS
318 Summer Lane
Birmingham B19 3RL
Tel: 021 359 4887/021 359 7359

Anderson, M., *Infertility: a guide for the anxious couple* (London: Faber and Faber, 1987)

Friedreich's ataxia

FRIEDREICH'S ATAXIA GROUP
Copse Edge
Thursley Road
Elstead
Godalming
Surrey GU8 6DJ
Tel: 0252 702 864

Haemophilia

HAEMOPHILIA SOCIETY
123 Westminster Bridge Road
London SE1 7HR
Tel: 071-928 2020

Jones, P., *Living with Haemophilia* (Lancaster: MTP, 1987)

Head injuries

HEADWAY: THE NATIONAL HEAD INJURIES ASSOCIATION
200 Mansfield Road
Nottingham NG1 3HX
Tel: 0602 622382

Slater, B., *A Positive Approach to Head Injury: guidelines for professionals and families* (Chichester: John Wiley, 1987)

Heart disease

BRITISH HEART FOUNDATION
14 Fitzhardinge Street
London W1H 4DH
Tel: 071-935 0185

Petch, Dr M., *Heart Disease* (London: BMA Family Doctor Publications, 1989)

Huntington's chorea

HUNTINGTON'S DISEASE ASSOCIATION
108 Battersea High Street
London SW11 3HP
Tel: 071-223 7000

Slatford, J., *Our Family has Huntington's Chorea* (COMBAT)

Hyperactivity

HYPERACTIVE CHILDREN'S SUPPORT GROUP
71 Whyke Lane
Chichester
West Sussex PO19 2LD

Taylor, E., *The Hyperactive Child: a parent's guide* (London: Martin Dunitz, 1986)

Hysterectomy

HYSTERECTOMY SUPPORT GROUP
11 Henryson Road
London SE4 1HL
Tel: 081-690 5987

Dickson, A., *Hysterectomy: the positive recovery plan* (Wellingborough: Thorsons, 1989)

Ileostomy

ILEOSTOMY ASSOCIATION
Amblehurst House
Black Scotch Lane
Mansfield
Notts NG18 4PF
Tel: 0623 28099

Wade, Barbara, *A Stoma is for Life* (London: Scutari Press, 1989)

Kidney problems

BRITISH KIDNEY PATIENT ASSOCIATION
Bordon
Hants GU35 9JP
Tel: 04203 2022

Camerson, J. S., *Kidney Disease: the facts* (Oxford University Press, 1986)

Leukaemia

LEUKAEMIA CARE SOCIETY
PO Box 82
Exeter
Devon EX2 5DP
Tel: 0392 218514

Meningitis

NATIONAL MENINGITIS TRUST
Fern House
Bath Road
Stroud
Glos. GL5 3TJ
Tel: 0453 755049

Menopause

WOMEN'S HEALTH CONCERN
83 Earls Court Road
London W8 6EF
Tel: 071-938 3932

Hunter, M., *Your Menopause* (London: Pandora Press, 1990)

Mental handicap

MENCAP: ROYAL SOCIETY FOR MENTALLY HANDICAPPED CHILDREN AND ADULTS
117–123 Golden Lane
London EC1Y 0RT
Tel: 071-454 0454

Mental health

MIND: NATIONAL ASSOCIATION FOR MENTAL HEALTH
22 Harley Street
London W1N 2ED
Tel: 071-637 0741

Burningham, S., *Not On Your Own: the MIND guide to mental health* (Harmondsworth: Penguin, 1989)
Edwards, H., *Psychological Problems: who can help?* (London: British Psychological Society/Methuen, 1987)

Migraine

BRITISH MIGRAINE ASSOCIATION
178a High Road
Byfleet
Weybridge
Surrey KT14 7ED
Tel: 09323 52468

Wilkinson, M., *Migraine and Headaches* (London: Martin Dunitz, 1982)

Miscarriage

MISCARRIAGE ASSOCIATION
PO Box 24
Ossett
West Yorkshire WF5 9XG
Tel: 0924 830515

Leroy, M., *Miscarriage* (London: Macdonald Optima, 1988)

Motor neurone disease

MOTOR NEURONE DISEASE ASSOCIATION
PO Box 246
Northampton
Northants NN1 2PR
Tel: 0604 22269/0800 626262

Multiple sclerosis

MULTIPLE SCLEROSIS SOCIETY
25 Effie Road
London SW6 1EE
Tel: 071-736 6267

Forsythe, E., *Multiple Sclerosis: exploring sickness and health* (London: Faber and Faber, 1988)

Muscular dystrophy

MUSCULAR DYSTROPHY GROUP
Nattrass House,
35 Macauley Road
London SW4 0QP
Tel: 071-720 8055

Myalgic encephalomyelitis (ME)

MYALGIC ENCEPHALOMYELITIS ASSOCIATION
PO Box 8
Stanford le Hope
Essex SS17 8EX
Tel: 0375 642466

Wilkinson, S., *M.E. and You: a survivor's guide to post-viral fatigue syndrome* (Wellingborough: Thorsons, 1988)

Osteoporosis

NATIONAL OSTEOPOROSIS SOCIETY
PO Box 10
Barton Meade House
Radstock
Bath
Avon BA3 3YB
Tel: 0761 32472

St John Dixon, A., *How to Avoid Osteoporosis* (London: Macdonald Optima, 1989)

Parkinson's disease

PARKINSON'S DISEASE SOCIETY
36 Portland Place
London W1N 3DG
Tel: 071-255 2432

Godwin-Austen, R., *The Parkinson's Disease Handbook: overcoming common problems* (London: Sheldon Press, 1984)

Patients' rights

COLLEGE OF HEALTH
St Margaret's House
21 Old Ford Road
London E2 9PL
Tel: 081-983 1225
PATIENTS ASSOCIATION
18 Victoria Park Square
London E2 9PF
Tel: 081-981 5676

Phobias

PHOBIC ACTION
Greater London House
547–551 High Road
Leytonstone
London E11 4PR
Tel: 081-558 3463

Mitchell, R., *Phobias: what they mean; how they occur; what can be done to treat them* (Harmondsworth: Penguin, 1982)
Vose, R. Hurst, *Agoraphobia* (London: Faber and Faber, 1986)

Postnatal depression

ASSOCIATION FOR POSTNATAL ILLNESS
7 Gowan Avenue
London SW6 6RH
Tel: 071-731 4867

Dalton, K., *Depression after childbirth: how to recognize and treat postnatal depression* (Oxford Paperbacks, 1989)

Premenstrual syndrome

NATIONAL ASSOCIATION FOR PREMENSTRUAL SYNDROME
PO Box 72
Sevenoaks
Kent TN13 3PS

Shreeve, Dr C., *The Premenstrual Syndrome* (Wellingborough: Thorsons, 1984)

Psoriasis

PSORIASIS ASSOCIATION
7 Milton Street
Northampton
Northants NN2 7JG
Tel: 0604 711129

Marks, Professor R., *Psoriasis: a guide to one of the commonest skin diseases* (London: Martin Dunitz, 1981)

Schizophrenia

NATIONAL SCHIZOPHRENIA FELLOWSHIP
28 Castle Street
Kingston-upon-Thames
Surrey KT1 1SS
Tel: 081-547 3937

Tsuang, M. T., *Schizophrenia: the facts* (Oxford University Press, 1982)

Smoking

ACTION ON SMOKING AND HEALTH (ASH)
5/11 Mortimer Street
London W1N 7RH
Tel: 071-637 9843

Carr, A., *The Easy Way to Stop Smoking* (Harmondsworth: Penguin, 1987)

Spina bifida

ASSOCIATION FOR SPINA BIFIDA AND HYDROCEPHALUS
42 Park Road
Peterborough
Cambs PE1 2UQ
Tel: 0733 555988

Welch, C., *Spina Bifida and You: a guide for young people* (Association for Spina Bifida and Hydrocephalus (ASBAH), 1985)

Spinal injuries

SPINAL INJURIES ASSOCIATION
Yeomans House
76 St James Lane
London N10 3DF
Tel: 081-444 2121

Fallon, B., *So You're Paralysed* (2nd edn, Spinal Injuries Association, 1987)

Stillbirth

STILLBIRTH AND NEONATAL DEATH SOCIETY
28 Portland Place
London W1N 3DE
Tel: 071-436 5881

Borg, S. and Lasker, J., *When Pregnancy Fails: coping with miscarriage, stillbirth and infant death* (London: Routledge and Kegan Paul, 1982)

Stroke

CHEST, HEART AND STROKE ASSOCIATION
CHSA House
123/127 Whitecross Street
London EC1Y 8JJ
Tel: 071-490 7999

Hewer, R. J. and Wade D. T., *Stroke: a practical guide towards recovery* (London: Martin Dunitz, 1986)

Sudden infant death

FOUNDATION FOR THE STUDY OF INFANT DEATHS
35 Belgrave Square
London SW1X 8QB
Tel: 071-235 1721

Murphy, S., *Coping with Cot Death* (London: Sheldon Press, 1990)
Knight, B., *Sudden Death in Infancy* (London: Faber and Faber, 1983)

Tinnitus

BRITISH TINNITUS ASSOCIATION
c/o Royal National Institute for the Deaf
105 Gower Street
London WC1E 6AA
Tel: 071-387 8033

Youngson, Dr R., *How to Cope with Tinnitus and Hearing Loss* (London: Sheldon Press, 1986)

Twins

TWINS AND MULTIPLE BIRTHS ASSOCIATION (TAMBA)
41 Fortuna Way
Aylesbury Park
Grimsby
South Humberside DN37 9SJ
Tel: 0384 373642

Zentner, C., *Twins: the parents' survival guide* (London: Macdonald, 1984)

Women's health

WOMEN'S HEALTH AND
REPRODUCTIVE RIGHTS
INFORMATION CENTRE
52–4 Featherstone Street
London EC1Y 8RT
Tel: 071-251 6580/6332

Llewellyn-Jones, D., *Everywoman: a gynaecological guide for life* (5th edn, London: Faber and Faber, 1989)
Phillips, A. and Rakusen, J., *Our Bodies, Ourselves: a health book by and for women* (Harmondsworth: Penguin, 1989)

Index